Carroll Fitzgerald Wilkinson
2003

#468
3.00

SurferGrrrls

Look Ethel!

An Internet

Guide for Us!

Laurel Gilbert and Crystal Kile

Seal Press

Seal Press
3131 Western Avenue, Suite 410, Seattle, Washington 98121
email: sealprss@scn.org

Library of Congress Cataloging-in-Publication Data
Gilbert, Laurel
Surfergrrrls : look Ethel! an Internet guide for us / Laurel
Gilbert, Crystal Kile.
    1. Women—Research—Computer network resources.
 2. Internet (Computer network) I. Kile, Crystal. II. Title
HQ1180.G55   1996   025.06'3054—dc20   96–13645
ISBN 1-878067-79-6

Printed in the United States of America
First printing, August 1996
10 9 8 7 6 5 4 3 2 1

Distributed to the trade by Publishers Group West
In Canada: Publishers Group West Canada, Toronto, Canada
In Europe and the U.K.: Airlift Book Company, London, England

Cover design: Kate Thompson
Cover photograph: Courtesy U.S. Army Photo. *Patsy Simmers holding ENIAC board, Gail Taylor holding EDVAC board, Milly Beck holding ORDVAC board, Norma Stec holding BRLESC I board.*
Back Cover illustration: Ellen Forney
Interior illustrations: Ellen Forney (unless otherwise noted)
Interior design: Stacy M. Lewis

Acknowledgments: Page 7: Photo © William B. Kile. Page 9: Photo © Robert Gilbert. Page 41, 45 and 49: Images and photos from TAP. http://www.cs.yale.edu/homes/tap/tap.html. Page 124: Photo provided by Rod Rehn. http://www.scifi.com/bionics/. Page 131: Logo designed by Sandra Guzdek. Used by permission of the Star Fleet Ladies' Auxillary and Embroidery/Baking Society. http://www.eecis.udel.edu/~masterma/ladies.html. Page 135: Photo from http://www.xfiles.com. Page 136: Photo from http://www.mgmua.com/hackers/. Page 137: Photos from http://www.dcs.qmw.ac.uk/~bob/stuff/tg/index.html. Page 177: Photo © Burns. Page 189: Photo © Rex Fly. Page 190: Graphic © 1996 EJL Productions, LLC. Page 201: Graphic © Janet Planet and Yes! Pigs Can Fly, Box 1613, Jackson, Wyoming 83001. Page 204: Photo of Adrienne Clemont from http://teddy.law.cornell.edu:8080/chezadri.htm. Photo of Elizabeth Muzzo © Gianni Muzzo. Page 207: Photo courtesy of Amy Goodloe. Page 215: Photo from Tana B. http://www.we.got.net/~tanab/. Page 230: Photo from Sassy. http://www.tumyeto.com/foxy/. Page 231: Photo © 1994 Danny Clinch.

Acknowledgments

People we gotta thank in no particular order:

Holly Morris, our editor, as well as designer Stacy M. Lewis, copyeditor Cathy Johnson and the rest of the women at Seal Press; Ellen Berry, Vicki Patraka, Annmarie Adams, Steve Krause and Annette Wanna-maker, Johnathan Macy, all the geeks in the BGSU Faculty/Grad Lab, the Spiderwoman e-list and other members of our respective online communities, and Kristen Golden, Barbara Findlen and little Grace (for starting the process without even knowing it).

✧ *Crystal:* Mom and Dad, Bill and Nora Kile, Jeff Schwartz, Chris Geist, Tom Klein, everybody in the Summer 1995 Computer and English Studies class, Rick Kill, all of the students in my Fall 1995 Women's Studies Intro and TV as Popular Culture classes, all of the students in my Spring 1996 Women's Studies Intro and Popular Entertainment classes, and Skip Lonas of Chattanooga Data Connection.

✧ *Laurel:* Robert Gilbert (for Timothy Leary and Chaos), Shauna Gilbert (for showing me how to be a grrrl), Jeff, Coby and Dean (for answering my questions), Mel, Caitlin and Wendy (for inspiration), and Westminster College (for Net access while traveling).

CONTENTS

CyborgCulture

Wired Women Hall of Fame

Outro

SURFERGRRRLS FAQ

Why did you write this book?

As of May 1996, the population of cyberspace is still overwhelmingly male. According to the latest numbers from CommerceNet Consortium and Nielsen Media Research:

> Males comprise 66 percent of users of the Internet. In addition, males tend to use the Internet with both greater frequency and duration than females, accounting for approximately 77 percent of the total usage. Males comprise 59 percent of the users of online services and are responsible for 63 percent of the total usage (http://www.commerce.net/information/surveys/execsum/exec_sum.html).

When users at .edu sites are removed from the Net census, the user ratio is more like 70 percent male to 30 percent female.

However, none of those figures tells us much about *how* women use the Net, and even less about how we are regarded in the cyberscape. Our goal is to demystify the Internet for women who are still squinchy or nervous about going online, to show them what is possible and to provide a mentoring resource for women who constantly find themselves helping other women get wired.

We wrote *SurferGrrrls* to show the world once and for all that women are a kicking, amazing, important part of Internet culture, not anomalies. We wrote it because women are using the Internet in personally and economically empowering ways, and their examples can inspire other women. And we wrote this book because even though women and girls from many walks of life are doing extremely fun, fabulous and useful stuff on the Internet, this myth still persists that the Net is a "guy thing" or a "geek thing" or a "white thing" or something only for the affluent, the businessman, or those interested only in the alt.sex newsgroup hierarchy.

You might notice as you browse through *SurferGrrrls* that we don't include many lists of Websites, URLs and the like. We decided not to do the typical Internet book thing because that kind of information becomes dated so quickly. Instead, we focus on telling you *how* to find what you want on the Net. We've also established a Website at http://www.sealpress.com/surfergrrrls/ which will feature updated hotlists and other features of interest to our readers. Visit soon!

Finally, so much of the way we think about the Internet has been determined by "manly" metaphors (the frontier, the highway) and by cyberpunk (we dig it, but it's not really a female-friendly vision in a lot of ways), that we decided it was time to take a look at the visions suggested by women's spaces on the Net, our participation in online culture and the sites and creations women offer to the developing Net at large.

We're not writing this book with the hopes that all men on the Net will magically disappear. We're not against men online, or against men, period. No matter what you've heard on the playground, that's not what feminism is about. Moreover, sexism on the Internet is no worse than it is anywhere else, and, thankfully, the number of cool, nice guys is at *least* equal to the number of jerks and trolls with hair-trigger keyboards and/or perpetual virtual hard-ons (um, actually those guys tend to talk mostly to one another, usually in alt.sex.whatever on Usenet). We've met some rad guys out there; on the other hand, we've also been involved in a few flame wars where we've been baited and attacked as "fucking feminists." We've also received some unwanted and crude solicitations and an occasional unwarranted "read the manual, you dumb bitch," but we prefer to look at these incidents as instructive. After all, it's good to know what folx really think of you, and the relative anonymity of the Internet inspires people to really let go and vent. Besides, sticks and stones may break your bones, but words you can *answer!* We're totally down with the geekgirl motto: "A keyboard is a greater equalizer than a Glock .45." What this means to us is that the Internet can be a powerful tool for communication and for dissemination of information that can help women and all peoples in the struggle for self-determination. The flip side of "divide and conquer" is, of course, "network and resist with every resource available to you."

The unprecedented thing about cyberspace is that it is a forum in which there is, theoretically, more than enough room for everybody. Women have to insist on and work for that reality, get technology in the hands of people who haven't had it before, and get our ideas, perspectives, art, priorities and information out there! Call us utopian, but the more the Net swells with the sound of many different voices, the more we'll all enjoy it and learn from it, and the more representative it'll be.

✧ What's with the "grrrl" thing?

✧ "Grrrl," a word coined by Bikini Kill singer and activist Kathleen Hanna, is a spontaneous young-feminist reclamation of the word "girl." It has proud analogies among many groups of women; in fact, "grrrl" was at least partially derived from a phrase of encouragement popularized by young American black women in the late 1980s: "You go, *guuuurlll!*" As we all know, when it is not being used to describe a woman under sixteen, the word "girl" often takes on pejorative, infantilizing overtones, suggesting silliness, weakness or insubstantiality.

"Grrrl" puts the growl back in our pussycat throats. "Grrrl" is intended to recall the naughty, confident and curious ten-year-olds we were before society made it clear it was time to stop being loud and playing with boys and concentrate on learning "to girl," that is, to be a proper lady so that boys would like us.

Riot Grrrl is a loosely affiliated group of young, generally punkish, take-no-prisoners feminists who publish zines, play in bands, make art, produce radio shows, maintain mailing lists, create Websites and sometimes just get together and talk about our lives and being women in contemporary society. "Grrrlishness" is at once cuddly and fierce, Hot-head Paisan *and* Hello Kitty, Lynda Barry's Marlys and Maybonne *and* Tank Girl, Susan Faludi *and* Winona LaDuke, Queen Latifah *and* Courtney Love!

We chose the title *SurferGrrrls* as a counter to the "nice girls don't hack around with computers" message that society (still!) sends out, despite the educational system's extensive lip service to getting girls involved with math and science. *SurferGrrrls* also acknowledges the great grrrl/girl presence already on the Net, from Stephanie Brail's *Digital Amazons* and Aliza Sherman's *Cybergrrl* Website to the searchable feminist database *Femina* and the Web zines *Foxy* and *Fat Girl*.

Moreover, we've coined a new grrrl-word, CyborGrrrl, in homage to the ways that feminist Donna Haraway, author of "A Cyborg Manifesto," prompts us to think about our online selves, the gendering of technology and our common cyberfuture. We'll talk about feminism and cyborgs in the CyborgCulture section of the book.

✧ **But doesn't that Beach Boys song "Surfer Girl" represent everything you oppose?**

Well, yeah. That's the idea behind culture-jamming the song and all those sixties beach movies and eighties surfpunk movies, and making a place for women in the cybersurfing metaphor. Surfer girls are all those chicks in bikinis who hang around on the beach and cheer and glom all over the surfer boys when they return from riding the big bad waves. Surfer *grrrls,* however, are us: the hot-chix, out-there, in the water, on the board, standin' up and gettin' wet. We are rad, we are bad, and we are on the boards (or modems) with the best of the boys. We *rock.* And we're not just surfer grrrls, we're *CyborGrrrls,* too. We actively negotiate what it means to be grrrls with computers . . . making the waves we surf. *SurferGrrrls'* theme song is the cover of "Surfer Girl" by Cub, a Canadian grrrl-pop band. You can find it on their first album, *Betti-Cola* (Mint Records).

✧ **So who are you, and what's your personal interest in this book?**

✧ *Crystal:* I started messing around with computers when I was in the seventh grade, way back in the disco era. Before school I used to hang out in the math room and play on the (get this) TRS-80 with 16K RAM and a cassette tape drive! Ahhh, 1979! One couldn't do much with that

TRS-80—write a few BASIC programs, play backgammon or blackjack—but I was hooked. Somehow I even talked my math teacher into letting me take the computer home on weekends. That winter my parents enrolled me in a Saturday morning computer class at the University of Tennessee at Chattanooga where I learned more BASIC and met my first mainframe. I learned a lot, but I was the only girl in both of those classes and felt really out of place, like a crasher in some sacred boy-space.

Crystal, age 4

Not only were most of the boys older than I was, but I wasn't into science fiction or role-playing games and had already manifested a real dislike for so-called progressive bands like Rush. I wasn't particularly interesting to boys, nor was I willing to suck up to them. A twelve-year-old girl, however smart or cool or interested, had no chance to participate fully in the overwhelmingly homosocial teen-boy would-be-hacker subculture of that time, nor was there anyplace else for her to go. *Blah.* So I spent a lot of time working alone at the terminals in the library, messing around with whatever interested or amused me.

✧ *Laurel:* I started messing with computers in junior high too, but didn't get serious about the whole thing until college. Today, my high school has a pretty impressive Web presence, and I feel lucky to have gotten the exposure to computers that I did, growing up in a small Utah town.

We learned BASIC, a programming language, in junior high. That "goto loop" was *sooo* endlessly fascinating. I mean, I could get the computer to talk to me; I could program it to have a conversation . . . granted, it had to be the same conversation over and over because I couldn't change the format or the machine would freak out. But I could teach it to interact on a really crude level. It was *interactive.* I noticed even then that the guys in the lab (and, it wasn't—oddly enough—all, or even mostly, guys in the computer labs in junior high) were trying to program shoot-em-up games while the girls were trying to make interactive games. Our assignment might have been to develop an educational game for younger kids; the guys would make "Asteroid Alphabet" while the girls would make "Bob Bunny Counts Carrots." It was my first introduction to the different ways gender impacts computer use.

✧ *Crystal:* By the time I got to high school, the culture-wide emphasis on computer literacy had emerged. We had a great computer lab full of Apple II+ machines, BASIC programming classes (but no Advanced Placement programming classes) and learned how to use word-processing programs. We had a lot of machines, but very little in the way of software and computer-savvy teachers (still a common problem in many schools), so there were limits to what we could do and explore. I was discouraged that even among my girl friends who dug computers (yes, finally!), crude role-playing games like Wizardry and Hitchhiker's Guide to the Galaxy were choice computer distractions.

I got my first computer—an Apple II+ with an ImageWriter printer—in tenth grade and started programming crude graphics and sound creations. I'll never forget pulling my first all-nighter, staying up to write a report on my beloved new machine, then waking up the house with curses and howls the millisecond after oh-so-geeked and exhausted me turned the computer off without saving the document! That's how I used my machine: I wanted to be able to write with it, make art with it. Because I sucked at math, I didn't fit into the "computer girl" stereotype of the time and there were no workshops or summer programs sponsored by defense industry research units designed around my interests or needs. My friend Beth also sucked at math, but she kept reaffirming her desire to be an engineer, so while she went off to learn FORTRAN and PASCAL, I kept lamely hacking around and giving my word processor a workout. By the time I graduated from high school, I was using my computer pretty much only for word processing.

It was the same story in college. Still, even though my computer remained a glorified word processor, I was turned on by the new Macintoshes popping up in friends' dorm rooms and labs. Around 1987 a friend bought an early IBM-PC clone and a modem (!) that he used to access the online service Prodigy. I was impressed, but didn't really foresee a day when I'd be able to afford to go online. I knew nothing about bulletin board systems (BBSs). They weren't a big thing in the South, and they certainly weren't a big thing among my artsy friends; we were into books, films and music. I hit bottom, in a manner of speaking, when I left my trusty, yet bulky Apple II+ at home during my senior year and, instead, bought an electric typewriter. It seems weird to me now, but at the time I even felt a little righteous about it. What *was* I thinking? I'm still not sure.

✧ *Laurel:* When I went to college, I got totally hooked on computers and discovered the world of cyberspace. The guy I was living with was really into computers, and it didn't take very long before I was lost in my own right in the late-night-online world of BBSs. I adopted the name "novice" because, well, I was one, and because when I had to make up my first alias, I had a "best novice debater" trophy on the wall in front of me. I had some (guy) friends who really pushed me along unknowingly . . . I was adamant about never, ever showing my ignorance in front of them. Early on, if one of them would start talking about computer stuff I didn't understand, I'd nod and go "uh-huh" and then figure out what they were talking about on my own. Not the easiest way to learn, for sure! These guys would be up until two, three in the

Laurel, age 4

morning doing "computer stuff," and I felt sort of left out. So finally, one boring afternoon, I sat down at *his* computer, fired up the communications program, dialed the number for my first BBS, and instantly became an addict. Soon, *I* was the one up until two or three in the morning. *I* was the one talking about people I'd never met as though they were my closest friends, and so on.

✧ *Crystal:* Even though it was woefully "antique," my Apple II+ got me through my masters program in popular culture studies and through the first year of my doctoral course work before it gave up the ghost. I turned it off one night after I finished writing a paper and it went into a coma. Using extreme measures, I managed to get it to power up a couple of times after that and was able to make hard copies of most of my writings, but its little power-pack was juiced out. *Sob. My baby!* Then I got a Mac LC II and a modem and discovered a whole new world. It was June 1992.

✧ *Laurel:* It wasn't until I got to graduate school in 1992 that I discovered the Internet. I knew more about computers than most people around me, so I started focusing on them. At first I had some . . . not problems, exactly, but a couple of male computer geeks in my department seemed to feel that because I wasn't as interested in the traditional canon of cyberpunk stuff as they were, I wasn't a *real* computer/ cyberspace geek.

✧ *Crystal:* I'd been reading here and there about the Internet, so I was totally geeked to get online. A friend loaned me her printout of that classic guide by Brendan Kehoe, *Zen and the Art of Internet.* After reading it and finally managing to log on to one of the university mainframes, I determinedly pestered a computer guru in one of the campus labs until he helped me. Within a couple of weeks of my first connection, I was fully functional . . . and totally addicted.

For a grrrl who'd grown up perversely thrilled by libraries and book and record/CD stores, the Internet (even then!) was absolutely mindblowing! And being able to access libraries around the world 24/7 was a grad student's dream come true. My experiences on the Net were totally in sync with a lot of the reading I was doing at the time: Foucault, Avital Ronell's *The Telephone Book,* Donna Haraway's "A Cyborg Manifesto," and *Mondo 2000.* Far freakin' out! Crystal was goooooonnnne, baby—gone through the mirror into the raging electron sea that birthed her e-alter ego, PopTart. Truly, I knew then how Batgirl must have felt the first time she zipped up her bitchin' Bat-boots and elbowed Robin out of her way! So from that point, I set about turning on all my friends, professors and students. In my Batgirl-as-Timothy Leary phase, I concentrated especially on my women friends, many of whom were technophobically hesitant at first, but who totally dug it after they made it over that initial hurdle.

✧ *Laurel:* It's kind of like a religious cult or the whole Deadhead thing. If you're already into computers and the Net, you know what I'm talking about. You've felt the quickening heartbeat at the sound of modems connecting. If you aren't yet into computers but want to be, you might feel poised on the edge of a community of cyborgs—half human, half machine—that constantly beep and buzz. Are they unfriendly, or are they just preoccupied? If you're not interested in computers and don't know what all the fuss is about, you might suspect (and rightfully so) that it's all a sick and twisted phenomenon, and that the masses of techno-geeks out there are totally brainwashed by being plugged in.

I've made it my mission in life (this stage of it, anyway) to get as many grrrls as possible using the Internet and thinking about how it can help them in whatever they do. My hands-down-most-fabulous experience has been getting my own mom wired. I left her alone with my computer and many pages of handwritten notes explaining how to get Netscape up and working, and when I came back . . . *bam!* I discovered my mother had fallen prey to the seductive whir of the hard drive and the glow of the monitor. *Sigh.* When I left her, she was unsure about the whole double-clicking business, and if the machine got a little too friendly with beeping or flashing lights she had to immediately take a smoking break on the porch to recover. But the last time I talked to her—and it was through e-mail—she had just discovered yet another fabulous Website and was sending me the address. Yup, my mom has joined the ranks of women enamored with the screen.

I feel almost perversely linked with the Net and computer stuff. Not only do I share a birthday with computer pioneer Admiral Grace Hopper—but I am exactly as old as the Internet. Well, kind of. We were both officially born in 1969.

✧ *Crystal:* Yeah, well I share a birthday with Jim Henson and F. Scott Fitzgerald. It's fitting: I'm just a wide-eyed cybermutant mutt given to wild mood swings! ;-) And I was in utero during the "Summer of Love."

Does all this help explain where we're coming from? Aw, enough background information! Turn the page, and start reading!

An Internet Glossary

for the Innocent and Eager

B efore we get started on our far-out tour of the *Net de la femme,* we have to all be speaking the same language. To help you get started, here's a basic list of terms we use throughout *SurferGrrrls* (and that you'll run into during your online jaunts). It can suck hanging out with a crowd that speaks some sort of "in language"—things get much easier as you learn the lingo. So, browse through this lighthearted romp of terms, concepts and definitions that we hope will make the cyberscape easier to navigate.

ARCHIE A software program that searches anonymous FTP sites for a particular file. The icon often has freckles and red hair. You need to know what you're looking for, and then tell Archie, who will search for it. *See also* FTP.

ARPANET (Advanced Research Projects Agency Network) The beginning of it all, the start of everything, the infant Internet. The U.S.

Department of Defense developed this network in the late 1960s in case the Russians attacked. They didn't, and the Net was born instead.

ASCII (pronounced "as-key") An acronym for American Standard Code for Information Interchange, a standard for computer representation of all letters, numbers, and symbols. Asking for an "ASCII file" is asking for simple type. There are 128 standard ASCII codes, that stand for upper- and lowercase letters, numbers, and symbols.

BACKBONE A high-speed line or series of connections that forms a major pathway for Internet traffic. The T3 line started in the early 1980s by the National Science Foundation is generally considered the Net backbone.

BANDWIDTH Though the word itself originally refered to the "umph" of a radio broadcasting signal, Net bandwidth is instead an amorphous concept of online space. Example of common usage: "That Website is such a waste of bandwidth!"

BAUD The baud rate of a modem is how many bits it can send or receive each second. Baud usually refers to the modem or translating hardware. A modem with a baud rate of 14.4 Kbps sends or receives 14,400 bits per second. *See also* Modem *and* BPS.

BBS (bulletin board system) A computerized meeting and announcement system where people can carry on discussions, exchange e-mail and make announcements to other users. Before the Internet caught on in the popular consciousness, BBSs were the "online world." There are thousands upon thousands of BBSs around the world, some of which are now also part of the Internet.

BINHEX (BINary HEXadecimal) A method for converting program or picture files into ASCII (text, or mimicking text) so they can be sent via e-mail. Electronic mail can only be sent as ASCII, but BinHex makes it possible for someone to send you a picture of their pet as an attachment.

BIT (Binary digIT) Basically a one or a zero. The smallest possible unit of computerized data; the entire electronic world can be reduced to the bits it is. Bandwidth and baud rate are measured in bits per second, or bps. *See also* Byte.

BITNET (Because It's Time NETwork) A network of educational sites separate from the Internet, although e-mail can be freely exchanged between the two. Listservs—or e-mail discussion groups—originated on BITNET. As the Internet grows, BITNET becomes smaller and smaller, and might eventually become subsumed by the Net itself. *See also* Listserv.

BOOKMARK To save the address of an exciting Web page so you can return to it at leisure. Most Web browsers have a built in bookmark feature.

BOT An abbreviation for "robot" usually used in IRC (Internet Relay Chat) to refer to what seems like a "real" person but is really a program. Bots can be "good," and welcome you to a channel, or they can be "bad bots" that send stupid, trite or nasty messages to everyone in IRC. Makers of Bad Bots are usually banned from IRC space. Don't make a Bad Bot.

BPS (bits-per-second) A measurement of how fast data can move across a network. A 28.8 Kbps modem sends and receives data at 28,800 bits per second.

BROWSER A software program that lets you view the sites out there on the Internet. The term usually refers to World Wide Web browsers, such as Netscape and Mosaic. Also sometimes called a "client program," to differentiate from the server software that stores or creates the information to look at with the browser.

BYTE (BinarY TErm) A set of bits that represents a single character in computer processing. There are eight bits in a byte, about a thousand bytes in a kilobyte, one million bytes in a megabyte, and so on, and so on. Data on the Web is measured in bytes; using a 28.8 Kbps modem, one megabyte takes five to ten minutes to download.

CHANNEL Because IRC (Internet Relay Chat) is so large and sprawling, people must create and join channels to talk to each other in small groups. Some channels are permanently available, while others are established temporarily for people to talk privately. *See also* IRC.

CLIENT A software program used to contact a server and get data from it. When you run software on your machine to retrieve e-mail, you are using an "e-mail client." Similarly, you need client software to "do" FTP, IRC or to surf the Web. Each client needs a server to interact with. It's a two way thang. *See also* Server.

CYBERSPACE The big bang, the whole enchilada, the "space" created by computer networks all over the world; William Gibson coined the term in his novel *Neuromancer,* and the world of computer networking picked it up and ran. It doesn't really refer to anything real or tangible, but everyone uses it as though it does.

DOMAIN NAME The name of an Internet site in words. Domain names always have at least two parts, usually three, separated by a "dot." The first part is specific and the last part is general; so in the domain name "Yahoo.com," "Yahoo" is the specific site and ".com" (pronounced "dot com" if you say it out loud) classifies it as a business site. The most common last parts are .edu (educational), .com (business), .org (nonprofit organization), and .mil (military site). Countries and states can have their own domain identifications, such as .uk (United Kingdom) or .de (Germany). *See also* IP number *and* URL.

DOWNLOAD To move files from a remote computer to your own, usually using file transfer protocol (FTP). *See also* FTP.

EFF (Electronic Frontier Foundation) Founded in 1990 by Grateful Dead lyricist John Perry Barlow, EFF is a nonprofit organization designed to ensure that the principles embodied in the Constitution and the Bill of Rights are protected as people use the Internet.

E-MAIL (electronic mail) Text messages sent from one person to another via a computer network. E-mail can also be sent to a large mailing list, which is called a listserv. E-mail doesn't have to be sent over the

Internet; if you and a friend work at Microsoft.com, you can send e-mail to your heart's delight and never use Internet bandwidth.

ENCRYPTION As e-mail (and other files) winds its way from you to your friends, anyone can grab it and read it. Encryption programs translate your messages to gibberish, which can be translated back by the receiver, keeping it private. *See also* PGP.

ETHERNET A common way of networking computers in a business, computer lab or classroom. Ethernet can handle about 10,000,000 bits per second and can be used with all types of computers.

FAQ (frequently asked questions) "Check the FAQ!!!" might very well be the most often screamed bit of advice in newsgroups and on listservs. FAQs are documents that list and answer the most common questions about a site or a topic. There are thousands of FAQs on thousands of subjects. FAQs are often collaborative in nature, written and added to by people who are tired of answering the same questions over and over again. Many listservs and newsgroups have FAQ-keepers who periodically post the FAQ to the group or maintain it on a Website.

FINGER An Internet software tool for finding people on other Internet sites. To "finger" someone is to find out if they are logged on at that particular moment or when they were last logged on. Saying "finger me tonight at eight" is not as obscene as it sounds. Some machines do not allow incoming "fingers." Too messy.

FLAME Noun: A message posted electronically with the intent of making people angry and starting a loud, obnoxious, ongoing argument, or "flame war." Verb: To post such a message. As nasty as it sounds, it's often pretty fun.

FTP (file transfer protocol) The most common and easiest way of moving files between Internet sites. FTP is a special way to log on to a remote machine in order to get or send files, pictures, movies, FAQs or programs. There are hundreds of "Anonymous FTP sites" on the Internet where you can log on anonymously and download programs, pictures or text . . . and fill up your hard drive rather quickly. As a noun, FTP refers to the transfer protocol, as a verb, to the moving of data, and as an adjective to a type of site on the Internet.

GATEWAY A machine that translates between two different networks. For example, America Online (AOL) is not, technically speaking, hooked up to the Internet proper, but it serves as a gateway for AOL users to access the Net. (Gateway is also a brand name for a certain bovine-spotted brand of computer. Moo . . .)

GOPHER Not just a fuzzy animal , Gopher refers to both the method and the programs used to find material on the Internet by accessing menus of folders and files. Although the World Wide Web is, in theory, a very similar service, Gopher clients are still popular and useful. The English Server at Carnegie-Mellon University, for example, is a huge database of articles and information available via Gopher.

Pointers to Internet Resources

Often, the best place to go for online information is online. Here are some of the cornerstones of "Internet How-To's."

NEW INTERNET USER FAQ
Frequently asked questions (and answers!) for new Internet users.
http://www.cis.ohio-state.edu/htbin/rfc/rfc1206.html

EXPERIENCED INTERNET USER FAQ
Frequently asked questions for the Internet user who is ready for more detailed information.
http://www.cis.ohio-state.edu/htbin/rfc/rfc1207.html

THE HITCHHIKER'S GUIDE TO THE INTERNET
The 1989 text by E. Krol: A classic.
http://www.cis.ohio-state.edu/htbin/rfc/rfc1118.html

ZEN AND THE ART OF THE INTERNET
Brendan P. Kehoe's 1992 classic Net guide is available online.
http:;//www.itec.suny.edu/SUNY/DOC/internet/zen.html

BIG DUMMY'S GUIDE TO THE INTERNET OR EFF'S GUIDE TO THE INTERNET
Though we usually don't go for anything that assumes we're a dummy, this was renamed "EFF's Guide to the Internet" in 1994.
http://alpha.acast.nova.edu:80/bigdummy/

GLOBAL VILLAGE TOUR OF THE INTERNET
A friendly site, the Global Village Tour is designed for the first-time Internet user.
http://www.globalcenter.net/gcweb/tour.html

BEGINNER'S LUCK
A list of helpful resources for the beginning Internet User.
http://www.execpc.com/~wmhogg/beginner.html

GETTING STARTED ON THE INTERNET
Answers why get online and how to proceed once you're there.
http://www.portinfo.com/faq/

HOP AND STICKY'S GUIDE TO THE INTERNET
A fun and useful place to start surfing.
http://www.ccnet.com/~yuval/hopstick.html

HACK The geekiest verb in the English language. In spite of its bad rep, "hack" simply means to playfully/obsessively attack a problem, machine or structure, learn by it and share what you learn. You can hack a building or your own brain the same way you can hack a password. One who hacks is, of course, a hacker.

HOMEPAGE The first document you encounter upon visiting a Website, usually with links to other pages within the same site.

HOST Any computer on a network that is available for other computers to use . . . a big-sister sort of thing. An Internet host machine often provides a variety of services—from World Wide Web access to e-mail— to a gaggle of other computers. Hosts can also be the main machine in a small network of terminals.

HOT JAVA The original World Wide Web browser that can read and interpret the Java programming language, allowing animation and interactive presentations—called applets—on Web pages. *See also* Java.

HTML (hypertext markup language) How the Web was won. HTML is the coding language used to create homepages for viewing using a World Wide Web browser. HTML is not a programming language; rather, it is a specific way of coding text so that a browser can "read" it, format it, create links from it and make it pretty. *See also* Homepage.

HTTP (hypertext transfer protocol) The way documents written with HTML get moved from one Internet site to another. HTTP is the most common and important protocol used for "surfing" the World Wide Web; Web browsers such as Netscape and Mosaic are clients that use HTTP to gather information.

HYPERTEXT Generally, any text that contains "links" to other documents, or other parts of the same document. Hypertext is interactive; you can "jump" to another Web page or site by clicking on highlighted text. But hyptertext isn't just the Web: you are also navigating hypertext when you use those funky kiosks at the mall to find the computer store.

INTERNET The massive collection of networks that use TCP/IP—the underlying standards that define the Internet—and that evolved from the ARPANet. The word "internet" can also be used to refer simply to any computers hooked together. But *the* Internet . . . well, that's another story. *See also* TCP/IP.

IP NUMBER The "dotted quad" given by an Internet service provider (ISP) to identify a machine on the Internet, for example, 129.1.2.2. *See also* Domain name.

IRC (Internet Relay Chat) If MUDs and MOOs are the heroin of Internet addiction, IRC is the downward spiral. IRC is a huge (and we mean huge) multi-user live chat network. There are IRC servers around the world to which you can connect your client IRC program; join or create a "channel" and chat away madly until the early morning hours. Channels can be public or private, and private messages can be sent. There *are* twelve-step programs.

ISDN (Integrated Services Digital Network) One of the newest and fastest ways to move data over existing phone lines. With a special ISDN modem and a connection hooked up by your local phone company, transmission speeds up to 128,000 bps can be achieved. ISDN makes "double connections" possible, i.e. you can talk on the phone *while* connected to your ISP. Information overload!

ISP (Internet service provider) The company that provides you with Internet access. An ISP can be large or small, local or national. Most offer PPP or SLIP accounts for either a monthly flat fee, a charge per hour, or a combination of both. *See also* PPP *and* SLIP.

JAVA A programming language similar to C++ that allows users to make animated icons, interactive presentations and other really fun stuff on Websites. A browser that supports Java "applets"—such as Netscape 2.0 or Hot Java—is necessary to see them in action. *See also* Hot Java.

LAN (local area network) A computer network in a relatively limited area, such as a building, lab, classroom or office.

LISTSERV A basic e-mail list. When you join a listserv, you get all the e-mail generated by the other listserv members, and you (supposedly) write back to the entire mailing list. Listservs originated on BITNET as an educational resource. Now, there are listservs on every conceivable topic from horses to politics, from queer theory to kite flying.

LURKER One who lurks. Someone who hangs out in a Net space but doesn't participate. People lurk on newsgroups and listservs by reading them but never responding, and in IRC by joining a channel but never typing anything. Usually, lurking is really frowned upon in IRC, but most listservs and newsgroups have a lot of lurkers.

MOO (MUD, object-oriented) One of several kinds of multiuser text-based role-playing environments played over a computer network.

MUD (multiuser dungeon or dimension) *The* hard-core Internet environment. If you or someone you know begins using the word "MUD" in conversation with a straight face, seek help immediately. A multiuser simulation environment, very Dungeons & Dragons-esque, but played by typing over a computer network. Some are for fun and games, while others are used for serious research, development or education. A significant part of MUDs is the ability to create "objects" that can be interacted with by other users, even if the creator is not there. This creates a text-based, virtual world that can be very addictive and amazingly fun.

MODEM (MOdulator + DEModulator) This all-important device attaches to your home computer and to your phone line, providing access to computer networks and the Internet by converting data to a form usable in telephone transmissions. A little slice of hardware heaven.

MOSAIC The first graphical World Wide Web browser available for the Macintosh, Windows and UNIX, all with the same interface. Mosaic triggered the popularity of the Web, and the basics of this nifty little program are the basis for nearly all popular Web browsers, such as Netscape.

NETSCAPE The most popular Web browser. Developed by Marc Andreessen (also the creator of Mosaic), Netscape is available for free use to anyone at an educational or government institution, and supports many advanced HTML features.

NEWSGROUPS Discussion groups on Usenet. Newsgroup names follow a basic, hierarchical form, such as alt.food.coffee or soc.women. scientists, and can be viewed with a news reader client program or through UNIX commands. Also called Usenet groups or Usenet news. *See also* Usenet.

NODE Any computer connected to a network.

PACKET A chunk of data on the Internet. All the data coming out of one machine headed to another is broken up into packets, each of which has the address of where it's going and where it came from. This allows data to travel to and from all the different machines on the Internet without bogging down any one line with any one group of information. *See also* Router.

PGP (Pretty Good Privacy) A free encryption software program developed by Philip Zimmermann in 1991. Because encrypting electronic communication is illegal in many countries, Mr. Zimmermann had to wage a lengthy legal battle after developing the software and making it available on a world-wide computer network. *See also* Encryption.

PLUG-IN A helper application available for Netscape (or any other graphical Web browser) to view multimedia files. Plug-ins are available for video (Macromedia's Director plug-in), real-time audio (Real Audio's plug-in), VRML and many other file types.

POP This abbreviation has two, unrelated meanings. (1) "point of presence," which is a location a network can be connected to; (2) "post office protocol," or the way in which an e-mail client gets mail from a server. If you have a PPP or SLIP account with an Internet service provider (ISP), you also have a POP account that arranges e-mail transfers between your machine and the rest of the Internet.

POST Noun: A message sent to a newsgroup or listserv that everyone can read. Verb: To compose and send such a message.

PPP (point to point protocol) The fastest, easiest and most common way a home computer makes a TCP/IP connection with a modem and regular phone line to the Internet. You must have either a PPP or a SLIP connection to use client software with a modem over a phone line. *See also* SLIP *and* TCP/IP.

PROTOCOL A set of rules or standards that allows computers to communicate, regardless of the hardware (Macintosh or PC), operating system (UNIX or Windows 95) or software (different e-mail clients).

ROUTER A computer or software program that handles the connection between networks on the Internet. The only thing routers have to do is make sure packets get to their destination address. *See also* Packet.

SEARCH ENGINE Any one of many databases of thousands of Web pages available for online keyword searches. You provide key words and the search engine returns related Websites . . . often thousands of them. Altavista (http://www.altavista.digital.com) is an extensive and popular search engine.

SERVER A computer or software package that provides service to "clients" on other computers. A computer can be a server for one service—as in "the big computer in the back is our World Wide Web server"—or, through administrative software, allow access by different clients—as in "what kind of IRC server software do you use on that big computer there?" *See also* Client.

SHAREWARE Unlike software you buy in a store, shareware has a "try before you buy" policy. You download shareware and try it for a short period; if you don't like it, you erase it. If you like it, you send the author a small payment and receive documentation and upgrading information in return.

SLIP (serial line Internet protocol) The original standard for hooking up a TCP/IP connection using a modem and a phone line. As PPP becomes more popular, SLIP is being phased out. *See also* PPP *and* TCP/IP.

SPAM Noun: Electronic "junk" mail that is trivial, off-the-point, blatantly commercial, annoying or a flame. Verb: to send such e-mail. You might hear someone brag "I spammed 100 newsgroups with my resumé," or complain "This list is *sooooo* full of spam lately. Can we get on with it?"

SYSOP (system operator) The person in charge of a BBS or Web server. Often, people say "Webmaster" and mean the same thing.

T1 The fastest, most common way to connect large networks to the Internet. Still not fast enough for full-screen, full-motion video, a T1 connection can nonetheless move data at 1,544,000 bits per second, or a megabyte in just under ten seconds. Pretty darn fast.

T3 A leased-line connection capable of carrying data at 45,000,000 bits per second. The Mother of all Internet lines, capable of transmitting full-screen, full-motion video. Fast, fast, *fast*.

TCP/IP (transmission control protocol/Internet protocol) The standards that underlie the way information travels on the Internet. Originally designed for UNIX, TCP/IP software is now available for almost every operating system.

TELNET The command and software used to log in to one Internet site from another. When you "telnet" to another site, you find yourself conveniently at the login prompt of that system.

TERMINAL The basic hardware needed to log in to a network: usually only a keyboard, a monitor, and some kind of wiring. Terminal emulators are software programs that make a home computer *pretend* to be a terminal, thus allowing it to log in to another machine and give commands from your remote location.

TERMINAL SERVER The machine whose job it is to answer the phones, working between the modems and the server or host machine.

TROLL Nickname for anyone on the Internet who spams consistently, makes inappropriate advances and comments, starts flame wars indis-

criminately and is an all around Net loser. Don't be a troll. *See also*
Spam *and* Flame.

UNDERNET A major IRC server, sometimes referred to as an IRC space
all its own. Undernet can be reached by hooking up to server
us.undernet.org in the United States, or uk.undernet.org in Europe. Although saying "meet me in undernet" sounds much more dark and
mysterious than "meet me in IRC," the two are similar.

UNIX A computer operating system, with built-in TCP/IP networking
capabilities, but without the friendly "graphical user interface" of
Macintosh and Windows. Real geeks speak fluent UNIX.

URL (uniform resource locator) An address of a document on the World
Wide Web. When you type in the URL of a Website into a Web browser,
the browser software knows where to go and what to do once it gets
there. An *http://* URL tells the browser to treat the site as a HTML
homepage; *mailto://* tells the browser to send a piece of mail, and *ftp:/
/* tells it to expect to retrieve a file.

USENET A rather anarchistic-seeming global network of public discussion groups called newsgroups, or Usenet news.

VERONICA (very easy rodent-oriented Netwide index to computerized archives) Whew! As a partner to Archie, Veronica is a constantly
updated database of the names of almost every menu item in all of
Gopher-space. *See also* Archie.

VRML (virtual reality markup language) Similar to HTML, VRML allows a specialized Web browser to navigate in 3-D space. Instead of
looking at a "page," you float or walk through a "room" (or any other
space) by clicking the mouse where you want to go next. Runs slowly
on even 28.8 Kbps modems.

WAIS (wide area information server) A commercial software package
that indexes information on the Internet and makes it available for
Internet-wide searches. An important difference between WAIS and
other search engines is that WAIS can pick out the "important stuff"

and then go find more stuff like it, insuring that all the stuff you get is the same relative stuff. It manages stuff well.

WAN (wide area network) A network of computers that covers an area bigger than a campus or single building.

WAREZ Illegal or pirated software traded on the Internet. Not a really common item, but sometimes prepubescent boyz throw around the term to show they're hot stuff, as in, "Pst, ne1 out there have warez 2 trade???!!!???"

WWW (World Wide Web) In simplest terms, WWW is a hypertext interface for the Internet that allows you to navigate it by pointing at and clicking on graphics and text. In looser terms, it's the "universe" of multimedia sites on the Net made up of hyperlinked texts, graphics and sounds that you access with a browser.

History

A BRIEF HISTORY OF

THE INTERNET

Though the Net didn't splash into the mainstream until the early nineties, it's been around for roughly twenty-five years. For over a decade, the Internet was a hangout reserved for only the highest breed of computer geek. Access was limited to a select few until the mid-1980s; the first freenet was developed in 1986, and it wasn't until 1988 that access was offered to anyone at an American educational, military or government institution (not just to computer scientists or electrical engineers). The first commercial provider (world.std.com) offered access-for-cash in 1990, and in 1993 and 1994, the World Wide Web and Mosaic (the first graphical Web browser) caused Net growth to explode at the rate of almost 350,000 percent (yes, almost *three hundred and fifty thousand percent!*) annually—nothing short of phenomenal.

The *early* history of the Internet actually goes back to the mid-1950s and the development of the Cold War, when the U.S. Department of Defense began planning a computer network that would be indestructible in case of nuclear attack. Such a network would have no central authority, and information would travel from one point to another along random paths—that is, if one path was destroyed, the data would find another route to get to its destination.

Thus, the Internet—or ARPANet as it was named—was born. ARPA (Advanced Research Projects Agency) had in mind a decentralized computer network since 1957, when the USSR launched Sputnik and the Cold War mentality took over. The agency started official research on a "cooperative network of time-sharing computers" in 1965, and four years later, the infant Internet was developed, hooking up four American universities—three in California and the University of Utah.

The baby Net instantly became a dedicated, federally funded, high-speed, electronic post-office. Seems that most people, when it came right down to it, were more interested in how fabulously *fun* this new technology was, and were not really worried about a sudden nuclear attack. For example, one of the first mailing lists was for . . . science fiction fans. So much for national security secrets.

The Internet grew, not because the United States was scared of the Soviets, but because a plethora of computer geeks had technology and time on their hands, and a vision of what a truly worldwide network could—and would—be. Almost instantly, the Net took on the personality of the people using it and began to mirror the development of the culture surrounding it. In short, the Net (growing up in the 1970s) is a Generation X-er. The development of the Internet has consistently followed the development of the generation that is just coming out of college to take—or reject—its place in the world.

As the twentysomethings hit colleges and universities, the young-adult Internet hit campuses, too. It's only in the last couple of years that corporations and businesses all over the world have wanted—often demanded!—both a Web presence and employees who are Net-savvy. And these jobs are often being filled by the Net's age-peers: recent college graduates.

We've all had too much of smug, mediaoid baby-boomers who make their sorid living stereotyping Generation X-ers as numb, dumb and toxic to the very fiber of civilization. We—your friendly Gen-X authors—think we will be vindicated by historians of the not-too-distant future who will more fully appreciate us as the first adult population to grow up thinking hypertextually (Sesame Street as pre-MTV in its three-minute structure). Pucker up and kiss us: We're postmodern, and the

The WELL

The WELL. You may have heard of it and are wondering what's up with this intriguingly-named service? Isn't it a California thang? A hardcore, cyberpunk thang? A new-wave *granola* thang? Well, here's the info to make an informed decision on whether or not the WELL is right for you.

Established in 1985, the Whole Earth 'Lectronic Link began as an offshoot of Stewart Brand's *Whole Earth Catalog* and is still considered one of the primary Internet hot spots for virtual hanging, intellectual cybercommunities, cutting-edge politics and the like. A decade of growth (in 1994, Rockport Shoes cofounder Bruce Katz caused quite a stir by purchasing the WELL) has done good things for this Internet service provider, and it now offers dial-up PPP access in many U.S. cities and abroad (in fact, over half the users on the WELL are from outside California). The WELL offers over 260 conferences on subjects ranging from art to parenting to spirituality. The conference Women on the WELL (WOW) covers any topic under the sun, all with a sort of *femme*-grrrl slant.

Of eleven thousand total users, approximately 20 percent are female. The WELL is for the newbies among us, too; included with your membership is the Whole Works Internet Toolkit, which walks all new users through the fine art of negotiating a PPP connection and setting up graphical software.

Comparatively speaking, the WELL is not the cheapest, but it is reasonably priced; service starts at $15 a month, with a charge of $2.50 per hour for any hours over five. If you're looking for a secondary account to telnet in to, the $15 monthly charge covers unlimited telnet and FTP access (save that cash, and have yourname@well.com as a cool secondary e-mail address, besides!).

If you're needing a Net fix and the WELL sounds intriguing, they can be reached at (800) 935-5885. Or better yet, check 'em out at http://www.well.com/ and poke around a bit. Even if you don't choose the WELL as your ISP, you'll find a lot of entertaining things at their Website, including the homepage of Electronic Frontier Foundation's John Perry Barlow.

Net is, too. We were both brought up on a steady diet of intertextuality, irony, self-reflexivity, interactivity, diversity, tribalism and autobiography.

The future will also bring a longer view of the (at present rather short) history of "nostalgia culture," especially in the United States. On one level—we'll call it the hypercommodified VH-1 level—to be under thirty-five and listen to only the Beatles, obsess over Kerouac, wear anything tie-dyed or even think about buying tickets to a Sex Pistols reunion tour screams of zombified cultural necrophilia. On another level—best exemplified by "sampling" both popular and obscure sounds or images in various media—nostalgia culture can also be about coercing collisions of past and present, time travel and consciousness poaching as stylistic appropriation as consciousness poaching, and that's way, way gone. Thinking hypertextually; it's fun.

In lieu of conclusion here, ponder this perfect little Zenternet nostalgia koan (we know you know the tune):

> "Conjunction junction, what's your function?
> I'm gonna get you there if you're very careful."
> (Bob Dorough, American Broadcasting Company Music, Inc., 1973)

A lot of sites on the World Wide Web discuss the history of the Net (we love that self-reflexivity . . . it's like having a TV screen on your back that plays your childhood movies), and quite a few real-world books and articles explore its history as well. But by far one of the more interesting, informative and downright extensive timelines is Hobbes' Internet Timeline (http://offworld.wwa.com/timeline.html). If our simple timeline here piques your interest in what the Net was doing when you were in second grade or when you turned sixteen, check out this site. Meanwhile, sit back and relax; we're about to take a trip down the Internet's memory lane.

1969

In the throes of the Cold War, ARPANet is established by the U.S. Department of Defense. The goal: to develop a communications network the USSR can't destroy or spy on. The first node is built at University of California, Los Angeles (UCLA), followed by Stanford Research Institute (SRI), University of California, Santa Barbara (UCSB), and the University of Utah.

1970

ALOHANet is developed at University of Hawaii.

1971

The number of nodes jumps to fifteen: UCLA, SRI, UCSB, University of Utah, Bolt Beranek & Newman (BBN), Massachusetts Institute of Technology (MIT), the RAND nonprofit institution, System Development Corporation (SDC), Harvard, Lincoln Lab, Stanford University, University of Illinois (UIU), Case Western Reserve University (CWRU), Carnegie Mellon University (CMU), and National Aeronautics and Space Administration (NASA)/Ames.

1973

The first international connections to ARPANet are established at University College of London (England) and the Royal Radar Establishment (Norway).

1976

Elizabeth, queen of the United Kingdom, sends e-mail.

1977

THEORYNet is created at University of Wisconsin for researchers in computer science.

1979

Usenet newsgroups are established, and the first MUD (multi-user dungeon) is developed at the University of Essex.

1981

BITNET ("Because It's Time NETwork") is established, providing e-mail and listserv servers.

1982

Prototype Internet is in place, with two hundred computers scattered nationwide. TCP/IP is established as the accepted protocol for handling data across the Internet.

1983

All military computers hook up, bringing the total number of machines to 562; ARPANet splits into ARPANet and MILNet. The name server developed at the University of Wisconsin, makes it unnecessary for users to know the exact IP number for an Internet site.

1984

William Gibson writes *Neuromancer* and coins the word "cyberspace." The Japan UNIX Network (JUNET) is established.

1985

The National Science Foundation hooks up to the Net and offers CSNet for computer science students, and the WELL (Whole Earth 'Lectronic Link)—a bulletin board system (BBS) and future Net service—is established by *Whole Earth Catalog* founder Stewart Brand in the Bay Area.

1986

NSFNET, with a backbone speed of 56 Kbps, is created by the National Science Foundation to connect supercomputer sites around the country, as well as research sites and schools near them.

1988

The NSF funds a new high-speed wide area network (WAN) and offers the use of the network to anyone with educational, academic or governmental affiliation. Total number of machines hooked up is over twenty-eight thousand. CERFnet (California Education and Research Federation Network) is founded, and the "Internet Worm"—a network computer virus—burrows through the Net.

1989

The number of computers hooked up to the Internet more than doubles to over eighty thousand, and AARNET (Australian Academic Research Network) is introduced.

1990

ARPANet is dismantled, and the Electronic Frontier Foundation (EFF) is formed to protect privacy, free expression and access to online information. Philip Zimmerman develops the popular encryption software PGP (Pretty Good Privacy). The number of computers more than triples to 290,000 machines, and the first commercial dial-up service is offered (world.std.com). The NSFNET backbone is upgraded to a T3 line, creating the backbone of the Internet as we know it today.

1992

The World Wide Web server is released by the Civil Engineering Research Network (CERN), making the development of Websites possible. Your authors go online.

1993

U.S. White House hooks up at http://www.whitehouse.gov/. Web searchers are developed (such as WebCrawler), Internet Talk Radio begins broadcasting and Mosaic is introduced as the first graphical interface Web browser, causing the WWW to expand by 341,634 percent.

1994

The twenty-fifth anniversary of the Internet is celebrated and the first commercial "spam" (junk mail sent to thousands of users) is endured by Net citizens. Estimates place the number of Internet users at over thirty million people and connected machines at 2.25 million. Netscape surpasses Mosaic as the graphical Web browser of choice.

1995

The National Science Foundation ceases to fund the backbone network, and the Internet is turned over to the commercial realm. CompuServe, America Online and Prodigy offer Internet access. Cyberporn creates major media hoopla and the U.S. Congress considers the Communications Decency Act. The Internet faces major commercialization as Web browsers become capable of multimedia and some Websites acquire commercial sponsorship. International service providers (such as CompuServe) face international censorship issues when the German government demands the removal of "obscene" newsgroups from the newsfeed.

Telecommunications Act of 1996 becomes law. This act includes
controversial "decency" provisions currently being contested in
Federal courts. "A Day in the Life of Cyberspace" is published online
at http://www.1010.org/.

PUTTING THE WOMEN BACK IN

COMPUTER SCIENCE HISTORY

The world of computing has always pretty much been the territory of men, right? Code cowboys have a lot in common with the men who used to jump on their horses and ride off into the purple sage with only a tin cup and a blanket; late nights with the monitor are cold and lonely. Hacking is hard on the back. Sometimes, the howling of wolves is echoed in the whir of the hard drive. Women don't understand. Women want warm, soft, touchy-feely sorts of interaction with other real-live human beings, not us-against-the-machine, late-night show-downs on the final frontier of technology. Women . . .

Argh! Can we rewind for a second, here?

Unfortunately, some stereotypes are more accepted and normalized than we like to admit. Even though women can "wear the virtual pants," gender stereotypes are alive and kicking, and are still powerful forces in shaping who we are in this digital world. Pick up any recent popular magazine, and the experts will tell you: There are so few women involved in technology and/or computers as to be nonexistent. *They*

Geekboys + CYBERMOGULS

It would be unfair, it would be *sexist* of us to ignore or "forget" the influence of nearly one-half of the world's population simply because of their gender. We wouldn't *dare*.

So here it is, grrrls, our top-ten list of influential men in computer science. We're sure there are other, brilliant males out there who have made a significant contribution to information technology, we just didn't have time to research—to tease out of the history books—their lives, their experience.

We're pretty sure someone, somewhere else, will do that job for us.

Marc Andreessen At the oh-so-young age of twenty two, lil' Marc cofounded Netscape Communications. While still in college, he loosed the Web browser Mosaic on us all, and the Web became a world wide phenomenon.

Tim Berners-Lee Thank this guy for developing many of the basic standards for online documents (such as HTML and HTTP) that are read by browsers to make up the World Wide Web.

Bill Gates Okay, okay. Microsoft guru Gates knows what people want. With MS-DOS and Windows to his credit, his marketing savvy can't be challenged, and Windows 95 makes some wonder if he understands the appeal of the Macintosh a little *too* well . . . for someone not working with Macintosh. He's been around since the mid-70s, and will probably be an influential type for a long time to come.

Steve Jobs Cofounder, with Steve "Mr. Mac" Wozniak, of *Apple Computer,* Mr. Jobs helped bring forth the magic Macintosh and its massive impact on computer science. The Mac ruled; Job's ill-fated NeXT machine didn't. Now Jobs is focusing on WebObjects, a product that allows a Web server to repackage data into an HTML document.

Thomas Kurtz Way back in the 1960s, Kurtz—with his pal, John Kemeny— ➡

say that the Internet—and computer technology in general—has always been a guy place and that women are unused to this virtual world. They're intimidated by it. Women must either be protected . . . or learn to "play like the boys." The few women who dare to mosey on out to the frontier of the Net must squelch their womanly nature and Take It Like a Man. Gulp.

Even some women seem to believe this. Witness this description of the Internet in J. C. Hertz's book *Surfing the Internet: A Nethead's Adventures On-Line* (Little, Brown & Company, 1995):

Not too many women in these here parts, scant discussion of philosophy and impressionist paintings, and *no* tea sandwiches. Rather, much of the Net exudes a ballistic ambiance seldom found outside post-apocalyptic splatterpunk video games. Someone should nail up a sign: "Now entering the Net. Welcome to Boyland. Don't mind the bodily fluids and cartoon-caliber violence. And if you can't take someone ripping your arm off and beating you with the bloody stump, go back to where you came from, girlie."

Excuse me? *Girlie?* Did she call us *girlie?* That's *grrrlie* to you, miss, with a *grrrowlll* that'll match any beating with a bloody stump. As if we or any other women we know regularly have tea sandwiches. *Humph.* Either we don't know the same women or we don't know the same Internet. The Net we know and love hasn't ever really resembled any Boyland we've imagined, and we've been in some pretty rough corners of virtual saloons.

In fact, maybe the whole idea of the Internet as "the final frontier" is set up around this little piece of (fabricated) history. Like any frontier, the Internet must be tamed and subdued before the women and children are allowed in. It's gotta be civilized; we gotta take out all the bloody stumps and the bad words before the innocents can come in and see what a fabulous new land our brave men have created and conquered. At least, that's *one* way to understand our mythical American frontier, and certainly the way the Net is categorized in the rhetoric surrounding the Telecommunications Decency Act of 1996.

Except everyone seems to have forgotten something here. This ain't no frontier, folks—we're making it up as we go along, not discovering something that was already there—and women have been involved in the process since the first modem made the little screeching sound that announced the virtual world. Even if you accept the frontier metaphor, computer technology is a frontier with the Amazons right up front, helping to break a trail for other women (and men) to follow. And it's not just the Internet that has a posse of CyborGrrrls as major contributors; women have been involved in the birth of the computer age since day one.

Ahhh . . . day one.

More Geekboys + CYBERMOGULS...

developed the BASIC programming language. Anyone who has a dark past in computing remembers the "goto" command. Enough said.

Drew Major Just out of college in 1980, Mr. Major accepted a consulting job with Novell Networks and stayed fifteen years. When the network operating system NetWare 3.0 shipped in 1989, Major was *the* major influence behind the most important upgrades. Networking is his biz.

Dennis Ritchie Although back in 1969 he promised the financial backers of his project a great, new word processor, Mr. Ritchie delivered the UNIX operating system, instead. Not satisfied with just UNIX (perhaps the most influential operating system of all), a few years later, Ritchie offered up the C programming language and compiler, too.

Bjarne Stroustrup This Scandinavian inventor offered up the programming language of Windows enthusiasts: C++, and started the object-oriented programming revolution.

Alan Turing Persecuted by the Brits for his homosexuality, "the founder of computer science" developed the concept of the "Turing Machine," which led to the first digital computer. See the Alan Turing Website at the Virtual Museum of Computing: http://info.ox.ac.uk/~wadh0249/Turing.html.

John Warnock Adobe Systems cofounder Warnock looks forward to the day when all platforms share a graphics and documents standard; for example, Adobe Acrobat documents can be read on any platform using free Acrobat Reader software. No more of this "I have a Mac, you a PC, what shall we *dooo!?*" whining.

Once upon a time, a long time ago, a little girl named Ada was born. Okay, perhaps it wasn't that long ago, just the beginning of the nineteenth century. And technically her name was

What Do Women Want Online?

Ask Rosalind Resnick (http://www.netcreations.com/rosalind/index.html), a veteran technology and business writer and online service consultant. She also hosts the NetGirl forum on America Online and e-publishes *Interactive Publishing Report*, a biweekly e-letter about the state of online newspaper and magazine publishing. In 1995 she conducted a major survey, sponsored by Apple Computer, to determine why women go online and what they want once they get there. For a big wad of cash you can order a complete copy of the report from the *IPR* Website, but here are some of her conclusions, for free!

- Most women are convinced to get online by friends or colleagues.
- On women's online agendas, communication with others ranks first (e-mail, posting to newsgroups or forums).
- Online shopping ranks dead last. Sixty-four percent of those surveyed had never bought a service or product online.
- Time and money are women's biggest barriers to getting online.
- Once they go online, women tend to log in frequently.
- Women *do* want virtual communities of their own.
- Most women value politeness and good manners online, and many favor policies against flaming.

Augusta, not Ada, but the gist is that this chick was born. What makes Ada's "once upon a time" important to our "once upon a time" is that this grrrl really set the computer revolution on its feet. She was Augusta Ada Byron.

Lord Byron (the famous English poet) married the intellectual but worldly Anne Isabella Milbanke in early 1815, and a respectable ten months later, Augusta Ada was born. Her parents split up soon after—often, being married to a romantic poet with a bad reputation makes that particular move seem inevitable—and Ada's mum was so disturbed by her association with the wicked poet, she encouraged little Ada to study mathematics (instead of poetry, you see). Perhaps encouraged isn't quite strong enough. Mama Anne Isabella firmly believed that ten-plus hours of arithmetic tutoring was *good* for the constitution of a five-year-old child. Ada had a fondness in childhood for ice skating and riding her pony, but a brief entry in the child's journal shows the folly of such wishes: "I was rather foolish in saying that I did not like arithmetic and to learn figures, when I did—I was not thinking quite what I was about. The sums can be done better, if I tried, than they are."

Little Ada was on *quite* a brainy-princess training course.

By the time Ada was a lovely young lady of seventeen, she had spent many years as an invalid because of a nasty attack of the measles. All this lying around in bed had done two things for our heroine. First, it gave Ada plenty of time to think about all the mathematical problems her mother and tutors assigned to her. During her years of ill health, Ada had even "invented" a flying machine of her own, apparently to spirit her away to sunnier locations. Second—of course—her years as a frail young thing had lent her the fair skin, large eyes, petite frame and long, dark locks that every princess needs. These two advantages led to two very separate relationships in Ada's adult life. Her beauty snagged her the hand of William, Lord King and Earl of Lovelace, which made Ada the Countess of Lovelace.

That wasn't the important happily-ever-after relationship for our heroine, though.

Ada also hooked up with Charles Babbage, one of the more famous of the obscure geniuses of the nineteenth century and a full twenty-five years older than Ada. What Babbage and Ada shared, however, was nothing that would mar our heroine's lily-white reputation or make her devoted husband jealous and angry. Babbage was in the process of creating the "analytical engine," and Ada was fascinated! Enamored! Titillated! Thrilled! Not by Babbage—none of that Barbara Cartland stuff here—but by *the first computer.*

In 1842, a write-up of Babbage's early analytical engine by a French writer named Menabrea appeared in a Swiss journal. Ada translated the article from French and showed her notes to Babbage, who was so impressed with her translation that he asked her to continue her notes on the engine, which she did. Eventually, the "notes" Ada was keeping turned into quite an important pile of papers in its own right and went on to describe theoretically the impact such a contraption as the analytical engine might have on humanity. For example, the engine itself was designed to sort of simply count things that were already there, but by improving upon the design a little bit and thinking ahead to what might be, Ada proposed a way that the engine might be used to create music (she was also really into music, by the way) by following rules

The Mother List of Internet Resources for, by and About Women

It's so easy to search the Web by keyword, we didn't devote much space in this book to those extensive hotlists that characterize some other Net books. Still, we thought you might be interested in pointers to a few of the more interesting and better known "Websites for and about women." Go get lost.

FEMINA: THE FIRST SEARCHABLE DATABASE OF ONLINE INFO FOR WOMEN AND GIRLS
Cybergrrl intends Femina to be the Yahoo! for women and girls.
http://www.femina.com/

ABORTION RIGHTS AND OTHER FEMINIST ISSUES WEBSITE AND THE WOMEN LEADERS ONLINE WEBSITE (MERGED JANUARY 1996)
This info and link-packed site, hosted by Laurie Mann, is the place to find all sorts of great stuff, including the lastest issues of Catt's Claws (an online feminist Washington-watch and culture-watch newsletter) and browse the Women of Achievement and History archives.
http://www.lm.com/~lmann/feminist/whereis.html

VOICES OF WOMEN HOMEPAGE
"Power tools for visionary women." Very comprehensive. Yeah!
http://www.voiceofwomen.com/

WWW SITE FOR WOMEN
Includes an illustrated guide to the Net, discussion groups and forums, a calendar of Net events of interest to women and a big directory of women's organizations, resources and businesses on line.
http://www.pleiades_net.com/

WEB WEAVERS
Sage "Galactic Web Empress" Lunsford's site about women on the Web and so much more.
http://www.best.com/~tyrtle/women.html

WEB-STER'S NET-WORK
Devoted to everything about women in/and information technology. Extensive hotlists.
http://lucien.sims.berkeley.edu/women_in_it.html

set out by a person—basically the earliest sort of programming language. Ada noted many other characteristics of the engine, too—characteristics that have become really important in the development of computers. For example, Ada was really fascinated by how people might interact with the analytical engine, and how the engine design could be changed to help people interact with it better. Basically, the first human-computer interface design issues were brought up by Ada Byron King more than a century before anyone at Massachusetts Institute of Technology's (MIT's) Media Lab got around to it.

You could say she was way ahead of her time.

More than one hundred years later, the U.S. Department of Defense trademarked the name "ADA" for the first computer language developed. Augusta Ada Byron King, Countess of Lovelace, was the proverbial mother of the computer. And what an absolutely fabulous mother she was, too.

But women's influence on the development of computers doesn't end with Ada. By the earliest twentieth century, other women were becoming heroines in their own rights.

Edith Clarke graduated from Vassar College, spent a brief moment at the University of Wisconsin and then went to MIT (now home of the ten-year-old Media Lab), becoming the first woman to earn a master's of science from MIT. Edith had been born a farmer's daughter in Maryland, and—like a lot of fairytale heroines—supported herself through those lean college years by working for the phone company (well, okay, then an engineering outfit, not phones *quite* yet). She took a summer job with AT&T in 1912, becoming a "computer assistant" (technically a "skilled mathematician") and, as often happens with summer jobs, liked the work so much that she didn't go back to school in the fall (though she later returned to MIT to study). Her career move led her into various positions, including professor of physics in Turkey, electri-

WOMEN'S NET
"A nonprofit computer network for women, activists and organizations using computer networks for information sharing and increasing women's rights." This is a truly global Website! Lots of useful, fascinating links to activists and organizations around the world.
http://www.icg.apc.org/womensnet/

WOMEN'S WAY
"Our intention is to create a space on the Internet for women's ways, a safe and comfortable space for women to speak their thoughts, perceptions, feelings, and experiences in their own authentic voices. We want to honor women's sensibilities, interests and concerns, creating an atmosphere in which women can share and connect." Hey, so far so good. A tip of the cap to Sandy Lillie, the brains and vision behind this undertaking. Sandy is also cofounder of Online Marketspace.
http://www.omix.com/womensway/

NRRDGRRL
If you have ever felt a kinship with Lisa Simpson, Velma (*Scooby-Doo*) or Marcie (*Peanuts*), this is the site for you.
http://www.winternet.com/~ameliaw/

SPIDERWOMAN HOMEPAGE
The homepage of the web-weaving Spiderwoman listserv. Hosted by Stephanie Brail of Digital Amazons.
http://www.primenet.com/~pax

WOMEN'S WIRE
The self-described slick, hip, interactive, online women's magazine.
http://www.women.com/

PLANET WOMAN
"Your guide to interesting, useful and fun women's resources on the Web."
http://www.america.net/com/prestige/planet/menu.html

WHERE THE GIRLS ARE
Susan Dennis's delectable site is allegedly the "girls and women" site most often mistaken for a sex site!
http://www.eskimo.com/~susan/girls.htm

FIRST POINTERS TO A WOMEN'S GUIDE TO THE INTERNET
Michelle's site was one of the very first "women's hotlists" out there.
http://mevard.www.mit.edu/people/mevard/women.html

cal engineering professor at the University of Texas, Austin and a stint as an inventor—like Ada herself—of another calculator/computer of sorts, the "graphical calculator." Clarke suspected that the technological revolution would need the manpower that only women workers could give and foretold the importance that the sheer numbers of female computer/technology users would have on the development of technology.

Also important in the story of computers is Evelyn Boyd Granville, the first African-American woman to receive the doctorate of mathematics from Yale University (in 1949). Her work with computer programming was essential to the development of the Mercury Project (the first U.S. manned space mission) and the Apollo Project. The women and men who have been catapulted into space owe the fact that the machinery can analyze the trajectory arc to Ms. Granville.

In the mid-1970s, a little upstart company called International Business Machines (IBM) started its SHARE users group and asked the members to establish the Human Factors Project to consider the human-computer interface in hardware and software design. Part of that first think-tank was Joan Margaret Winters, who had been working in Cornell University's computer services department designing applications for the manuscripts and archives department. By 1978, Ms. Winters was the deputy manager of the IBM/SHARE Human Factors Project, and by 1983, she was the project manager.

Other notable women in computing are Alexandra Illmer Forsythe, who coauthored a number of textbooks for use in computer science departments nationwide, and Margaret Fox, a member of the U.S. Naval Reserve, who was also chief of the Office of Computer Information in the National Bureau of Standards Institute for Computer Science and Technology. Note, please, that none of these women were put off by the "cold, hard steel" of the machines they worked with. The stereotype of the lack of women in computer technology just doesn't hold up under historical investigation. We almost-twenty-first-century wired women have plenty of female role-models to look to, not the least of whom is the most excellent Rear Admiral Grace Hopper.

Born in 1906, Grace Murray Hopper joined the U.S. Navy in 1944. She came into the service with a doctorate in mathematics from Yale University and ten years' teaching experience at Vassar College. Her initial assignment was to figure out how to use computer technology (this is in the late 1940s, folks!) to calculate ships' positions. After World War II, Ms. Hopper left the navy, but continued to work with computer systems at Harvard, where she was involved in the development of the Mark I, the first large-scale digital computer (and we mean *large:* fifty-one feet long, eight feet high and eight feet deep . . . and performing a whopping three additions per second).

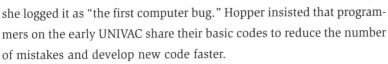

Hopper also worked on the Mark II and III and helped develop the UNIVAC I, where the dry Hopper wit perhaps shows up best: Upon discovering a moth in the UNIVAC I, she logged it as "the first computer bug." Hopper insisted that programmers on the early UNIVAC share their basic codes to reduce the number of mistakes and develop new code faster.

By the early 1950s, Hopper was busy developing the COBOL programming language and building the first compiler (a program that interprets code written in English to a binary form the computer can understand)—the A-O. Other scientists and engineers had scoffed at the idea that there might be a way for people to "tell" computers in English (not an endless binary loop of zeroes and ones) how to do something over and over and over, but Grace Hopper plowed right in and proved it could be done by developing exactly what Ada Byron King had seen as the potential for computers. Using the UNIVAC I and II, Hopper showed that it was possible for engineers and operators to use basic commands in English to tell the computer what to do. In 1952 she made the UNIVAC "understand" twenty commands issued in plain English. She believed people could learn to communicate with these new technological wonders, even if they did not exactly understand the complex underlying electrical wizardry; she was the first to see the computer as a democratic possibility, not just an elitist boy-toy. She was, it seems, one of the first to insist that computers could have a user-friendly interface, created with good programming code. Let's face it, grrrls, both Apple and Microsoft owe her a big debt of gratitude.

In 1969, Admiral Grace Murray Hopper was honored with the first Computer Science Man of the Year Award. In 1973, she became the first American—and the first woman of any nationality—to be named Distinguished Fellow (!) of the British Computer Society and in 1991 she received a National Medal of Technology. Hopper was also an incredibly prolific speaker, addressing more than two hundred audiences of young computer students and engineers in her lifetime. She died in 1992 at the age of 86.

Right now, more women than ever are becoming computer literate not only as programmers, developers, designers and users, but as philosophers as well. Women are making major contributions to the ways we view computers, how we interact with them and how they change our lives. Human-computer interface design—how we interact with computers—has its own call-sheet of very important women; a few of our favorites are Sherry Turkle, Allucquere Rosanne (Sandy) Stone, and Brenda Laurel.

Sherry Turkle (found on the Net at http://web.mit.edu/sturkle/www/) holds a combined doctorate in sociology and personality psychology from Harvard, and is now working at MIT and with the Media Lab. She's done work with identity in the virtual environments of MOOs and MUDs and her recent book *Life on the Screen: Identity in the Age of the Internet* (Simon & Schuster, 1995) is a must-read for anyone interested in what happens to computer users as they become immersed in screen-life.

Similarly, Sandy Stone at the ACTlab, University of Texas, Austin, does a lot of worthwhile thinking and teaching about technology and people. She's currently an assistant professor in the department of radio/TV/film at the University of Texas, Austin, and just published *The War of Desire and Technology at the Close of the Mechanical Age* (MIT Press, 1995). She also does a traveling "theoryperformance" piece on cyberspace and the transhuman (transformed human, as in transsexual). Check out Sandy at http://www.actlab.utexas.edu/ ~ sandy/ for more information.

Brenda Laurel, despite her Ph.D. in theatre from Ohio State University, is now researching the development of computer-mediated virtual worlds at Interval Research Corporation in Palo Alto, California. She edited *The Art of Human-Computer Interface Design* (Addison-Wesley, 1990) and authored *Computers as Theatre* (Addison-Wesley, 1993); neither book is necessarily popular reading, but they are both fascinating and useful if you're interested in how people interact with computers.

One of Laurel's latest projects, *Placeholder* with Rachel Strickland, was featured at the 4CyberConf in Banff, Alberta. In *Placeholder*, the users enter a virtual world, choose one of four beings to become—a fish, a snake, a crow or a spider—and then interact with one another and the virtual world. The *Placeholder* project highlights one of Laurel's concerns about the use of computers: the different ways in which we now have to interact with nature in the digital age. As well as a writer and researcher, Laurel calls herself an artist (well, of course), traveler, hiker, environmentalist and storyteller.

We hope that we've grabbed your attention and piqued your interest in finding out (lots!) more about how influential women are in the development of computers, technology, and the virtual world. All this and more can be found online at The Ada Project (TAP). Read all about TAP and its creators in the following pages and then hop right on over to the website and check it out. We're sure you'll find a few heroic women with major technology fetishes to look up to; we did.

TAP DANCING

If there is one place online to get the inside story of women and computers, then http://www.cs.yale.edu/homes/tap/tap.html is it. TAP is The Ada Project, named—appropriately enough—for our own, our first, our favorite computer foremother: Augusta Ada Byron King, Countess of Lovelace. The brainchild of Yale University computer science students Elisabeth Freeman and Susanne Hupfer, The Ada Project splits its energies evenly among preserving and popularizing the history of women in computing, considering contemporary issues related to gender and computing and providing the latest information about educational and occupational opportunities for women in computer science. The Ada Project is definitely a Website that belongs at the top of any woman's hotlist.

◊

Name: Elisabeth Freeman. **Age:** 29

Name: Susanne Hupfer. **Age:** 30

Geographical Location: New Haven, Connecticut

Machines: SunSparc Workstations

Elisabeth Freeman

Where did you get the idea and inspiration for The Ada Project?

From attending the Grace Hopper Celebration for Women in Computing and getting very psyched about being there, surrounded by more women in computer science than we knew existed, and by our idea that we should somehow collect interesting tidbits from the various mailing lists that we are on, and our discovery of how cool the Web is. We each filtered through our own collections of information as well as looked through mailing lists, Gopher sites, and Websites, threw it all together at our own Website, and then gradually started organizing it.

Susanne Hupfer

What has been the response to TAP?

Across the Internet the response has been great; we regularly receive feedback from people—not just women—who have found TAP a useful resource. We also receive questions, requests for help in finding information, and suggestions.

So, how old were you guys when you started messing around with computers?

Elisabeth: Seventeen.

Susanne: Sixteen.

How did that come about?

Elisabeth: A friend had a home computer (from Radio Shack!). Over the summer, I messed around with it. I thought "writing loops" was really cool. Then, the following semester, I took my first computer class in college.

Susanne: My high school began offering computer science classes when I was a junior. I took an introductory class which involved BASIC programming on Radio Shack TRS-80s, wrote some very primitive graphics programs, and was hooked!

Did you ever deal with sexism in computer labs or stores, or in other computer-related places?

Susanne: I've occasionally encountered disturbing attitudes among male contemporaries. There seems to be a backlash against any inroads made by women in the computing field; when a successful woman is encountered, she is sometimes viewed suspiciously as someone who got where she is because of gender rather than her capabilities. Not only is that untrue; I find such attitudes disturbing and belittling, having personally experienced that hard work and persistence precede any accomplishment.

Elisabeth: I have met some students along the way—as well as one or two people in the industry—who feel that women will never be as good at programming as men (or as good as men at any technical endeavor). This kind of attitude has not affected my own progress (in terms of getting into schools and getting fellowships) as much as it affects my confidence when I hear people talk like this.

Do you think the way you approach computing differs from that of your male friends, classmates or co-workers?

Elisabeth: Yes. In my experience, women tend to question their abilities more than men do, and their confidence is easier to shake. Men will charge right ahead on a project and believe that what they are doing is the *right* way to do it. But another thing I've noticed is that women tend to be more well-rounded than men, and thus do not spend every waking minute in front of a computer (of course, there are exceptions to every generalization!). Personally—because I try to spend time doing other, noncomputer things—sometimes I find myself feeling guilty for that, even though I would never *want* to be the kind of person who does nothing but computer work.

Susanne: I think males tend to be more willing and able to conform to a "hacker" mentality in which interaction with the computer tends to rule much of one's waking hours. I haven't met many female computer scientists who fall into that category. Though they are willing to work and play hard at computing, in general, I think women have a real life "off-line," as well.

What did you do with computers before you discovered the Internet? When did you go online?

Susanne: I mostly just programmed for class assignments and used e-mail to communicate with friends. I didn't "discover" the Internet until graduate school, when I started reading Usenet newsgroups and communicating through e-mail with friends at other institutions.

Elisabeth: I went "online" a long time ago in terms of communicating with other people. I first had access to communication via talk and e-mail on BITNET, and then the Internet as an undergraduate (around 1984 or 1985). At that time I was using PRIME and IBM mainframes at school, so my use was somewhat limited by that. Soon, however, I moved to UNIX machines and had fuller access to the Internet (telnet, FTP, et cetera). Once on a UNIX system, I never went back, and I've had full Internet access ever since. Other than using computers to do my school work, I also use them to write "fun" programs, and of course to exchange e-mail, read Usenet, and, now to surf the Web and create Websites.

What resources and/or people have been really helpful to you?

Susanne: Some professors have been really encouraging along the way. I've also benefited greatly from being hooked into "virtual communities" of female computer scientists, especially the Systers listserv [e-mail list].

Elisabeth: I worked as a lab manager at the computer science department at the University of Kentucky for several semesters, and I think it was very helpful in learning a lot of aspects of computer systems that were different from what I was learning in my classes. Many professors and students through my school years have been especially encouraging, and—most of all—my husband, Eric, who is also in computer science.

What's been your best experience using the Internet?

Elisabeth: Developing TAP with Susanne. It's been a lot of fun to learn about and keep up with Web developments by actively collaborating on a project that I hope will help a lot of women. Also, of course, keeping in touch with friends who live far away via e-mail, "talking," and exchanging online info, including pictures of each other, et cetera.

Susanne: My most rewarding Net experience has been developing and maintaining The Ada Project with Elisabeth. We have received a lot of positive feedback on TAP. People find it a very valuable site, and that has made working on it truly worthwhile.

What words of encouragement do you have for other women getting involved in computer science and the Internet?

Elisabeth: Stick with it! Don't let anyone with a bad attitude get you down—find someone with a good attitude, and listen to them, instead. Find a female mentor with a positive attitude and an understanding of the needs of women in computer science—which can be really isolating and lonely sometimes—and talk with her.

Susanne: The world of computers and the Internet is an exciting place, and there is definitely room (and a need) for female "info-pioneers" and computer scientists out there! Computing is not necessarily an easy field in which to succeed, and there may be many discouragements along the way, but you should persist because the personal and professional rewards can be great.

What do you want to see for The Ada Project in the future?

We would like to see TAP expand to be a more comprehensive information Website. We'd also like to incorporate a serious search/database mechanism. While we'd like it to continue to be an "index" of women's resources on the Web, we also want to develop and offer more original content addressing more topics related to women and computing. For now, with our limited resources, keeping up with just women in computer science is a handful!

How To's

HARDWARE TALK,

SOFTWARE GOSSIP

Okay. So you're interested in this whole "going online" business. You don't have a machine of your own though, or maybe you're not sure if the computer you inherited two years ago from your little brother is up to the task of taking you where you want to go. You want to know what's necessary? What's the best? What ought you avoid and what can't you live without? And how do you deal with all those . . . those . . . parts?

Pssst. Here's a little secret. Everyone—at one time or another—has to learn those parts. Replace the whatsit with the 14.4 Kbps modem, the thingamajig with the 4-megabyte 70-pin RAM chip in your vocabulary, and you're well on your way to mastering the language of computers and taking your place among sister-geeks everywhere.

Regardless of your platform choice—both Macintosh and PC (short for Personal Computer, the name IBM coined for its microcomputers in the early eighties and which now refers to any machine built with an Intel-compatible chip) are appropriate, fun and useful for getting

FROM THE POPTART DIARIES:
THE DEATH OF A MODEM

3 August 1995

I didn't even *know* that a lightning strike on a phone line could zap a modem. When that big thunderstorm hit day before yesterday, I ran right in and unplugged my computer, but it was too late: The same hit that took out my answering machine mortally wounded my modem as well.

I *knew* it was a goner. First I had problems connecting, and there was lots of line noise on the screen. Finally, that dreaded "no carrier" message appeared no matter what voodoo resuscitation techniques I tried. *Uh-oh.* I checked out everything. Plugged in. Turned on. I even broke open the manual. Damn. No way around it. It was dead. I had to replace it.

So, the next day—after I'd attempted a few more heroic measures over the carcass—off I went to the local computer store, dead modem in hand. The very nice and helpful salesman explained to me that, *yes indeedy,* from what I described, my modem had been zapped through the phone line. He sold me a new 14.4 Kbps modem and I whistled my way out into the sun.

Brain in neutral, I came home and hooked the new modem up and logged on . . . or tried to. Damn. Time to look at the manual. Wait. Why is this manual discussing "configuring your U. S. Robotics modem in *Windows*"!? Preliminary tears of frustration pooled in my eyes. I checked the box: it was indeed a Mac modem— but it seemed this was one of those modems that had to be told exactly and explicitly what to do. *Argh!* Letter and number soup time! AT&F&A3&B1&H1&R2&D0&C1X4S0=0S7=90— and so on, and so on. It made no sense, it wouldn't connect, and I swear the thing was laughing at me. ➤ ➤ ➤

online—you need a minimum configuration depending on what you want to do. If all you're interested in is sending and receiving e-mail, then an older, cheaper and slower machine is okay . . . though as you dabble in the online world you'll probably want to upgrade to bigger and faster eventually. Both a Macintosh Classic (the old, "all in one" Macintosh system) and a 286 (a PC built with one of the slowest x86 processors) are capable of retrieving e-mail from another machine (a server) with a 2,400 bps (or even a 1,200 bps!) modem. Neither of these machines, however, are able to offer the full spectrum of the Internet experience.

Platform choice is a personal choice. Your Net-obsessed authors are split down the middle; Crystal works almost exclusively with Macintosh and Laurel has a PC thang going. However, we've both come to an uneasy peace that each other's platform has its merits, too. The Macintosh is an amazingly easy machine to set up and maintain. Hardware and software "problems" are rare, and the machine rates number one in customer loyalty. On the other hand, a PC is cheaper—byte for byte—and the individual parts are easy to purchase and upgrade. Certain types of computer geeks prefer the PC because *they're in charge.* While a Macintosh makes many of the decisions *for* the user, a PC's hardware and software quirks can be worked around by an ingenious geek. Regardless of your personal belief (and many people compare platform choice to religious faith), both PCs and Macintoshes are capable of getting you online with style.

In order to make a PPP (point to point protocol) or SLIP (serial line Internet protocol) connection—which is the connection needed to run graphical Web browsers and the like—you need a minimum of 4 megabytes of RAM and a 14.4 Kbps modem. To really enjoy the interactive and graphical aspects of the Web, you're going to want 8 megabytes of RAM and perhaps a 28.8 Kbps modem; this is the minimum configuration of most new machines (as of early 1996). Of course to really make things fly, keep increasing your RAM and keep your eyes and ears open for ISDN (Integrated Services Digital Network), ADSL (Asymmetric Digital Subscriber Line) or cable modems/connections in your area, which can move data at up to 128 Kpbs. Beyond RAM and connection speed, here are our minimum recommendations for an Internet-friendly machine:

CPU

The CPU—central processing unit—measures in megahertz how fast your machine processes information. PCs are built with an Intel-compatible chip, either the x86 (286 is slowest, while the 486 is faster), the Pentium or the Pentium-Pro. Because the Pentium-Pro is built to take advantage of only the newest "32-bit" software, it isn't usually the best buy for a home user, who uses a lot of older and upgraded "16-bit" software. (Windows NT is really the only operating system that can take full advantage of the Pentium Pro.) The 286 is the only processor speed incapable of making a PPP (point to point protocol) connection—the type of connection you'll want to run graphical Web browsers and the like.

Macintosh CPUs are either based on the Motorola 68000 series CISC (Complex Instruc-

I'm a Macintosh girl and an Apple loyalist. And I drive a Honda (an almost wholly unproblematic car). Laurel, on the other hand, is a PC clone girl and drives a Volvo. That is, she is (she has to be!) much more hardware savvy than I: she regularly takes the cover off of her computer and fiddles around inside with the cutest set of tiny computer tools. I know I could immerse myself in a manual and handle a PC if I ever *needed* to, but I still prefer to plug stuff in and have it work almost-transparently. And this modem *wasn't*.

I *finally* sorted my way through the modem commands, figured out how to configure my software to work with the new modem, and got the connection working. Then, crisis past, I felt really sheepish. Who was I to be working on this book you're reading if something like hooking up this new modem could send me into techno-fits?! Or maybe that's precisely the point: *No one* is ever beyond those sorts of frustrations. What matters is how you deal with them. Even if you're a Mac person (like me), you need to develop a basic understanding of your system components (hardware and software), a style of computer troubleshooting and problem-solving, and at least a tolerance for the trial and error of hacking away at a problem. However you do it, you need to learn to think with your computer.

The moral of the story: Cursing, crying, fiddling and feverish consultations with geek friends over seemingly arcane manuals are all totally permissible, even *de rigueur*. Throwing up your hands in despair over the slightest little thing is not. Back to it, grrrl.

tion Set Computing) processor or the IBM Power PC RISC (Reduced Instruction Set Computing) processor (the same type of processor found in high-end servers and workstations built by Sun Microsystems and Silicon Graphics Inc.). Macs running one of the original 68000 processors (original Macs, the SE, Mac Plus) cannot support a PPP connection, but Macs running the 68020 processor (or better) can. The speed of your computer actually depends more on the amount of RAM than the processor speed, but a Pentium- or RISC-based processor offers that extra *"oomph."* Sometimes an older machine can accept a CPU upgrade, offering an increase in processing power for fewer bucks.

HARD DRIVE

Your hard drive is where data (programs and files) is stored. Because it's so *tempting* to download every fabulous file and program you find while surfing the Net, a large hard drive is a wise investment. We know people who get by with older, 40 to 80 megabyte hard drives, however if you're buying new or upgrading, 500 megabytes should really be the minimum you consider. Often, the operating system alone takes up 50 to 100 megabytes, and you'll want room for other things, like a word processor or games as well as your Internet software. Hard drives up to 1.5 gigabytes (1,500 megabytes) are not uncommon in new machines.

MEMORY (RAM)

Sometimes, new computer users confuse RAM (random access memory) with hard drive space; while hard drive space is where data is stored, RAM is where data is manipulated. The more you have, the more you can do. Graphical Web browsers such as Netscape need a *minimum* of 4 megabytes, and often run painfully slow with any less than 8 megabytes. Fortunately, memory is easily upgraded on a need-more-*now* basis. Start with 8 megabytes if you can, and add from there.

MONITORS

Monitors are measured in many different ways—screen size (measured diagonally), refresh rate (how often each pixel is replaced by a new one; a low "refresh rate" causes the flickering screen that drives us crazy), dot pitch (how many pixels there are per inch; a smaller dot pitch means a finer-looking picture), resolution (how many pixels are on the screen) and number of colors (anywhere from 16 to millions of colors are available). The minimum we recommend for a home/Internet machine is a 15" monitor, with a refresh rate of at least 72 Hz and a dot pitch of at least .28. To support 256 colors at a resolution of 600 x 800 pixels (a configuration that works well for most Web browsing), the video adapter (the card inside the computer case that hooks the monitor to the system) must have a minimum of 1 megabyte of RAM. More RAM on the video adapter means more colors, a higher refresh rate and higher resolution. Figuring out video adapters and monitors is often difficult; we recommend you read a few issues of your favorite platform's magazines for more information.

MODEMS

The modem makes the connection between your computer and the phone line . . . and the online world. Many computers come with an internal modem—a card inside the machine with the phone jack on the back of the computer. If you don't have room for an internal modem (or feel uncomfortable installing one), an external modem that hooks into a port on the back of the machine works well, too. In the early, *early* days of telecommunications, 300 bps (bits per second), 1,200 bps and 2,400 bps modems were standard. Now that the multimedia capabilities of the World Wide Web are so popular, a 14.4 Kbps modem is our minimum recommendation. A 28.8 Kbps modem is even faster.

SOUND CARDS AND SPEAKERS

Let's face it: The Web is about multimedia, and that often includes sound. Most new PCs and all Macs come with a sound card installed and speakers attached. If your PC doesn't, don't panic but *do* be aware that sound cards are not always easy to install; ask your mentor for help and/or plan to spend a few days with the manual. Shopping for a sound card or speakers is similar to shopping for a stereo—you want to be able to listen before you buy.

CD-ROM AND OTHER STORAGE DEVICES

Although a CD-ROM drive isn't necessary for surfing the Web, it's a nice addition to any machine. Most software programs (especially the *big* ones) are sold on one CD-ROM instead of ten or more floppy disks, making installation and storage easier. Many CD-ROMs are useful, important or just plain fun to have—games, encyclopedias and clip art collections all come on CD-ROM. Starting in 1996, some high-end CD-ROM drives have recording capability, meaning you can theoretically "burn" or create your own CDs, but most CD-ROM drives don't allow you to save your data. There are a number of other personal storage devices, however. Tape drives are either internal or hook up to an external port and are great for storing unused data (they're not so great for running programs, because they are much slower than hard drives). Both the Iomega Zip Drive and the Syquest EZ Drive have made big splashes in early 1996 as storage devices; the drive installs either internally or to an external port, and 100 megabyte (Zip) or 135 megabyte (EZ) disks are accessible just like floppy disks, only bigger.

PRINTERS

In order to share info gleaned online with your non-wired friends, write letters to family or submit "hard copy" papers to professors, a printer is an important addition to your computer desk. Depending on your budget and your needs, you might get by with a used dot matrix (that "pounds" out the image or letters like a typewriter), an inexpensive inkjet printer (tiny jets of ink create the image or letters), or a laser printer (which "burns" dry ink on the paper surface and offers the finest looking print). Today, color inkjet printers are fun, useful, popular and dropping in price. Buying a printer is a personal matter; go to your favorite computer store and check the samples of the printers that fall within your price range and need.

DESKTOPS, NOTEBOOKS/ LAPTOPS AND PDAs: SIZE MATTERS.

It's a fair assumption that the majority of Internet users use a desktop machine—a computer that isn't really portable. Many people are discovering the advantages (and disadvantages!) of small-sized, on-the-go computing, however, and today's notebook computer offers most of the power of the average desktop at ten pounds or less. The obvious advantage is portability. Whether checking e-mail from a hotel room or surfing in bed, a notebook is your everywhere computer solution. The flip-side includes price (notebooks *are* expensive), limited upgradability, a greater chance of having your machine stolen, lost or broken and (sometimes) a smaller keyboard and monitor (which can be uncomfortable for long-term use). Both the Macintosh and PC come in numerous notebook configurations; if you find a desktop system that seems perfect, rest assured that for more money, you can have the mini-version.

The division between "laptop" and "notebook" means very little in today's world of computing. Originally, a laptop was slightly bigger than a notebook; now most portable computers are in the five pound range and easily fit in a briefcase or book bag, so the distinction isn't important. "Notebook" is appropriate for any of them.

Buying a notebook is a personal thing; you may want the smallest, sleekest machine possible and be willing to sacrifice extras like a CD-ROM drive. On the other hand, you might want a replacement for your desktop and be willing to carry around a few extra pounds; it depends on you. Don't settle for less out of a new notebook than you would from a new desktop, though . . . insist on 8 megabytes of RAM, a 500-megabyte hard drive and the largest, brightest display you can afford.

The newest development in small-scale personal computing is the personal digital assistant (PDA). Sort of a glorified, electronic day-planner, PDAs offer pen (not keyboard) computing, compatibility with PCs or Macintoshes and (some of them, at least) the ability to send e-mail and access the Internet. A PDA isn't a replacement for a desktop or notebook computer, but they *can* be useful and are fun little gadgets.

SOFTWARE, THE INTERNET AND BEYOND

Spend an hour in your favorite computer store and you'll realize there are a *lot* of software programs out there. Infinite combinations of programs can work together to make your computing and online experiences easier. Our advice? Start small and cheap—perhaps by checking out "lite" versions of major software programs—and go from there. All new computers come with the operating system (OS) installed (Macintosh installs System 7.5, and new PCs almost always come with

Windows 95), and often include a selection of other programs for you to try. An older system may have an older OS installed, which is fine. Get to know as many operating systems as you can. A cross-platform grrrl is prepared for anything.

OPERATING SYSTEMS
Windows, DOS and Windows 95

Windows 95 is the newest of Microsoft's inventions, and has quite a few advantages over older versions of Windows (the dial-up networking tool offers a simple, easy, one-step PPP or SLIP connection), but really needs 8 megabytes of RAM and a large hard drive to be effective. Windows 3.1 (or Windows 3.11 for Workgroups) isn't obsolete, and takes less RAM and hard-drive space. Windows 3.1 isn't, however, an operating system; it requires DOS (which *is* the OS) to run. Windows 95 is actually its own OS, although it is "backwards compatible" with DOS programs.

Macintosh System 7.x

System 7.5 features an appropriately snazzy version of the beloved Mac graphical interface. If you plan to run a PPP connection on your machine, you must have at least System 7.0. A new Macintosh OS is scheduled for late 1996.

ANTIVIRUS PROGRAMS

Kinda like condoms, the time for antivirus programs is *before* you go online. Viruses are programs (usually attached to a file) that do awful things to your machine if you inadvertently run them. Some viruses are more annoying than harmful; they might change the date or time of your system clock. Others are devastating; they can erase your entire hard drive or corrupt each file you open. An antivirus program checks files for "infection" and lets you know if a virus is found so you can delete it. Some newer antivirus programs work seamlessly with your Internet software, checking files as you download them instead of waiting for you to tell it to. We recommend consistent use of reliable antivirus software; better safe than sorry.

INTERNET SUITES

An Internet suite is a collection of Internet software for use with the ISP (Internet service provider) of your choice. Internet in a Box and

Netmanage Chameleon are both suites you might purchase. The advantages are obvious: You don't have to search out individual programs and set-up is usually pretty easy. The disadvantages? You *pay* more—many client programs included with a suite are available in a shareware or freeware version on the Net—and you don't have the choice of which clients to use. An Internet suite includes a dialer, a Web browser, e-mail and FTP clients, and often finger, Gopher and IRC clients, too.

DIALERS

A dialer program simply negotiates the connection between your computer and your ISP. If you purchase an Internet software suite, the dialer is included. If you prefer to search out your favorite Net software elsewhere, however, you may have to search out a dialer too. There are many different dialers for each platform, so (again) it's your choice. Ask your mentor or check out a few platform-specific magazines or books for suggestions.

WEB BROWSERS

Netscape is the hands-down favorite Web browser at the moment, but Mosaic (the first graphical, cross-platform Web browser) pops up now and again as a licensed version in an Internet suite. Netscape needs a minimum of 4 megabytes of RAM, and (as usual) we recommend 8 megabytes for anything beyond molasses-slow surfing. There are many other browsers available, so if Netscape isn't working for you, look around for another one (or two, or three!) to try.

CLIENTS

Many different clients are shareware and are available for downloading online and some—such as the Usenet news reader Free Agent and the "lite" version of the e-mail client Eudora—are free for personal use. We include our favorite clients elsewhere in *SurferGrrrls*, but encourage you to try as many as possible to find your favorites. If you purchase an Internet software suite, clients for e-mail, FTP (file transfer protocol), reading news and IRC (Internet Relay Chat) are included. People have their favorites, so try as many as possible before you pick the ones you want to use.

◊

UTILITIES

Utilities are usually available online as shareware or freeware and are the tiny "can't do without" programs that you'll collect as you become familiar with your computing needs. Popular utilities for Internet use include LView (for viewing graphics files), VMPG (for viewing videos on the PC) and PKZip/Unzip (for working with PC compressed files). Other useful utilities might include alarm systems (that beep when it's time to go to work, perhaps) or screen savers (a graphic that appears on your screen when you're not using your computer).

HEY, CAN I GET HURT PLAYING THESE REINDEER GAMES?

OF COURSE, HONEY. Most everyday activities, even if they seem as safe as rolling out of bed, are "dangerous" in some way, including computing. We need to be mindful of that and insist on the development of "hardware helpers" that are easy on our poor, vulnerable wetware (bodies). Think about it this way: Don't cars have seat belts, airbags, adjustable seats and steering wheels? We need to protect ourselves at our desks, too.

A good, general Website for folks concerned with the potential dangers and risks of the human-computer interface is The Risks Digest (http://catless.ncl.ac.uk/Risks/), the collected, select proceedings of the Association for Computing Machinery forum on risks to the public from computers and related systems. (It's not as dry as it sounds!) You might also want to follow the conversations on the Usenet newsgroup comp.risks. Briefly, there are three areas of potential illness and injury you should be aware of as you point-and-click and clack-and-peck away at the keyboard.

The most common serious problem you're likely to encounter is hand and wrist strain, the Net-surfing equivalent of "surfer's bumps" (calcifications on the knees of surfers caused by all that kneeling). See, the human hand and wrist are elegant structures, and the average computer keyboard and mouse abuse them most terribly. It's hardly surprising that the most common career-threatening malady among computer geeks and "pink collar" workers is carpal tunnel syndrome, a repetitive strain injury of a nerve that runs through a "bone tunnel" in your wrist to your hand caused by continual limited-range movement—like keyboarding or mousing. When that nerve becomes inflamed, some combination of pain, numbness, weakness and "locking" of your hand can result. It's most unpleasant. Trust us—we both have firsthand experience. In many cases, the problem can be alleviated by using an ergonomically designed keyboard and/or mouse, through physical therapy and by wearing one of those funny-looking braces, but extreme cases may require cortisone shots into the carpal tunnel or surgery to make the tunnel wider. *(Yowch!)* Before your wrist starts aching, or if it's throbbing as you read this, scoot on over to A Patient's Guide to Carpal Tunnel Syndrome (http://www.cyberport.net/mmg/cts/ctsintro.html) and check out the wealth of info available there.

Yeah, we slouch too, but bad posture and improperly designed chairs and desks combined with long hours in front of the computer can lead to back and neck problems, eyestrain, stress and depression. Even little things can help: Get in the habit of stretching a little at intervals during a long session at the computer, make sure your refresh rate is set as high as your video card and monitor allow and set the screen colors of your communications and word-processing software to minimize eyestrain. As more and more humans get wired, hardware and furniture companies will have to better incorporate ergonomics—the science of maximizing productivity and minimizing discomfort—into the design of our computer environments. After all, no one expects all tennis players to use the same size racquet grip!

MORE → → →

MORE REINDEER GAMES

To find out how to make your setup friendlier in a few simple relatively inexpensive moves, check out The WEBster: Ergonomics and Computer Injuries site (http://lucky.innet.com/~kathiw/ergo.html).

A question raised frequently (especially by women) concerns the potential health risks of long hours spent in front of VDTs (video display terminals, a fancy abbreviation for "monitors"). As early as 1985, Sweden and Canada gave pregnant women whose jobs required them to spend significant periods of time working around VDTs the option to change job assignments temporarily "just in case." Still, despite documented clusters of adverse-outcome pregnancies among "pink collar" workers using VDTs all over the United States, no scientific connection has been established between radiation from VDTs and miscarriage or birth defects. Or between cancer and radiation from VDTs. If you're still plotting to snitch one of those lead aprons from your dentist's office, know that the X-ray, ultraviolet and electromagnetic radiation emitted by your computer screen is comparable to the radiation emitted by other household appliances. That is, your computer is no more dangerous than your refrigerator or alarm clock. Completely reassured? We're not.

Think for a moment about the potential economic impact of millions of low-paid "pink-collar" data-entry and word-processing workers demanding safer working conditions and be a little paranoid with us, okay? Remember how long it took for Them to admit that asbestos causes cancer? So, add The EMF (Electromagnetic Frequencies) Health Report (http://infoventures.com/emf/contents.html) to your list of bookmarks, and position your monitor so that it is approximately one and one-half to two feet from your body. And if you're still uneasy, see-through shields that attach to your monitor and block a significant amount of EMF are available from many computer retailers.

We love our computers. But it's frightening to note that in the screenplay adaption of his short story "Johnny Mnemonic," William Gibson spun an AIDS-crisis allegory around an imaginary disease called Neural Attenuation Syndrome (aka NAS or the Black Shakes). The stricken folk of Gibson's cyberfuture died slow and painful deaths from the effects of electromagnetic radiation on the myelin sheaths that protect every nerve in the human body. Fiction is usually stranger than reality, but we still think it's a good idea to protect yourself, stay informed and compute safely.

Computer Terms

Ya Need ta Know

The first rule of being a computer geekgirl—we'll say it again for those who didn't catch it the first time—is know thy machine. You can get away with not knowing squat about a Cray supercomputer—unless you happen to be running one—but you must be able to identify your own machine in order to get help, upgrade, buy software or hardware add-ons, and generally do nerd-type stuff. PCs and Macintoshes each have their own vocabulary and quirky terms, and there's a general *computerese* that applies to all microcomputers. Here's a list of terms you might come across in your quest to become acquainted with your hardware and software.

AUTOEXEC.BAT (PC) The file your computer reads to find out what software programs you want loaded, such as antivirus software and Windows. When you start your computer, the config.sys and autoexec.bat are run automatically. It's important to keep a backup of your autoexec.bat file in case your computer crashes.

.AU (Mac) A file suffix (what Mac-types call the letters after the "dot" in file names) indicating a sound file that can be downloaded and played by most Mac sound software.

.BMP Short for BitMaP, a basic graphics file, or picture. This is the extension (the three letters after the "dot" in PC file names) you'll find on files that can be used as backgrounds, or "wallpaper" on the screen.

CD–ROM (compact disk–read only memory) A removable storage device. Unlike a floppy disk (which can be erased), a CD-ROM's data is permanent. Many large software applications are sold on CD-ROM, since each disk holds approximately 650 megabytes of data.

CONFIG.SYS (PC) The file that tells your computer what hardware to look for and set up. If you have a CD-ROM or a sound card, for example, their drivers will be set up when your machine runs the config.sys file, right before the autoexec.bat. An important file to back-up occasionally.

.CPT (Mac) A suffix indicating a file is compressed using CompactPro (shareware available at any good Mac archive). Sometimes the suffix is cpt.hqx. (Don't panic: CompactPro also decompresses BinHexed files). *See also* .hqx.

CPU (central processing unit) The brain of your computer. The CPU is an integrated circuit on a single silicon chip. CPU chips include the 486 and the Pentium for the PC and the RISC-based for the Mac/PowerPC. A chip's processing speed is measured in megahertz (MHz); the higher the megahertz, the faster your machine can process information.

CURSOR The blinking thing on your screen. Or the arrow. Or the waving Elvis, if you have a special cursor installed. Basically, it's where your mouse is, or where you're typing on your screen.

DEFRAG As hard drives read and write information, they scatter bits all over themselves. To "defrag" a hard drive means to run a program that cleans up the mess and puts all the bytes back where they belong.

Running a defragmenter every so often will keep your machine running faster.

DEVICE DRIVERS (PC) The small software programs that allow pieces of hardware to communicate. For example, the printer driver (often included with Windows, but sometimes on a separate disk that comes with the hardware) allows the printer to "hear" when a word-processing program tells it to print something.

DESKTOP What you see on the screen when all programs are closed but the machine is still running Windows or the Mac OS (operating system, like System 7.5). Often, a desktop will have wallpaper and icons which act as shortcuts to programs.

DOS (PC) (also, MS-DOS) Officially stands for disk operating system. Back when Microsoft was just an upstart young thing from Seattle (pre-grunge), it licensed DOS to IBM and other PC makers, and it became the best-selling computer operating system. Windows came next. The rest is history.

FONT A typeface. There are serif and sanserif ("sans" meaning "without") fonts. Serifs are the fine lines at the ends of the letter's major strokes. You can download *oodles* of beautiful and fun fonts for the Mac or PC from any good shareware archive.

GUI (graphical user interface) DOS and UNIX are operating systems that require you to type commands. Windows and the Macintosh OS are GUIs, meaning they have toolbars, icons and other graphical elements.

HARDWARE All the physical stuff. Keyboard? Hardware. Disk drive? Hardware. Monitor? Hardware. Can you pick it up, drop it and stick things into it? Can you break it? It's hardware.

.HQX (Mac) A file suffix indicating BinHex compression. CompactPro will un-BinHex files. *See also* .cpt.

ICON A small symbol on the screen that represents a program, a command, a function, etc. For example, click on the Microsoft Word icon, and that application opens. Click on the arrow that points left on a Web page, and you'll (usually) return to the previous page.

IRQ (PC) There are so many IRQ numbers, and each device uses one. If something you've just hooked up doesn't work, chances are it's an IRQ problem. This one will require either hours with a manual or a super-savvy hardware friend.

LPT PORT Where your printer plugs in. The port itself is called a parallel port or plug, and the computer thinks of the printer as being on LPT1, or "online printer #1."

MOTHERBOARD The big, green board covering the bottom of your computer case (or side, in a tower system) where all the main electronic circuits, the processor and empty slots (for memory, the video card or drive controller) are located.

MOUSE A handheld input device that replaces some keyboard commands. Trackballs and touchpads (popular on notebooks) perform the same function.

MULTIMEDIA Loosely speaking, anything that combines two or more media (mediums), like visual images and sound, film and text, etc. A multimedia computer system usually has a CD-ROM drive and enough memory and the right hardware to handle sound files, movies and full-color graphics.

OPERATING SYSTEM DOS, Windows 95, UNIX, Macintosh System 7.5 and the like, that runs when you turn your computer on. The OS sends commands to the computer and helps create files, run applications, print documents, et cetera.

RAM (random access memory) RAM is the memory that determines how much information the computer can work with and how fast it completes tasks. The more RAM you have, the faster things will work and you'll be able to run more complex programs. RAM, however, is *temporary* memory; as soon as you shut down your computer, it's gone, unless you store your data on a permanent storage device such as a hard or floppy disk.

REFRESH RATE (PC) How fast the monitor refreshes the pixels (picture elements) on the monitor. The Macintosh has a pre-determined refresh rate and resolution; you can't change (or improve) it. However, if your PC monitor seems like it's "flashing," you could upgrade your video card to support a higher refresh rate.

RESOLUTION The number of pixels or dots your screen has. The higher the resolution, the sharper the image. Again, the resolution of the Macintosh monitor is pre-determined, but the PC's resolution can be changed, depending on the system's video card.

ROM (read only memory) The most vital information about your computer is stored in ROM chips. The ROM allows your computer to remember the time and date and how to access the hard drive when you turn it on.

.SIT (Mac) A file suffix indicating the file has been compressed using a shareware program called Stuff-It. *See also* .cpt *and* .hqx.

TSR (terminal and stay resident) A program that gets loaded into memory when the OS starts and stays there so it can be activated instantly. Examples of TSRs are virus checkers, the double-space drive compressor program and screen savers. TSRs can also use tons of memory.

VIRTUAL MEMORY In Windows and on a Macintosh, it's possible to supplement your RAM with virtual memory. When you use virtual memory, the computer sets aside a portion of the hard drive it can read and write to as though it were *verrrry* slow RAM. Using virtual memory allows you to run programs and work with files that need more RAM than you've got, but it takes up hard drive space and is really slow to access.

WALLPAPER The background color, pattern or graphic you have behind all the icons on the screen. Hint: using a huge, full-color photograph of your cat might make your desktop look good, but it ties up a *lot* of memory.

.ZIP (PC) A file extension indicating a file is compressed with one of the many "zipping and unzipping" programs. A couple of versions of this shareware program are available online, so if you find a file with a .zip extension, don't panic . . . use the same shareware to unzip it.

SO, LITTLE LADY...YOU'RE LOOKING TO SIGN ON WITH AN INTERNET SERVICE PROVIDER?

Now that everybody, her grandma and her little sister want to get online (or they will want to as soon as you finish with 'em!), Internet service providers (ISPs)—local, regional and national alternatives to commercial services like America Online (AOL), Prodigy and GEnie—are popping up all over the place. This means that individuals and families close to large and even medium-sized cities can have local dial-up access to a full range of Internet services for a reasonable fee, usually a flat fee between twenty and forty dollars per month. People who travel a lot should look into national ISPs, which offer local dial-up numbers in most cities. Fees for business connections vary based on the type of connection you want, but the basic transaction is the same. Internet service providers make money by leasing dedicated direct, networked data lines from telecommunications companies, and then sell-

Access for the On-the-Go Grrrl

If you travel a lot, a national ISP might be the choice for you. The following ISPs provide national PPP/SLIP access and have both a URL and an 800 number for your convenience.

BBN PLANET CORPORATION
http://www.bbnplanet.com/
800-472-4565

EARTHLINK NETWORK
http://www.earthlink.net/
800-395-8425

GLOBAL ENTERPRISE SERVICES, INC.
http://www.jvnc.net/
800-358-4437 X 7325

HYPERCON
http://www.hypercon.com/
800-652-2590

IMAGINE COMMUNICATIONS CORPORATION
http://www.imagixx.net/
800-542-4499

NOVALINK INTERACTIVE NETWORKS
http://www.trey.com/
800-274-2814

PORTAL INFORMATION NETWORK
http://www.portal.com/
800-433-6444

QUESTAR MICROSYSTEMS, INC.
http://www.questar.com/
800-925-2140

TRADERS' CONNECTION
http://www.trader.com/
800-753-4223

ing their subscribers access to these data lines, a certain amount of "storage space" on the ISP machine(s), and some features and content local to the ISP.

If you're really lucky, you live in a city/area where citizens operate and maintain a freenet—a *very* low-cost (if not totally free) access provider, sort of like a telecommunications co-op. Some freenets offer complete Internet access; others don't offer much at all, so if you discover a freenet in your area, make sure it meets your needs. And, yeah, people who don't live in a freenet area can establish accounts and telnet into any freenet anywhere. Getting involved with your local freenet is a great way to meet some of your more dedicated nethead neighbors and to learn more about the Internet. Find out if there's a freenet in your area at http://is.rice.edu/~kevin/freenets.html. If that site disappears or moves, or if you just want more information, call the National Public Telecomputing Network at (216) 498-4050, or write them at info@nptn.org or P.O. Box 1987, Cleveland, OH 44106-0187. NPTN is dedicated to helping communities establish freenets, so the truly ambitious among you might want to look into starting one in your town.

Commercial online services like America Online and Prodigy are fine for people who want some initial hand-holding in cyberspace, who like the safety of features like the supervised children's chat forums, or who don't have any other providers available to them, but lots of people find these services limiting, *expen$ive* and hard to use to truly access the Internet. (That's right. When you log on to AOL and get that "Welcome!" message, you're in AOL space, not on the Net. You can get to the Net from commercial services, however.)

If we didn't enjoy unlimited Internet access as an academic perk, both of your friendly, Net-obsessed authors would access the Net via an ISP or freenet. A lot of students and employees at institutions and corporations which restrict Internet access use their academic and work accounts to telnet to remote ISPs, where they maintain Websites or participate in SIGs (special interest groups) available there. Folx who telnet into remote ISPs must still pay a fee, but it is usually less than the fee for dial-up users. For example, Crystal used to pay $9.95 per month for an account on MindVox (a really great NYC ISP) in order to telnet in and hang out in its forums, and the WELL offers unlimited telnet access at $15 a month. A limited account on a remote ISP is great for creating an e-mail persona or alias. For example, when we send mail or posts to Usenet from our school addresses, readers know or can find out a *lot* about us; janedoe@mindvox.com could be *anyone* from *anywhere!* Only her ISP billing department knows for sure.

Lots of great lists of ISPs and ISP Websites are available on the WWW. To get an idea of the information a stand-up ISP offers its potential subscribers, check out the Website of zoom.com, a woman-owned ISP in Fremont, California (http://zoom.com/). If you have Net access, but are shopping for a new provider, here are some good places to start looking:

THE LIST (ISPS LISTED BY AREA AND COUNTRY CODES)
http://www.thelist.com/

NERD WORLD—INTERNET PROVIDERS (LIST)
http://www.tiac.net/users/dstein/nw57.html

US INTERNET SERVICE PROVIDERS LIST (BY AREA CODE)
http://www.primus.com/providers/

CANADA INTERNET SERVICE PROVIDERS META-LIST
http://www.herbison.com/herbison/iap_canada_meta_list.html

All ISPs are not created equal, and you should know how to shop smart. That's why we've come up with some tips and a list of questions to ask an ISP representative before you turn over your credit card number to her and say, "Sounds good; sign me up." Before you go searching, figure out exactly what your needs are, and write them down. Then you can start comparison shopping to find the ISP that provides *exactly* what you need for the fewest dollars. There are many excellent ISPs out there, but with the recent Net boom, some losers are springing up as well. A good rule of thumb: Your ISP should be at least as reliable as your cable TV system or primary means of physical transportation. As with most other things, ask your mentor(s) for advice on specific ISPs in your city, region or country.

THE BASICS

1 Is the ISP financially and organizationally stable? What is the likelihood that it will be in business a year from now? How big is its subscriber base? **Tip ➤** Cut new ISPs some slack, but try to gauge the commitment of the primary players.

2 Does the ISP offer the full range of Internet services—e-mail WWW, Gopher, Usenet news, telnet? Is a full Usenet news feed available? If not, which groups are available? Can you tailor your service contract so that you don't have to pay for stuff you don't use?

3 Can you put up your own Website? What are the "community standards" of the ISP? Can you be as wild/provocative/gross as you want, or are there limits?

4 What's the fastest dial-up speed the ISP can handle? **Tip ➤** Even if you plan to connect at 2,400 bps (perfectly acceptable for e-mail), the max speed that the ISP can handle should be no less than 14.4 Kbps. 28.8 Kbps is becoming the new standard as prices for modems with that capacity drop.

5 How much dial-up capacity does the ISP have? How hard is it to "get in" during peak hours? How vulnerable is the ISP to hardware and software problems? How long does it usually take to resolve these problems? **Tip ➤** There's absolutely nothing more annoying than that busy signal on the other end of the line when you have work to do, e-mail to send and sites to surf, so be sure the rep is giving you straight talk when she answers these questions.

6   Are SLIP and/or PPP connections available? You need a PPP
    (point to point protocol) or SLIP (serial line Internet protocol)
    connection to be able to run graphical Web browsers like
    Netscape; PPP or SLIP allows your personal computer to use
    TCP/IP (standard Internet) protocol with a high-speed modem
    (9,600 Kbps or faster) over a regular phone line. **Tip ➤** If you're
    really into graphics, video and sound, ask if the ISP has any
    plans for offering ISDN connections (digital connections that
    make "true" multimedia possible at home at 64 Kbps) once the
    price falls.

7   Can you telnet in to your account and use UNIX commands to
    manipulate files? **Tip ➤** This may seem geeky to you now, but
    may very well become important to you later, especially if you
    want to get into authoring Websites.

8   Does the ISP offer some sort of help facility accessible via either
    e-mail or phone? Is it staffed by knowledgeable, patient, polite
    folx? **Tip ➤** Make it clear that you're not at the support staff's
    mercy and that you won't put up with attitude. They are there
    to help *you.*

GEEKY QUESTIONS TO HELP YOU SORT THE GOODIES FROM THE BADDIES

Tip ➤ If your mind draws a blank at the terminology, flip back to
page 20 for a peek at the glossary.

1   Is the ISP using the best, most up-to-date equipment available—
    modems, routers, switches? **Tip ➤** Ask this question even if the
    answer is meaningless to you. Listen for hesitation. Use your
    psychic powers of perception, and if you're really interested in
    their answer, research.

2   How close, network-wise, is the ISP to a major Internet back-
    bone (that is, a branch of the much touted, but still "informal"
    information superhighway system)? Ask to see their network
    topology maps. **Tip ➤** As magical as the speeds of the Net seem,

all data travels on physical networks. If someone tries to tell you that physical topology doesn't matter and/or starts looking around shiftily and talking about a "virtual backbone," run away, run away!

3 What is the speed of the provider's backbone links? That is, what is the total bandwidth the provider has to the Net (think "lanes of traffic")? **Tip ➤** Insist on a dedicated T1 (1.544 Mbps) connection. Beware fractional T1 lines. Beware leased-line 56 Kbps and 64 Kbps connections—they can be clogged by just a few 14.4 Kbps or 28.8 Kbps dial-ups. Be aware that your connection to the network will only be as fast as the slowest link. If there's a 56 Kbps line somewhere between you and a T1 node, your data will bottleneck and only move at 56 Kbps (major traffic jam). Large corporations and universities usually have T3 (45 Mbps) connections. If an ISP won't give you straight info on speed and bandwidth, you don't want to deal with them. Run away, run away!

4 How many external backbone links does the ISP offer? **Tip ➤** Ideally, the provider should offer several direct (called "dedicated"), high-speed connections to other network providers—the more the better. If the ISP offers only a single connection to the backbone, get a suspicious look on your face or tone in your voice and ask how often it fails and how long the connection is usually down.

5 Is the ISP's technical staff large enough and experienced enough at running TCP/IP data networks to be able to handle the usual problems and organizational situations? **Tip ➤** Present this scenario, and check their reaction: If the system goes down while two of the top propeller-heads are at a professional conference in another city and one is on vacation in Fiji, can the skeleton staff of propeller-heads fix it within a reasonable amount of time?

6 Is the ISP network operations center staffed by at least one *competent* person 24/7/365 (that is, all the time)? **Tip ➤** Staffers "on call" don't count. Insist that there always be someone there who

understands what's going on and *knows* what to do if things go bad. Sysops rule the cyberscape; make sure you're hooked up with a good bunch.

7   Are DNS (domain name server) and DNS-reverse present and working on all PPP ports and machines? Insist on this; it means that your provider machine recognizes name addresses like www.bgsu.edu, not just numerical IP addresses like 128.27.22.3. If DNS is present, it will be a lot easier to connect to remote machines (say, when you're surfing the Web) and for others to access your Website.

Well, with this information in hand, you are ready to hunt down your own ISP. If you're not in a major metropolitan area and can't find an ISP that meets all these requirements, you're better off with something than nothing, but keep your eyes open for either improvements to the ISP you choose or for another competitor to show up and offer what your service doesn't. Remember, you are paying for the service (even we are paying, via tuition and fee charges, for our "free" access); like any other service you hand over cold, hard cash for, shop around and find the best.

Your Mentor, Yourself

Yes, you can set up your system and get connected and acclimated to the Net all by yourself, little lonewolf, but it'll be a whole lot less *fun* than it could be and probably a whole lot more *frustrating* than it should be. So, how do you find this special person, this initiator, this mentor? S/he may be right under your nose. Netheads (especially the females of the species—imagine that!) are drawn out and almost literally sent into a helper-frenzy by even the simplest pre-newbie or newbie inquiry (especially from other women).

It is true that in this way Net culture has a lot in common with the idealized, pre-Altamont drug culture of yore: The imperative "dial up, log in and turn on" carries with it the understanding that you will help newbies as you yourself were helped. We know it sounds goopy, but it's true! If someone you know has been bugging you to get online for a long time, take her/him up on the offer of help and watch those geek eyes light up!

If you don't have any close friends who are online, the next time you're at a party and see a bunch of people gathered around your host's computer, insinuate yourself into the gaggle and let folx know that you're geeked and in need of knowledge/aid. You'll get phone numbers, e-mail addresses and advice from *at least* two or three people. In fact, they'll probably sit you down right there and give you a Net demo.

Ideally, your mentor should run the same platform as you (Mac or PC). Even more ideally, you two should use the same service provider because the most difficult task when you first log on is figuring out the specifics and little tricks, quirks, lore and shortcuts native to your ISP.

Getting online involves a pretty darn *steep* learning curve, but soon you'll be paddling about, posting here and there, searching and surfing the Web like a happy otter and wondering what you were so nervous about. At that point, it's time to take on a few students of your own. (And they'll turn on two friends. And so on. And so on . . .)

As you proceed through your particular nethead journey, you will encounter all sorts of mentors, teachers and collaborators, many of whom you'll only meet out there in the cyberscape. But even if you eventually outstrip your mentors skill-wise, you will always have a special place in your heart for those first people who shared their expertise and software with you, who sat down with you and showed you how to read Usenet on your system, who helped you subscribe to your first e-list or create a .sig file when you were all but in tears, or dragged you along on your first visit to Bianca's Smut Shack. This sort of informal mentoring system that has evolved within Net culture is the *foundation* of all cyberspace community! So, keep it going when the newbies begin to come to you for assistance and inspiration. It will happen.

SOME BASIC,

ANTICIPATORY Q & A

Because each ISP and computer has its own little quirks, we can't begin to answer every specific question related to the tasks we outline in the CyborGrrrl Scout merit badge section. What we *have* done is answer some of the more basic questions sure to come up during your introductory online jaunts. We've also included lots of pointers to helpful Websites and other resources. Good luck!

◇ **There was communications software packaged with my modem. Is that all I need to go online?**

◇ Well, it depends. A terminal emulator will connect to a UNIX shell through your ISP and will probably accompany a new modem. If you want to run client software—such as a graphical Web browser or an IRC client—you'll need some extra software to make the connection. Many commercial services (America Online, Prodigy, GEnie, et cetera) distribute their own specially designed, service-specific, easy-to-use software. If you decide to work via a PPP connection, however, you will need a dialer: One is included in Windows 95 and Macintosh System 7.5, and shareware dialers are available. Another option is a commercial Internet suite which includes a dialer, a Web browser, an e-mail client and other Net software and works with your ISP.

⋄ **So I signed up with an Internet service provider, and they told me I had a SLIP/PPP connection. Huh? What do they mean? What good is it? What do I do now?**

⋄ Congratulations! You have just put yourself on the Net in the best possible way. PPP (point to point protocol) is a way of implementing Internet Protocol (IP) and other networking protocols using a phone line and a modem. When you dial in to your ISP and make a PPP connection, the TCP/IP software allows your personal computer to interface directly with the Internet. This means you can navigate the Net in full-screen, graphical, point-&-click comfort. Assuming your ISP gave you instructions to set up the connection itself, all you need now is the client software. You'll definitely want a Web browser, an e-mail client and a Usenet reader, and you might even want a finger client, an IRC program and an FTP client. If you don't want to go the expensive Internet-in-a-Box route, you can download a whole suite of communications shareware and freeware from the following anonymous FTP sites (which are great places to start looking for *any* sort of shareware or freeware you might need):

- archive.umich.edu
- ftp.ncsa.uiuc.edu
- cica.indiana.edu
- sumex-aim.stanford.edu
- wuarchive.wustl.edu.

Make sure that you download the latest releases of whatever programs you choose. Here are our personal favorites:

◊

	Mac	PC
E-mail	Eudora Lite	Eudora Lite
World Wide Web	Netscape Navigator	Netscape Navigator
FTP	Fetch	WS_FTP
Usenet	NewsWatcher or Nuntius	Free Agent
Chat/IRC	ircle	mIRCv32
Telnet	NCSA Telnet	Trumpet Telnet
Gopher	TurboGopher	HGopher

✧ **I have an ISP, but MegaService X keeps sending me disks and promising ten or more free hours of online time. I am both annoyed and *sooo* tempted. Are there hidden costs?**

✧ You generally have to give commercial services a credit card number before they let you in, even for free trials. But heck, grrrl, if the phone number isn't long distance (check and make *sure*), take those free hours! While you're "inside," think like a poor college student scavenging free food at a cocktail party. You can download *lots* of goodies in ten hours! Wooo! Then if you don't find any long-term reason to keep the account, make sure you cancel your subscription as soon as those magical hours are up.

✧ **How can I find lists of listservs I might be interested in joining?**

✧ Be on the lookout for new listserv announcements in Usenet groups and on existing listservs, as well as on Websites and in magazines and journals. Looking for a listserv devoted to a specific topic/issue? Here are some "lists of lists" you can check out:

JOAN KORENMAN'S LIST OF GENDER-RELATED E-LISTS
Korenman is perhaps best known on the Net as moderator of WMST-L (Women's Studies list) and as Webmistress of the WMST-L archive site. In other words, she's got the inside skinny on everything even vaguely feminist-y.
http://www-unix.umbc.edu/~korenman/wmst/forums.html

TILE.NET'S SEARCHABLE LIST OF INTERNET DISCUSSION GROUPS
Excellent! Actually allows you to subscribe to lists on the spot using the "mailto" function of your Web browser. Includes a list of the one hundred most popular e-lists on the Net.
http://www.tile.net/tile/listserv/viewlist.html

LIST OF PUBLICLY ACCESSIBLE E-LISTS
Maintained by Stephanie daSilva.
http://www.neosoft.com/internet/paml/

LISTWEBBER LIST OF ACADEMIC-ORIENTED LISTSERVS
For the student in all of us.
http://www.lib.ncsu.edu:80/hGET%20/staff/morgan/listwebber.html

PROGRESSIVE ACTIVIST MAILING LISTS
Networking for change.
http://welcomehome.org/rainbow/lists.html

With some exceptions, most listservs are run by mailbots (not "real" people) which reflect posts to all subscribers of the list. When you want to join a listserv, send a subscription message to the e-mail address of the listserv, listproc or majordomo . . . not to the list itself! The subscribe message should be "subscribe [listname] [your name]." So if Jane Toughgrrrl wants to subscribe to chix-l, she might mail a message to listserv@fake.com that says "subscribe chix-l Jane Toughgrrrl." If you do something wrong, you'll usually get an automated e-mail message back from the mailbot telling you how to subscribe successfully.

Never send "please, pretty please add me to your list" messages to the list itself; you won't get anywhere and people will laugh at you. You don't want that.

Oh, and another tip: Delete .sigs from all messages you send to mailbots, listservs, listrprocs and majordomos. They can cause the bots to gag.

✧ **Help! I subscribed to this really high-volume listserv and don't want to be on it anymore! I tried to unsubscribe, but it didn't work. What do I do? How come I can't convince them to quit sending me mail?** *They're following me!*

✧ We're going to let you in on a little secret: The most annoying and cursed people in the listserv world are those who post "subscribe" and *especially* "unsubscribe" messages to a list itself instead of to (depending on the list) the listowner or the appropriate listserv, listproc or majordomo. This *really* cheeses off other subscribers who struggle with teensy mail quotas or who are forced to pay for e-mail based on volume. To save yourself and others from gigantic headaches, every time you subscribe to an e-list *save* the welcome message you get with the rules, regulations, instructions and (usually) instructions on how to interact with the mailbot that handles the mailing list. Save it! Then

SOME BASIC, ANTICIPATORY Q & A

scribble down the instructions (yes, by hand) in your handy CyborGrrrl Scout notebook. Occasionally, a bug in the mailbot will refuse to unsubscribe you from a listserv. That is the only time it might be appropriate to post to the list at large. *Really.* We're serious about this. Good listowners occasionally post instructions to unsubscribe (and how to retrieve archives, et cetera). If you're still confused, it is only appropriate to e-mail the list owner privately, admit you are not paying attention and request that she send unsubscribe instructions.

✧ **I can't find a listserv for a subject I'm interested in. Assuming that I have done my homework and there just isn't a listserv out there, how do I go about starting one?**
✧ At first thought, starting a listserv seems like a huge, perpetually ongoing responsibility. After you learn the basic listowner routine, though, it's not really that big of a deal. Nor is it at all permanent! If your listserv really takes off, and you find yourself too busy to deal with it or bored by the whole thing, you can hand list-owning duties off to another member of the listserv and let her run it from her site. Or if the topic is narrow enough, your list may just fizzle out when a good flow of discussion stops.

You can start a simple listserv merely by sending a message out to all your friends and asking them to reply to everyone who received it and not just to you. No one but you and your friends need be involved. If you want more people involved, you can still operate a small listserv or forum right from your own e-mail account. Announce a topic in some of the places you hang out (or just among a few people you know), then create a list of "subscribers" in your e-mail "address book" and zap messages you get to the rest of the folx on the list. This is a little labor intensive, but it's a great way to have private group discussions, thwart unwanted eavesdroppers and (should this be a potential problem) intercept harassing messages.

If you want to establish a more stable and bigger mailing list, check with your ISP. Many ISPs make listserv, listproc and majordomo utilities available to customers who want to start a list. As a listowner, you have to learn the administrative duties associated with running the list (it's not difficult) and probably sign a contract with your ISP agreeing to their administrative guidelines. Your list can have either wide-open subscriptions and submissions, or you can control who subscribes and/

or what messages get posted to the group. The latter may be useful if you run a list about a sensitive or controversial topic and are not interested in dealing with gratuitous flames or trolls. Depending upon the availability and cost of data storage space at your ISP, you may or may not be able to maintain an archive of messages posted to the list. No matter how you choose to make your list, *congratulations!* You've created another corner of the cyberscape!

◇ How do I add one of those personalized messages to the end of my e-mails and Usenet posts?

◇ Tags at the end of e-mail messages and Usenet posts are called .sig files. If you're on a UNIX system, create a file called .signature and type in your message, ASCII drawing or pithy quote. Otherwise, check your e-mail client help documents or ask your mentor how to do this. Most newsreaders and mail programs will automatically append the contents of your .sig file to any messages you send. Remember, .sig files over five or six lines are totally frowned upon in the Net community: They take up bandwidth and are seen as annoyingly self-indulgent. Keep your .sig file small, with your e-mail address, your URL or your job/school description and perhaps a *short* favorite quote.

◇ What are all those funny combinations of symbols sprinkled throughout e-mail and Usenet posts I keep reading? What does = ^) and > ;] mean?

◇ Hold the book in front of you and drop your head to your left shoulder. See the little faces? Those are "emoticons" or "smileys."

Emoticons are but one example of the weird creativity the Net demands of us. Their mission: to pump a little inflection into affect-defi- ... xt-based communications and alert your readers to your ... Until you have become embroiled in a flame war because ...sinterpreted or took offense at a message you meant sarcastically or as a joke, you can't fully appreciate the importance of these weird little ASCII glyphs. Too much is almost as bad as too little, though. Use emoticons sparingly, or you will seem like a scary emotional ketchup burst and people will avoid you.

=^)   Means something like "I know I'm being a little obnoxious by pointing this out to you, but accept the criticism in good spirit" (wide open eyes + pointy nose + big smile).

>;]   Might be used to indicate a mean-spirited joke (evil eyebrows + wink + smug, tight smile).

:)   The universal midget (no nose) smiley. "I'm kidding," "Happy happy, joy joy" or "Have a nice day." Meaning depends on context.

;)   The midget wink.

:-]   Dopey grin.

:-P   Tongue out at you!

:-\   Ambivalent.

:-0   Total surprise or a scream.

=-(A long, sad face.

8-)   "I'm a happy _____ (_____ smarts).

:-!   "I

=0+   "

>=0+   '

=)0+

New s _____ p any number
of smi _____ List of Smileys
(http _____ faves because
it all _____

⬦ H _____ et, but it's no
lon _____ d it?
⬦ _____ .dejanews.com).
Yo _____ ears by keyword.
St _____ odstock.stanford.
edu:2000/News/_____ mber, while you're
browsing around in Usenet, you can mail any choice bits to yourself (or
anyone else!) just as easily as you can reply to a message. You should
also remember that the advent of indexed Usenet databases means that

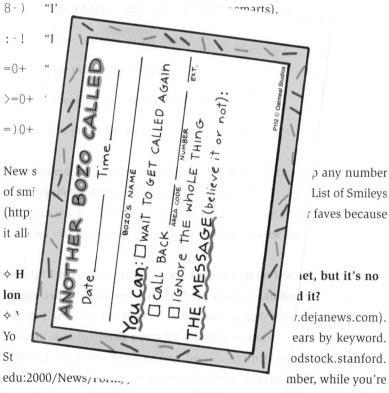

anything you post to any Usenet group can now come back to haunt you. (It also means that you can spy on friends, enemies, relatives and lovers.) Posting intimate details of your life to a Usenet group is most decidedly not a good idea.

✧ **Help! My site's newsfeed doesn't include a newsgroup I really want, and the sysop (systems operator) at my ISP can't or won't add it for some reason!**

✧ For purposes of this answer, we'll assume that you're not talking about a ClariNet newsgroup (clari.[whatever]). The ClariNet hierarchy comes into an ISP on a special, expensive, licensed feed and is available from relatively few providers.

If your sysop refuses to pick up a regular Usenet newsgroup, two things could be up. The group might not yet be available from the "upstream" network from which the feed for your ISP flows. In that case, you could ask your sysop to put in an add request upstream. The scarier scenario is when the ISP owners/operators censor entire sections of the feed (say, the alt.sex hierarchy) because they find those groups offensive, immoral, upsetting, et cetera. Unfortunately, this can happen upstream too, and then it can be *very* hard to do anything about it. If this is the case and you're bugged, check out the Banned Newsgroups FAQ (http://www.cs.rmit.edu.au/etext/FAQs/Banned.News.FAQ).

There are alternative ways to access full Usenet feeds from your account. The Usenet Information Center Launchpad at the University of North Carolina (http://sunsite.unc.edu/usenet-b/home.html) call tell you everything you ever wanted to know about Usenet, including where to find "public Usenet feeds." Perhaps the easiest way to access a full newsfeed is to zap over to Zippo Dot Com (http://www.zippo.com).

✧ **I can't find a newsgroup on my favorite topic. I've checked everywhere and one just doesn't exist. How do I start a newsgroup?**

It's incredibly easy to start a "local" Usenet group. Just send mail to your sysop asking her/him to "create" yoursite.whatever. Only people local to your ISP will access that group, but, hey, that's the idea! If you decide that absolutely everyone must have access to some support group you want to start—let's call it soc.women.who.sleep.too.much—things are somewhat complicated. There are two ways to start up groups that will reflect around the world. If you want to start a group on a hierarchy other than alt.*, you must go through the formal Usenet referendum procedure. Ideally, all new Usenet groups are formally proposed by an individual or group, and then voted on by whatever users are most interested in/affected by the proposal. When a formal proposal passes, you can count on the group being picked up by lots of sites. You can avoid the "formal" process by starting up an alt.* newsgroup on your home provider. As you advertise it far and wide, people will begin to request that their sysops add it to their newsfeeds, and the group will slowly creep over the networks like a slime mold. Neat, huh? Learn how to create an alt.* group at http://www.math.psu.edu/barr/alt-cre-ation-guide.html.

Another option: Become a Usenet squatter. Is nobody posting to alt.fan.naked-guy anymore? Grab some folx and rededicate the group to a whole other topic. Voilà! You have renovated a little corner of the cyberscape.

✧ So, how do I find stuff on the World Wide Web if I don't already know where it is?

✧ By using these really easy-to-use online search engines and indexes. The titles and texts of almost all documents on the Web are searchable by keyword. Fire up your Web browser and go to one of these sites:

METACRAWLER
Instead of maintaining its own internal database of sites, Metacrawler actually refers queries to other search tools like Lycos, Yahoo, AltaVista and InfoSeek, then compiles the results. What a nifty idea.
http://metacrawler.cs.washington.edu:8080/

ALTAVISTA
Fast and huge. It also allows you to search Usenet News posts.
http://altavista.digital.com

WEBCRAWLER
Developed at the University of Washington, this search engine is one of the best.
http://webcrawler.com/

INFOSEEK
Perhaps the speediest, most comprehensive search engine out there. Except for the most simple Website retrieval, searches will cost you. Still, for people in certain professions, InfoSeek's services are a bargain!
http://guide.infoseek.com/

YAHOO!
Started by a couple of now-wealthy Stanford grad students, Yahoo! is widely recognized as one of *the* starting points for Web exploration of almost any topic.

Search or browse . . . everything is organized hierarchically. Intuitive, fun, inevitable and now in a Japanese version (http://www.yahoo.co.jp).
http://www.yahoo.com/

LYCOS
This search engine has over three million pages indexed, so you get back tons of hits. Brought to the cyberscape courtesy of Carnegie-Mellon University.
http://lycos.cs.cmu.edu/

EINET GALAXY
Known more for its subject catalog than its searches, Galaxy is still a useful search engine to ferret out sites to browse.
http://galaxy.einet.net/

✧ **I need to research a rather obscure subject, and my library doesn't have enough information. Everyone is talking about using the Internet for research . . . but why? How? Where?**

✧ Great global bookmites! The Internet has forever changed how we do research—Virginia Woolf would totally *freak!* In addition to allowing access to collection catalogs, many libraries also make a limited range of research databases and resources available to remote patrons. The Library of Congress is online at http://lcweb.loc.gov/homepage/lchp.html. After you whet your research appetite there, try out Netlink (http://honor.uc.wlu.edu/net/catalogs/). If your Web browser supports telnet, you can jump from this page to just about any publicly accessible library catalog in the world. No, we're not kidding. This is great for students with access to interlibrary loan services.

✧ **What does "anonymous FTP" mean? What do I do when the remote machine asks me for a login name and password?**

✧ Anonymous FTP allows any user on the Net to download files from a public site. In return, users must tell the remote machine who they are:
Login: anonymous
Password: [your e-mail address]

✧ **My mentor said to download a certain file. How do I figure out what files are available from which anonymous FTP sites?**

✧ Everything's ARCHIEd. Everything, that is, that you can access via anonymous FTP. The ARCHIE system stores the names of files available on anonymous FTP servers around the world. Remember, ARCHIE indexes files according to file name, so if you're on the hunt for a particular shareware program, search by name, not type of application. The SURANET ARCHIE Guide (http://www.sura.net/archie/Archie-

Usage.html) can tell you all you need to know. Other places to explore are the ARCHIE Request form at Rutgers (http://www-ns.rutgers.edu/htbin/archie) and http://phaethon.cti.gr/archie.html, a Greek (as in country) ARCHIE browser. Way remote, but very nice.

✧ What is compression software and why do I need it?

✧ Compression software allows you to "unpack" files (software, images, sounds, et cetera) you download from various archives. To save space and conserve bandwidth, archive keepers compress uploaded files using one of several compression formats, and you must decompress or expand these files on your hard drive before you can run, view or listen to them. Conversely, you can also use these software programs to compress files before you upload them or send them to someone else.

Mac users need CompactPro (handles files with .cpt and .hqx suffixes) and Stuffit (.sit). The .sea suffix denotes a "self-extracting archive," or a file you don't need compression software to open. PC users need pkunzip and/or WinZip to decompress files with .zip suffixes. You can download shareware versions of these programs from your fave software archive.

✧ I'm having a bear of a time figuring out Internet Relay Chat. Some of the manuals indicate that I should just be able to type "IRC" at my UNIX prompt and kick right in, but my sysop says I have to get and compile my own "client" or telnet to a public server. I can never get in to those public servers! Help!

✧ Ah, IRC. Future conspiracy theorists are likely to argue that the cyborg Entities Who Run Things made a secret, tortured decision to make accessing this global cocktail party as difficult as possible in order to prevent the brightest and weirdest among us from flunking out of school, losing jobs, destroying relationships, hatching weird plots with likeminded malcontents halfway around the world, "misusing" critical resources and limited bandwidth, and generally getting nothing done. This is partly true, but heck, we'll tell you how to do it anyway. Mutants need toys! For a fuller explanation of why this is true, see *The Happy Mutant Handbook: Mischievous Fun for Higher Primates* by Mark Frauenfelder, Carla Sinclair, Gareth Branwyn and Will Kreth (Riverhead Books, 1995) (http://www.putnam.com/putnam/Happy_Mutant/).

Folx use IRC to hang out with e-mail friends in real time, to celebrate with far-flung friends and families on holidays, to discuss all sorts of serious and frivolous matters, to conference, to "perform" Shakespeare plays and (yes) to troll for sex. Anyone can start a "channel" and dedicate it to a topic, and that channel can be open to all interested parties . . . or restricted to only the folx you want to let in. In other words, once you learn some basic commands (see local help files or http://www.bastad.se/ ~ ryding/pub/irc/irccom.txt), IRC can be a blast even if all you do is lurk and channel-hop.

If you have a UNIX shell account with at least 2.5 megabytes free, you can download and compile a freeware IRC client (a version of irccle) by issuing this simple command at your usual prompt (watch spacing, no period at the end!): telnet sci.dixie.edu 1 | sh. Honest. Issue that command, sit back and wait for about twenty minutes while the software automatically downloads, decompresses and compiles. Amazing. Simply amazing. After that, IRC will be as easy as reading your e-mail. Just follow the help prompts, and be sure to print out a list of basic IRC commands.

If you have a PPP connection, there are a number of graphical IRC clients available for both PC and Mac. Once you download, uncompress and install one, you're on your way. Popular IRC servers include irc.dal.net, us.undernet.org and irc.eskimo.com. When we say popular, we *mean* popular, though, and sometimes IRC is simply so busy you'll have to get your online kicks elsewhere because there are no available login ports. If you're desperate, keep trying.

Confused newbies and longtimers alike should browse Paul Graham's one-stop IRC info-ganza (http://urth.acsu.buffalo.edu/irc/WWW/ircdocs.html). You'll find all kinds of FAQs, client and server info, stuff about graphical IRC clients, links to IRC channels with Websites and logs of conversations from long-running IRC channels.

You have been warned: IRC is perhaps the most mind-sucking thing in the whole wired world. Enjoy!

✧ What about MUDs and MOOs? Aren't they the same thing as IRC?
✧ Not at all. Remember Dungeons & Dragons and the whole role-playing game craze of the 1970s? Maybe you don't have *personal* fond memories of odd-shaped dice and calculating characters' stamina, but it's important to understanding the MUD/MOO phenomenon, so sit up and pay attention.

Early in the development of the Internet, a couple of stereotypes surrounded those first computer geeks: One, they all wore horned-rimmed glasses, and two, they were all dungeon masters of various levels. Some stereotypes don't hold up under historical examination but others have their basis in truth: Many of these early geeks realized the Net would be an *amazing* place to play disembodied role-playing games and create text-based fantasy worlds. Multi-user dungeons (MUDs) sprang up, and users all over the world logged in for real-time, text-based role-playing games over the Internet. Today, there are hundreds of available MUDs you can telnet to, rescue fair maidens and collect gold coins. Check out The MUD Connector at http://www.absi.com/mud/mud_home.html for information and a continuously updated list of running MUDs.

MOOs are actually a much more recent Net phenomenon, and literally mean "MUD Object Oriented." Playing in MOO-space is unique because the user can manipulate the "space" by creating rooms and objects other users can interact with. Two of the more influential (and, IOHO, fun) MOOs are LambdaMOO and MediaMOO. LambdaMOO (telnet://lambda.parc.xerox.com:8888) is built on the premise of a house. Users create their own rooms—where the virtual character "sleeps" and personal objects are kept—and share common spaces, such as the hottub and the kitchen. If your taste for online interaction leans towards the serious and intellectual, get your daily dose of MOOing at MediaMOO (telnet://purple-crayon.media.mit.edu:8888). Started by Amy Bruckman at MIT, MediaMOO is a virtual space for academics and media professionals to interact with each other and learn first-hand of this whole MOOing business.

Many text-based virtual words exist on the Internet, and they are fascinating places to interact with others and enjoy online space. The realization that you're spending time in an imaginary space you can conceptualize by reading descriptions and interacting with other people is a heady experience.

❖ **I got flamed. Totally *singed*. How can people be so mean and stupid!? I'm so agitated and mad I could . . .**

✧ Whoa, grrrl. Simmer down. Now, unless you made some major, unintentional gaffe (in which case you should immediately make nice with the newsgroup or listserv), let the medium work *for* you. Among the grooviest things about lists and Usenet is that you can take that extra five minutes (or five hours) to think of the perfect comeback (while you do other things, of course).

Since you'll need them only occasionally and because they can double as responses to street harassment, we suggest stocking up on pithy, infuriating or disorienting, kick-in-the-chest one-liners along the lines of "Give it up, baby. I eat your contempt like love." Brief is best, but be creative. Rage on! "Get a life" is not an acceptable response to anything, ever. Got it? It's much more cathartic to *hex* someone who repels you: "May legions of screeching possums rain down upon your next cross burning/Aryan race-actualization seminar, buddy. And then may they come to my house for an afterhours so I can reward them with a huge sack of grapefruit rinds." Understatement and unspoken threats are good too. Keep calm. Be ultra-reasonable. Be literate. And know when to just walk away.

✧ **But I'm *serious*. This creep is really *bugging* me. I'm almost scared for my virtual self. Now what?**
✧ The thin electron lines separating e-harassment, e-pranks and e-war are often fuzzy and hard to define. Sometimes things can get out of hand in the cyberscape. Sometimes people are just playing around, sometimes not. If you find yourself being harassed or threatened (not just flamed, but *persistently* harassed or threatened by a truly unreasonable or scary person), the first thing you should do is send e-mail to the person's sysop (sysop@obnoxious.org, for example), forwarding a piece of particularly choice e-mail or a Usenet post from your harasser along with your complaint. This puts the sysop and others on notice that one of their subscribers has been naughty, and the person will be reprimanded, in some cases to the point of losing his/her account with that ISP.

✧ **What is an anonymous remailer and why would I want to use one?**
✧ Anonymous remailers are nice for a variety of reasons. Sometimes it's just too freaking dangerous to send e-mail or post to a Usenet group

a crucial bit of info about an issue, an incident or yourself using a real, traceable e-mail address. Anonymous remailers like the legendary anon.penet.fi are the way you get around this, and every time you use one you should thank the committed souls (lotsa true cyberpunks) who, risking persecution/prosecution, live the First Amendment and make these cloaking devices available to the rest of us. Abuse a remailer (by sending a mail bomb, for example) and you will find your numerically designated account terminated, babe. More info on anon remailers can be found at the Community ConneXion remailer info page (http://www.world.net/%7Epirovich/remail.htm). This funky little site was set up to protect and foster Internet privacy and offer access at reasonable rates, and you'll find all sorts of remailer details and options explained and linked here. For more information about individual remailers, send mail to the following addresses: help@anon.penet.fi, help@vox.hactic.nl, and/or mg5n+remailer-list@andrew.cmu.edu, or finger remailer@soda.berkeley and/or remailer@chaos.bsu.edu. Good luck.

◇ **How can my little sister send me e-mail from catwoman@ tuffgrrrl.org when her e-mail address is really jane@freezing. midwest.edu and she doesn't own what is called a "virtual domain"?**

◇ Basically, what she's doing is tricking the name server of a machine, saying, for example, her name is tuffgrrrl.org, not other.machine.com (or whatever). Some machines won't let you play this game; just bang around until you find one that will. Here's how:

1) Telnet to port 25 (the STMP server) of a remote machine.

        <email>telnet other.machine.com 25

2) Tell the machine its "new" name and hope it doesn't insist that its name is . . . well, whatever its name really is. If it does, you've gotta look for another machine. (Note: HELO is not a typo.)

        HELO tuffgrrrl.org

3) Set up the fake (watch spacing!).

        MAIL FROM:catwoman@tuffgrrrl.org
        RCPT TO:your.victim@aol.com
        DATA

4) Type in your message. When you are ready to send it, type a period on a new line, hit the return key, then type "QUIT."

```
[blah blah blah blah]

.

QUIT
```

Voilà: fakemail. Practice sending some to yourself first.

✧ Some jerk just spammed a bunch of newsgroups with a list of "101 Ways to Rape a Woman." I'm peeved. What to do?

✧ Exercise your first amendment rights; engage in group actions with friends and cohorts. An effort organized by some Bryn Mawr netchix resulted in Cornell University being deluged by so much e-mail object-ing to a widely reposted list of the "Top 75 Reasons Why Women (Bitches) Should Not Have Freedom of Speech" message originated by four lame-o testosterone-challenged undergrad men calling themselves "The Four-Players of Cornell" that the university was forced to deal seriously with the matter. Justice On Campus, a free-speech organiza-tion, has compiled a great page on the Cornell incident (http://joc.mit.edu/cornell.html). You hardly need a cast of hundreds of thou-sands to pull a move similar to the one organized at Bryn Mawr; a handful of friends will suffice for most personal matters. What matters is a show of solidarity.

✧ How do I keep up-to-date about social, legal and cultural issues related to the Internet and life online?

✧ Welcome to Netizenship 101. Now is the time for all good netizens to add these links to their bookmark files:

THE ELECTRONIC FRONTIER FOUNDATION
Our voice and yours in the service of the Constitution in cyberspace. Even if we don't exactly dig how they deploy the frontier idea sometimes, we stand up for what they stand for. Anytime. Anyplace. Excellent reading room and resources, including the *EFF Extended Guide to the Internet*. Up-to-date reportage on the latest legal, political and social controversies flaring up on or around the Net. Very important stuff.
http://www.eff.org

COMPUTER PROFESSIONALS FOR SOCIAL RESPONSIBILITY
CPSR is a "public interest alliance of computer scientists and others interested in the impact of computer technology in society." Be sure to check out their section on gender issues and computing/networking.
http;//www.cspr.org/home/

WIRED AND HOTWIRED

Wired and its sister online venture not only have their fingers on the pulse of emerging technoculture as a whole, but have had an immense stylistic influence on the look of the online world. You'll love them, you'll hate them, you'll love them. Useful and unavoidable. The online version of *Wired* is available at the HotWired site.

http://www.hotwired.com/

INTERNET WORLD

Along with some really good articles, this magazine site features elaborate monthly hotlists.

http://www.iw.com/

ROBERT SEIDMAN'S ONLINE INSIDER

Offers a weekly summary of events in the consumer online service industry, as well as links to a number of related sites and online publications.

http://www.clark.net/pub/robert/

✧ **How do I make a homepage of my own? I mean, I don't know anything about computer programming, and it just looks so *hard!***

✧ Most emphatically *untrue*. HTML is *fun*. Trust us. First, when you "code" homepages, you are not actually "programming," but, rather, simply coding and formatting text and links to other files and sites so a Web browser will be able to "read" them. To get the general hang of things, scope out the source code of other people's pages: Use your browser to "view" the "document source," usually found under "edit" if you're using a Mac or a PC running Windows. There is a lot of online support for Web page creators. We have listed a few of the more helpful ones below. As we write this, the first practical applications of VRML (virtual reality markup language—which allows construction of *Myst*-like 3-D Web spaces) and Java (which allows online animation among other things) are up and coming. Woo! But, first things first. If you are in the market for a how-to book, Laura Lemay's *How to Teach Yourself Web Publishing Using HTML in a Week* (Sams Press, 1995) seems to be everyone's hands-down favorite. You will still want to check out these sites, though:

A BEGINNER'S GUIDE TO HTML

http://www.ncsa.uiuc.edu/General/Internet/WWW/HTMLPrimer.html

THE WEB DEVELOPERS VIRTUAL LIBRARY

http://WWW.Stars.com

LEARN TO WRITE CGI FORMS

http://www.catt.ncsu.edu/users/bex/www/tutor/index.html

MAP MARKER HOMEPAGE (IMAGEMAP
http://www.dl.ac.uk/CBMT/mapmarker/HOME.html

✧ **I want to put up a homepage, but I don't really know what to put on it. It just looks like fun . . . do I really *have* to think up something to say?**

✧ Three words are important to you at this point: *content, content, content!* Okay, we've all heard it from supercilious friends/relatives/teachers: "Why should anybody bother to get into that Internet stuff? Books/pencils/paper/the telephone/face-to-face interaction is/are better, and besides, I've heard there's really not that much good, useful stuff out there, just a bunch of porno."

Sure, there is some legitimacy to the popular bitch that there are millions of channels on the Net (especially the Web) and nothing on, but people who sniff and take this tack miss the whole point. First of all: this isn't *television*, fer goshsakes! The number-one nethead imperative is learn, learn, learn, create, create, create, build, build, build! After a certain point, one should not just *use* the Net, one should *invest* in it by making enticing spaces and archives/resources for others to enjoy as you, dearie, enjoy theirs. That's just part of the responsibility that accompanies being part of the larger cyberspace community.

That said, when you're constructing your personal, business or organizational Website, your focus should be on providing a decent bit of original content and on organizing your links topically or in some other way that makes them useful to your visitors. All good personal Websites have a healthy bit of ego involved in them (that's what makes surfing personal sites so much fun), but their creators don't allow self-absorption to *overwhelm* the tone and usefulness of the pages—they just allow their personalities to suffuse whatever they do. Check out Janet's Rocky Mountain Homepage (http://www.interealm.com/p/ratzloff/jan/), and notice how her personal information and original content color her external links to information about Colorado, Wyoming, horse stuff and other aspects of the "Western lifestyle." Very nice! As far as original content goes, well, that can be anything from a really wired interactive game or feature you created to scans of paintings or drawings you've done; creative page-design; hypertext versions of stories, essays or poems you've written; video or music you've composed or pages devoted to your favorite obsessions or causes. Whatever.

Just keep your content-to-links ratio fairly low! Trust us, people will love you for it, be inspired by your work and throw all sorts of virtual flowers and kisses into your in-box. One more thing: if your ISP tries to enforce some sort of cheesy and oppressive "standard-design" Web page policy, *revolt!* You don't have to take that.

SurferGrrrl Scout

Merit Badges

Every Internet service provider and every user's assemblage of communications software is a little different and has its own peculiarities. The purpose of this section of the book is not to "teach" you everything you need to know about getting and being online, but to map the territory of the Internet, define the skills and know-how you need to navigate and contribute to it, set and suggest some goals and provide pointers to how-to information available online.

Remember to refer to the earlier sections of the book if and when the techie talk starts making you dizzy or nauseated. As your intrepid leaders, we have tried to anticipate and answer many of the questions you may have and offer some survival tips and useful site pointers.

As you complete each task, skill or project for each badge, initial it. We encourage everyone to interpret, decorate and display their badges as they see fit!

◊

GremmieGrrrl

(A gremmie is a wanna-be surfer)

Objective: To assemble the hardware, software and connectivity I need to explore the Internet.

_____ I have acquired a mentor who is able and willing to answer my initial questions and/or help me configure my communications software. (Don't fret if you're all on your own initially; teachers will appear.)

_____ I have researched my Internet service provider options (including freenets) and picked the ISP and type of connection that are best for me. Or, I have signed up for Internet access offered by my school or employer.

_____ My computer has the necessary RAM to allow the type of dial-up access I have selected.

_____ I have a modem that is compatible with my operating platform (Mac or PC). **Tip ➤** Modems capable of recieving and sending 28.8 Kbps of data are currently the industry standard. If you are buying new, go ahead and spring for one of those. You need at least a 14.4 Kbps modem to be able to run a graphical Web browser effectively.

_____ I have communications software appropriate to the type(s) of connection(s) I want to make.

_____ I have the information I need to configure my communications software and log on (dial-up numbers, speed, parity, password information, IP address, et cetera.) **Tip ➤** If you are connecting to a service provider via a PPP or SLIP connection, you may also need to know how to write a log-on script. A total newbie on a quest to establish a PPP connections should, as they used to say in *The Girl Scout Handbook*, "get an adult to help you with this skill." No kidding, grrrls. This is where a mentor begins to come in really handy.

_____ I have installed an *up-to-date* antivirus program on my hard drive. The risk of picking up a virus on the Net has been grossly exaggerated in the media, but you must inoculate your machine before you head out into the big, bad world. Heck, you should be running an antivirus program if you *ever* stick floppies from friends or colleagues in your soft drive. You don't know where that floppy's been!

Newbie

Objective: To log on to my Internet service provider and to learn and practice some basic skills.

_____ I know my e-mail address, e.g., newbiegrrrl@myprovider. com or janedoe @campusnet.bigu.edu.

_____ I have decided on a log-on password and memorized it. For security reasons, it does not include my initials, my name, my birthday, or any other readily available data about me. **Tip ➤** Some ISPs require that your password include a number, symbol and/or capital letter. If your ISP refuses your new password, make sure you are using proper syntax.

_____ I have successfully configured my software, familiarized myself with its features and connected to a remote computer (your ISP).

_____ I have changed my password and understand how my ISP handles password security matters (some services ask users to change them once or twice each year).

_____ I have a reasonably secure notebook or journal for keeping track of addresses, shortcuts, tricks, information about how to sign on and off the e-lists to which I subscribe, and other miscellanea I need to remember.

_____ Using ISP service orientation documents, online menus and help functions or the help of my mentor, I have figured out how to send and receive electronic mail messages using my preferred mail reader.

_____ I have successfully subscribed to an electronic mailing list or discussion group.

_____ Observing proper netiquette, I lurked for a few days before posting a message to the list in order to get a feel for what goes on in the group, what's acceptable and what's not.

_____ I have briefed myself on the basic rules of netiquette, and promise to play nice as long as others respect me as well. **Tip ➤** There's a helpful netiquette site on the WWW at http://www.cis.ohio-state.edu/hypertext/faq/usenet/emily-postnews.

_____ I have briefed myself on safety on the Internet. (Check out the Oklahoma University Department of Public Safety pages on how to protect yourself, your money, your heart and your kids at http://www.uoknor.edu/oupd/inetmenu.html).

Complete at least two of the following. Every ISP is different. Just do the best you can with what's available to you:

_____ I have made a telnet connection to one of these sites: The WELL (well.org), NASA Spacelink (spacelink.msfc.nasa.gov) or Prairienet (prairienet.org).

_____ However randomly, I've visited at least ten sites on the World Wide Web using either a text-based browser or a graphical browser like Netscape.

_____ I have figured out how to read Usenet news on my site.

_____ I know that Gopher isn't only a type of rodent, but a directory-based, text-based information server, and I have explored Gopher on my home site. **Tip ➤** Try typing "gopher" at your cursor prompt. You may also explore Gopher sites using a WWW browser—the World Wide Web has pretty much replaced Gopher anyhow.

_____ I have logged onto an anonymous FTP server and dowloaded a file from a software, image, sound or text archive to my home directory or hard drive. **Tip ➤** If you are running a UNIX shell account, you also must consult your communications software manual and figure out how to download the file to the hard drive on your personal computer. Common protocols include Kermit, XModem, YModem and Zmodem.

Navigator

Objective: To become knowledge-able and comfortable using the most common Internet applications and learn how to be able to find almost anything I need or want to know.

_____ I can now access *all* of the following features of the Net available from my ISP: World Wide Web, Usenet news, Gopher, telnet and FTP.

_____ I have learned how to post articles and replies to Usenet newsgroups.

_____ I have learned how to save Usenet posts in my home directory and e-mail posts to myself and others.

_____ I know how to navigate directly to specific sites on the World Wide Web.

_____ I have used a search engine to research and locate sites on the WWW.

_____ I know how to use the "bookmark" or "hotlist" function on my Web browser.

_____ I have figured out how to save e-mail messages in my home directory on my ISP or on my hard drive.

_____ I have figured out the easiest way to print out e-mail messages and other text files on my specific system/printer. **Tip ➤** Mac and Windows 95 users, take advantage of the select and copy/print features on your systems when doing this.

_____ With the help of my mentor or newsreader help docs, I have figured out how to subscribe to my fave Usenet newsgroups and/or write a short UNIX program to get my fave newsgroups to come up in the order I prefer.

_____ I have figured out how to use the address book function in my e-mail program.

_____ I have figured out how to make a .sig (signature) file on my system.

_____ If I am a university student, I have figured out how to access my school's library and have explored the online resources and databases available there. If I am not a university student, I have inquired as to whether any local public or university libraries are accessible to the public via telnet or the WWW and, if so, have visited there.

_____ From my mentor/friend or via anonymous FTP, I have acquired copies of the latest versions of the most common compression software.

_____ If necessary, I successfully decompressed the file(s) I downloaded and/or configured my browser to automatically decompress files.

Mentor

Objective: To use my newfound powers for good by helping someone else get online.

_____ I have thanked _my_ mentor(s) profusely.

_____ I have agreed to mentor a gremmie girl or guy who has asked me for help getting online. Or, I have actively seduced someone I think would enjoy being online but isn't.

_____ My mentee has earned her or his Gremmie badge.

_____ My mentee has earned her or his Navigator badge.

_____ My mentee has outstripped my training and taught me a groovy Net trick or two.

◊

Netizen

Objective: To become conversant with the larger social, economic and political issues surrounding the ongoing development of electronic networks, including the Internet, especially as these matters impact on women's access to the Net, on freedom of speech, privacy and security online and on patterns of social or "flesh" interaction.

_____ I keep a close eye on discussions of the social and political impacts of the Internet, remaining mindful of the irony that electronic networking (especially all forms of telecommuting!) has a tremendous potential to isolate me from other individuals in my flesh communities.

_____ I have flesh-met at least one colleague/friend I linked up with on the Net. **Tip ➤** Safety first. Never meet a Net bud for the first time in a private place.

_____ I have spent some time thinking about what the Internet is and what directions I think its development should take.

_____ I am aware of the various censorship issues that have emerged— such as the early 1996 case of CompuServe pulling the plug on "obscene" newsgroups and forums because of complaints in Germany—as the Net truly becomes global.

_____ I stay well briefed about issues of girls' and women's access to and use of electronic technology and networks and can give my own "girls/women and the Internet" spiel (to girls, women, businesspeople, policymakers, civic organizations and the like) when asked or when it seems appropriate.

_____ I have spent some time poking about in the Electronic Frontier Foundation archives (http://www.eff.org/). There you will find information and pointers to information about most of the issues outlined here.

_____ I keep an eye on how the popular media portrays the Net, especially when they sensationally demonize the Net and it's population.

_____ I have considered the matter of government regulation of Internet content—including "cyberporn"—and am able to clearly articulate my views on the issue. **Tip** ➤ Web search with the keywords "Communications Decency Act" and "Internet censorship."

_____ I have considered the issues surrounding copyright law in cyber-space.

_____ I know about the Clipper chip controversy. **Tip** ➤ Check out the HotWired and _Wired_ Privacy Guide at http://www.hotwired.com/clipper for more info.

_____ I know what PGP (Pretty Good Privacy) encryption is, and am familiar with the arguments for and against it.

_____ I have at least a fundamental understanding of how the provisions of the Telecommunications Act of 1996 impacts the development and delivery of electronic resources and on the future of the Internet and individual network access. **Tip** ➤ See, for example, http://bell.com/hrconf.html.

_____ Especially if I'm a parent or teacher, I've considered how to best help children and K-12 students navigate the Net, yet avoid sites/discussions I believe are inappropriate for them.

_____ I have added the e-mail addresses of my congresspeople and a few other bigwigs to my address book.

_____ I have sent e-mail to my elected officials on some "Internet and society" issue that is important to me.

_____ I know the address and phone number of at least one organization in my area that accepts tax-deductible contributions of used computer equipment and/or makes equipment available at low cost to individuals or groups for training, enrichment and educational programs. Check out the state-by-state and international directory of computer donation programs from Parents, Educators and Publishers group (http://www.microweb.com/pepsite/Recycle/recycle_index.html), Goodwill (http://www.ocgoodwill.org/computer.html) and Computers for Others (http://cpcug.org/user/laurence/recycle.htm).

Weaver

Objective: To design and compose my own personal homepage on the World Wide Web.

_____ I know whether or not my ISP allows users to put up homepages, and, if it does not, I have explored other options. **Tip ➤** Some .edu sites may place restrictions on who can put up pages on their server. If you're at an .edu site that does not allow this, seek out a telnet-accessible ISP and, for a small monthly fee, put up your pages there. Physical location of your Web server is not an issue.

_____ I have figured out how I want to write/edit my page, either using an HTML editor, doing HTML markup in my word-processing program and uploading the document as a text file or doing markup and editing within my UNIX shell.

_____ I've figured out what I need to do within my ISP home directory to be able to put up a Web page. **Tip ➤** You may need to create a special directory (mkdir) and execute a couple of other UNIX commands to allow public access to your HTML documents.

_____ I have found a few Websites I really like design-wise and downloaded the marked-up source code to my hard drive. **Tip ➤** Checking out other people's pages is the best way to really learn HTML (hypertext markup language), VRML (virtual reality markup language), Java and whatever else becomes fun and possible as the Net continues to mutate.

_____ I have found a current HTML style guide I really like and added it to my bookmarks. **Tip ➤** Check out http://www.sandia.gov/ sci_compute/html_ref.html

_____ If I have decided to use a HTML editor, I've shopped around and found the shareware or off-the-shelf program that best suits my needs.

_____ I have visited some of the many excellent "homepage design, resources, tools and goodies" pages on the WWW and picked up some tips, ideas and maybe an image or two.

_____ I have acquired some basic graphics skills, such as scanning images, messing with or creating images in paint/graphics programs or converting other graphics formats to .gif and .jpg format. **Tip ➤** If you don't have access to a scanner or graphics software, just do madly fabulous things with color, typography and perhaps sound!

_____ Because everybody just hates "Hi. I'm Jane! Here are some links and a picture of my dog/girlfriend/boyfriend/inflatable-lizard!" pages, I have put some thought into the design and content of my page.

_____ Okay, I really followed through on that last part. My page is not boring and generic: it is _me_ (whoever I want to appear to be)!

_____ Yay! I have "finished" and debugged my page, uploaded it to the appropriate directory in my ISP home directory, and successfully accessed it on the network. **Tip ➤** Some people like to run their pages through an HTML-checker like Weblint (http://www.unipress.com/weblint/) before debuting them in public.

_____ I announced/registered my pages in at least a couple of places, for example, comp.infosystems.www.announce, on the WWW with Femina (the Yahoo for women!) or such places as the WWW birthday server and Yahoo!

_____ I solemnly vow to check and update my page(s) _at least_ every month or so, taking special care to fix or remove broken/down links.

_____ I have joined or regularly check out some sort of e-forum for Web weavers. **Tip ➤** Lots of sites offer local newsgroups for people who maintain pages on their server. There are a number of e-mail lists and Usenet forums devoted to the WWW.

_____ If I can do it from my ISP account, and if I want/need this degree of interactivity on my page, I have figured out how to do forms and write cgi-bin scripts.

_____ If I can run them from my account, I have figured out how to do imagemaps (images that contain links to different pages or sites).

◊

CyborGrrrl

Objectives: To start and/or moderate an electronic mailing list, a Usenet group or chat forum and to put up a nonpersonal page on the World Wide Web.

_____ I have helped at least three girls or women get online or become comfortable online. Or, I have planned and facilitated some sort of formal or informal introductory/instructional forum about the Internet for a group of women and girls in my community.

_____ I have started an e-mail list about some issue or topic I am really interested in or concerned about. Or, I have begun a Usenet newsgroup.

_____ I have put up a Web page for an organization I'm involved in, about an issue or topic I care passionately about, or for my business. (X-tra CyborGrrrl karma points if you put up material especially for/about women and/or girls!) **Tip ➤** Some local/regional ISPs may be willing to provide you with some free storage space in return for designing and maintaining a page for a local group or nonprofit organization. Be sure to inquire!

Okay, now! Wearing your most comfy dinking duds (bunny slippers optional!), spin around like Wonder Woman for a few seconds, place one hand on your machine, one hand over your heart and repeat after us. Ahem . . .

The CyborGrrrl Oath:

We are wired women. We would rather be cyborgs than goddesses. We have made a special vow to help guide our sisters, our mothers, our daughters and our friends into a cyberscape of their own. We promise to support them— however initially technophobic—as they apprentice themselves in that realm. We live by the geekgirl code: "The

keyboard is a greater equalizer than a Glock .45." We are wired in to Chaos and Gaia. We swell the listservs, we proliferate in the Usenet groups, we weave the Web, we chat and MOO, we upload and download, we help build and nurture our chosen online communities. We help imagine and create new applications and forms, always looking to that next horizon, always thoughtful about the interface of embodied humankind and the electronic projection of the highest mental faculties of our species. In the name of global good and human freedom, we vow never to surrender the Internet and its successors to dangerous, self-perpetuating myths of the technological incompetence of women.

Congratulations, CyborGrrrl!

WELCOME TO THE WIRED WORLD

1994 was the year of Information Highway Robbery, the year that the Al Gore government, the megacorps and the mainstream media went gaga over the notion of Cyberspace, a vast interconnected latticework of info-comm exchange made up at that time primarily of words, but also including games, music, pictures, moving pictures, and soon thereafter, virtual realities.

The now legendary pre-1994 Internet was a miraculous tribute to spontaneous self organizing and whatever was left of the cowboy spirit of wide-open space and wild freedom that had been America (at least for the white boys). It was a miracle born of Pentagon bucks— a self-organizing system of (at that time) incomprehensible complexity stretching across the globe. But now, these lawless regions populated by n
erd-cowboy outlaws and cranks were about to be claimed, legislated, bought, commodified, fenced in and settled. By mid-1994, everybody's dad had a modem. And dad rilly liked Newt Gingrich's plans for the Net. UH OH! HERE *COME THE NORMALS!*

—*St. Jude and RUSirius,*
How to Mutate and Take Over the World (Ballantine, 1996)

Okay, grrrls, there you have it: the critical mass of the Internet in 1994. Then we had 1995 and the Netscape extensions and multi-media revolution, the continued Communications Decency Act fiasco, Aaron Spelling shutting down the unofficial *90210* Website, and Keanu Reeves lending his baby-browns to Gibson's *Johnny Mneumonic*. And 1996 brought blacked-out Web pages when the Telecommunications Act was signed by President Clinton in February. No matter what, no matter when, we're sure of one thing: The landscape of the Internet changes . . . quickly and constantly.

Recall our (and *Wired* magazine's) patron saint Marshall McLuhan and know, oh young CyborGrrrls, that our different cultures are not only influenced by, but are essentially *created* by their media. What we mean in a nutshell is that the Net and our off-line lives are hopelessly intertwined and your quest for knowledge along the CyborGrrrl Scout path is not just to learn the difference between bits and bytes, but to become familiar with the history and current events of the Internet. Cultural trends don't develop in a vacuum, and we're hoping this lil' section will give you a push towards your own deep and meaningful relationship with the emerging cyberculture.

There are two main concepts here: On the one hand, culture influences the Net. *That's* evident in the often thwarted attempts of U.S. government officials to impose a strict, local, moral standard upon a mutating, cosmic, world-wide medium. It also pops up in the weird ways people try to mold the Net to established categories, such as by the rise of "online soap operas," (for a particularly gak-y example, try The Spot at http://www.thespot.com/). On the other hand, the developing Internet has crept into the cultural (un)consciousness of the last two decades or so, and has done much towards creating what we see as the postmodern, cyborgian, non-linear world we're livin' in. Jaime Sommers was a hip chick in the 1970s when the Internet wasn't exactly a household world, and yet her whole sleek bionic self was a not-so-indirect response to the emerging love affair between people and machines. We think there's more (much more!) to becoming a wired woman worthy of her badges than installing Netscape and showing a grrrlfriend how to surf the electric waves. Wired women are aware. They're hip to the strange ways this whole new world influences how we live, think and act; they're actively engaging with fascinating thoughts in their own minds and with other people. To put it simply, wired women aren't just wired into a network, they're wired into the collective soul of the culture(s) of the network. Wired women think, talk, read, wonder, learn and teach. They argue, consider, change their minds, and grow. They write, build Web pages, send e-mail, read newsgroups and hang out in IRC channels, MUDs and MOOs. They have opinions and let people know—on and off-line—what those are, sometimes rather loudly.

Here are a few of our opinions. Nothing really technical here, no machine innards, keyboards, or modems, just some food for thought.

OMIGOD! I THINK I MIGHT BE

AN...INTERNET ADDICT?!

Does the thumpa-thumpa of your heart speed up a little at the unmistakable sound of a modem connecting to a remote machine?

Do you ever go on downloading binges, ending up with megabyte upon megabyte of interesting but perfectly useless stuff, which you then have to purge from your hard drive when your head clears?

Do you regularly find yourself logged on into the wee hours of the morning?

Do you become markedly agitated and/or surly or snippy when your Usenet newsfeed goes down for over twenty-four hours?

Do you often start out to do a specific research task, but end up doing inane keyword searches?

Do you update your Website more often than you wash your dishes?

Do you find yourself spending more than two hours a day responding to personal e-mail? Aimlessly surfing the Web? Hanging out on IRC? In chat rooms?

Do you use or abuse diet Coke, No-Doz, tobacco, Mountian Dew, double espressos, et cetera, to facilitate your nocturnal online habits or to "get you through" school or work the next day?

Do you use emoticons even in handwritten communications? ;-]

Do your friends and family yell at you because your phone line is *always* busy?

I f you answered "yes" to more than two of these questions, well, *welcome sistah*! What took you so long? Unless you're running up long-distance or service-provider bills you simply cannot afford, seriously neglecting your family, friends, work, studies or pets, or are "living" 24/7 in a MOO zone, don't pay any attention to the growing media rumble about Internet addiction. Just shrug it off as yet another all-too-predictable, sensational manifestation of the War on Some Drugs-style policing of consciousness by People Who Mean Well, But Just Don't Get It. IOHO, when applied to the Net, the Twelve Steps just don't make *any* sense at all except as some particularly dippy, fearful, millennial Luddite vision totally inappropriate to life on the New Edge.

The global commercial, educational and interpersonal embrace of the Internet marks an epoch-breaking shift in human consciousness and interaction. From here on out, almost everything is going to be different. Thoughtful people from all walks of life *need* to spend significant amounts of time building and exploring the cyberscape and thinking and reflecting on what kind of "there" is created there. The new age of interactive, online multimedia will demand much more of us intellectually, intuitively and spiritually. Think about it: "Net potato" is a contradiction in terms simply because the Net is all *about* mutation, proliferation and affiliation. It's not about sharing a mass experience with thirty million other people. So, instead of thinking in terms of addiction, think about all that time you spend online as critical participation in a rapidly evolving democratic and aesthetic experiment, and try to *live* it that way. And insist on your right to free speech and privacy online; successful demonization of the Net and its people (as addicts, as perverts, as deviants, as deck potatoes, whatever) is the first step toward panoptical surveillance and control of our every virtual move.

So you think we're kidding? We're not. For example, Dr. Kimberly Young of the University of Pittsburgh at Bradford has founded The Center for Online Addiction, a research and counseling organization which offers seminars to schools and businesses about how to deal with Internet-addicted students who are "suffering" academically or employees whose "productivity" is down as a result of dancing with the digital monkey. There's also a Website for so-called "CyberWidows" (http://web20.mindlink.net/htc/4_1.html), women whose relationships with husbands and lovers suffer from Internet-intensified communication breakdown. (Hey, why isn't there a Cyber*Widowers* group? Huh?) You can get still *more* info on the subject and find out how to join the Internet addiction e-mail list—how's that for irony?—at the Internet Addiction Disorder Website (http://clio.iucf.indiana.edu/ ~ brown/hyplan/ addict.html or http://www2.nano.no/ ~ tombo/iad.html).

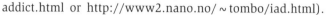

Finally, if any of you Macheads out there prefer to deal more privately with your "problem," know that you can download a copy of a shareware program called Addiction Manager (http://www-personal. umich.edu/ ~ gherrick /AddMan.html). It's sort of like Net Nanny for grownups.

Not exactly a pretty picture, is it? To soothe your Net-jonesing, jokester soul, may we suggest a visit to The Webaholics Page (http://www.ohiou.edu/ ~ rbarrett/ webaholics/ver2/)? Though often pedestrian or outright revolting, it's frequently so studded with stunning stuff that it's almost cool. *Good*-cool, that is. Check out the always changing hotlist of fifty Websites suggested by the latest visitors; it's a convergence point for many different sorts of netheads (some sites are NC-17ish). And after six-plus hours of hard-core surfing and endless cups of java (the liquid kind), don't ever let 'em say we told you so.

Living Dolls, Evil Fembots

and Cyborgs (Oh Yeah!)

In the affluent haven of Stepford, Connecticut, all is not well. The family men have bonded into a "Men's Association" which manufactures a nearly indistinguishable, though ineffably more glamorous, robot replica of the members' wives, allowing the husband to personally kill his wife and simultaneously acquire a mechanical replacement. The artificial substitute is preferred not only for its better looks and longer shelf life, but also for its more compatible personality, superb sexual performance, and superior housekeeping abilities.

—Jane Caputi
describing the film version of *The Stepford Wives* (1973)
in her book *The Age of Sex Crime* (The Popular Press, 1987)

They gave her looks, brains, nuclear capabilities. Everything but an off switch.
— from the media campaign for the film *Eve of Destruction* (1991)

E ver notice how the Western world tends to make machines "female?" Conveniently subject to "male" will? Well, this tendency betrays a lot about how we construct and interpret the relationship between technology and femininity. Take, for example, The Enola Gay, the B-29 from which the first atomic bomb was dropped on the Japanese city of Hiroshima, and Christine, the dream car of Stephen King's novel of the same name. Both machines . . . both women. The plane was named after Enola Gay Tibbets, the pilot's mother: World War II pilots regularly named their aircraft after women back home, equating their weapons of war with "what we're fightin' for": Mom, apple pie and Betty Grable. Christine, on the other hand, is the allegorical trophy girlfriend (the car of any teenage boy's dreams) who, rather than remaining a docile concubine, makes unreasonable (?) and jealous demands on her using, abusing master. In both cases, the guy's powers are directly proportional to those of his "mechanical bride." In this man-machine psychodrama, it's these feminized machines who keep "the phallus" under lock and key. The machine is the ultimate lover-bitch who must be romanced, maintained, coerced, disciplined and deployed by her master/creator to further *his* aims.

Many contemporary popular fictions elaborate this fantasy of woman-plus-machine controlled by men in very explicit terms. As Jane Caputi's summary of *The Stepford Wives* and as the promotional tag line for the film *Eve of Destruction* suggest, these are extreme "anti-feminist" containment fantasies which insist that powerful men use their technological control of women to keep society working the way it *ought* to. "Women's lib" fermenting among the wives? Replace 'em with machines programmed to fulfill each husband's every socially prescribed desire. A powerful, potentially destructive female android without an off switch? Unacceptable within any patriarchal logic! *Robocop?* That's more like it.

It is in the context of this sort of anti-feminist male hysteria that a full array of "electronic Eves" (and Liliths) have flooded popular culture since the 1960s. There is a long history of "living dolls" (or what Jane Caputi calls classic "icon[s] to patriarchal/pornographic culture") in literature and in Hollywood flicks—take, for example, *Cherry 2000* (1988), a cult movie in which a spunky Melanie Griffith pales in comparison to mass-produced, endlessly obliging android concubines and wives. And do we even have to mention *Blade Runner* (1982), *the* film (based on a story by Phillip K. Dick, one of *the* authors) which introduced the cyberpunk ethos and style to a mass audience? On one level, the whole film is about the physical (and emotional) dangers of living with elusive female "Replicants." (Happily, some escaped and formed the punk band Priss and the Replicants!) By no means do these women-machines inhabit only the fringes of popular culture. Consider these innocent, even cute boob-tube offerings:

MY LIVING DOLL

(CBS, 1964-65)

This short-lived sitcom starred Julie "Catwoman" Newmar, a super-brainy, bodacious babe who ties with Diana Rigg for most inspiring grrrl pop cult role model of the 1960s, in her first TV role. Newmar plays "Rhoda" (a.k.a. AF 709), a thinking, walking, talking robot pro-grammed to do anything—yep, *anything* (wink, wink, nudge)—she is told. When her creator, Dr. Miller, is called away on important military business overseas, the base psychiatrist, Robert McDonald, "adopts" her. The psychiatrist, who is a bit unsettled because he failed to notice that Rhoda was a robot upon their first meeting, sets about training her to be the perfect "mature" woman, one who is demure, does what she is told, speaks only when spoken to, and is sparkly and charming on command. Rhoda has some different ideas, though. See, even though she is 37-24-36, even though she can type 240 words per minute, Rhoda suffers from an odd malaise, a problem with no name . . . Unfortunately for her, that beauty spot on her back is a camouflaged off-button. And the shrink isn't afraid to use it. Ha ha, ha ha. Ha. Sigh. The series is even more interesting when compared with its much more successful, sister "magicoms," *I Dream of Jeannie* and *Bewitched*.

THE BIONIC WOMAN

(debuted on *The Six-Million-Dollar Man*, 1975; spin-off ABC, 1976-78; based on the Martin Caidan novel *Cyborg*.)

My Living Doll, 1970s-California-military-research-establishment-style. Jaime Sommers, former tennis pro and memory-wiped (oh, okay, *brain-damaged*) almost-wife of Colonel Steve Austin (The Six-Million-Dollar Man) becomes one of the country's top-secret agents/weapons. The "bionic woman" storyline on *The Six-Million-Dollar Man* was supposed to end when Jaime rejected her bionics and "died" of a massive clot in her brain, where the bionic systems interface lies, but the character was so popular, especially among young girls, that the character was "re-vived," then given her own series.

In addition to her work for the OSI (Office of Scientific Intelligence), Jaime still finds time to hold down a job teaching grades 7-9 at an Air Force base school where a classroom of tough service brats respond to her empathetic-but-tough style with respect and love. Of course the fact that she can scribble three hundred words per minute, tune into conversations taking place almost a mile away and has a hand that doubles as a Swiss Army knife gives her a bit of an advantage over the rest of the teachers.

Jaime Sommers (Lindsay Wagner) was so active, so empathetic, so *California natural* and, yes, seemed so *liberated.* The millions of girls and women (but especially girls) watching each week—us included—were more than willing to look right past the "Bride of Frankenstein" subtext and the fact that Jaime had to maintain good relations with her "makers" to assure her continued survival (she couldn't just run to Radio Shack for parts). We embraced her as some sort of feminist heroine without really grasping the paternalism involved. Say what you will, Oscar Goldman calling Steve Austin "pal" was different from his calling Jaime Sommers "babe."

Oh, and we can't forget Jaime Sommers's archenemies, the dread Fembots! In several episodes of the series, Jaime must do battle with a former bionics researcher turned mad scientist who has created a mini-army of radio-controlled, Stepford-esque bots and set out to replace key OSI personnel with their cyber-look-alikes. Only Jaime knows that the evil bots are not "real" women (whatever *that* means) because their transponder frequency creates feedback in her bionic ear. Highly attenuated cyborgs are so perceptive! And what great chick-fight scenes!

At least in the last episode of the original series, Jaime goes AWOL and renegotiates her contract with the OSI. "I need a *life,* Oscar!" No kidding, babe. We like the fact that the made-for television movies which continue the *Bionic Woman/Six-Million-Dollar Man* saga into the 1980s and 1990s reveal that Jaime goes to graduate school someplace in California and gets a doctorate in clinical psychology. Can't you just imagine her sitting in on lectures by Donna Haraway? Moreover, we learn in these movies that bionic technology has evolved in the direction of bio-enhancement rather than outright replacement, and that Jaime is involved in counseling the new bionic people (including Sandra Bullock in an early role). In the final movie, *Bionic Ever After?* (1994), Jaime

LIVING DOLLS, EVIL FEMBOTS AND CYBORGS (OH YEAH!)

overcomes another rejection crisis—caused this time by a maliciously implanted computer virus wreaking havoc with her systems—and, her memories of their love restored by a concussion (!), finally marries Steve Austin. To every cyborg a happy ending. Check out The Bionic Website at http://www.scifi.com/bionics/

SMALL WONDER

(Twentieth Century Fox, 1985-89, in syndication) Quite possibly the most grating half-hour series ever produced. Ever. Do you understand: *Ever*. Concept: *My Living Doll*, family values-style. Premise: A research engineer secretly develops an android that looks like a ten-year-old girl, dresses her in a pastel party-dress with puffy sleeves, sneaks her out of his lab at United Robotronics and brings her home to live with his family. As he, his wife and son work out the bugs in VICkIe (Voice Input Child Identicon), situation comedy, of course, ensues. The kid's a hybrid of a Fembot and Alf, only—and understandably—she's hyperkinetic, hysterical and annoying, and is played to neurotic, exhibitionist, barely-pubescent, beauty-contestant, high-strung brat perfection by Tiffany Brissette. No matter what crisis Vickie's super-strength, megabrain or various malfunctions cause during each episode, the engineer and his family never shut her off because they can just *tell* that daddy's little masterpiece is becoming more and more of a "real" little girl (well-behaved, well-mannered, helpful, docile and cooperative) every single day. Besides, Vickie is less

Hey There, Barbie Girl!

We love her, we hate her, we love her, we hate her, we love her, we want to shake that vapid smile off her face, buy her some steel-toed boots and give her a copy of *The Beauty Myth*. We love her. She drives us crazy! Oy.

BARBIES GALORE! JENNIFER WARF'S BARBIE PAGE
http://silver.ucs.indiana.edu/~jwarf/barbie.html

THE BARBIE COLLECTOR PAGE
http://deepthought.armory.com/~zenugirl/barbie.html

HACKER BARBE'S DREAM BASEMENT APARTMENT
Hacker Barbe, is a kissin' geek-cousin of Mattel's Barbie.™ Step into her wiggle room: "The pink Sun workstation in the corner, the little containers of takeout Szechuan scattered across the floor, her 'Don't Blame Me, I Voted Libertarian' T-shirt—it's on every little girl's Christmas list!" Ha ha ha!
http://www.catalog.com/mrm/barbe/barbe.html

THE MISS AMERICA ORGANIZATION
For chicas seriously inspired by Barbie. Yeah, we know: It's a scholarship pageant. Yeah, the recent Miss Americas have certainly been much more than T&A. That's fine, that's great, but this whole mindset has spawned sick, perverse crap like Miss Tiny Tot contests, and we just can't be down with that damage.
http://www.missamerica.com/

annoying than boy-crazy neighbor Harriet who has a big crush on Vickie's "brother." Is it even necessary to say that the intense emphasis on Vicki's "proper" socialization plays *very* creepy. Do we even need to point out that the real acronym of the secret project is "vici" ("I conquered")? Oh, and did we forget to mention Vickie's evil-twin prototype, Vanessa?

Love Is All Around

Courtney Love's got a modem, and she knows how to use it. Like that should surprise anyone. Sure lots of "stars" sign on to do those ridiculous chat room "interviews" on the commercial services, but scant few communicate broadband on the Net. Perhaps in part because she's the most vilified chick on the Net (with the possible exception of Hillary Rodham Clinton), Courtney Love actually does. In mid-1994 she began beaming out from aol.com under a variety of handles, and her posts to the Hole folder on America Online trickled out to the Net from there. Now, for privacy reasons, Carol Mariconda, a Love friend and creator of the Usenet group alt.fan.courtney-love and keeper of the group FAQ (http://www.mordor.com/rcmaric/clfaq.html), posts Courtney's rants, remarks and responses directly to the Net. No, it's not a hoax. No, it's not just some publicity thing. Grumpies and those she makes shrivel up and wilt attempt to bust her style, grammar and spelling as irrefutable proof that she is 1) illiterate, 2) dangerously insane, 3) still on major drugs, 4) had Kurt murdered and 5) must be *stopped*, but back on our planet, we crown her queen of netspew-of-consiousness whipsmartfemmeinistbitchbabeness.

THE DROWNSODA HOLE WEBSITE
Ralph Smith's little den of devotion is a beautifully-designed website. You can read the Courtney AOL posts in the "Hole Articles + Interviews" section.
http://www.albany.net/~rsmith/hole.html

THE KURT COBAIN SUICIDE INVESTIGATION PAGE
So you thought we were kidding? This site seriously contends it was a conspiracy: HE was *murdered* and SHE was behind it. Classically predictable, no? Even Yoko didn't have it this rough after she "broke up the Beatles."
http://www.muohio.edu/~carmance/kurt/index.html

DAVID PERLE'S NIRVANA HOMEPAGE
Includes a great section refuting the murder accusations. Really, this whole affair is *so* instructive.
http://www.lookup.com/Homepages/59218/home.html

MANN AND MACHINE

(Fox, 1992)
Futuristic series in which tough, cynical cop Bobby Mann (David Andrews) is partnered with buff and beautiful android partner Eve Edison (Yancy Butler). Only she doesn't "do" human emotions. Or sex. He is frustrated. She is very cute and otherwise malleable. Oh, is he frustrated. And confused. Sci-fi T&A fare with a mercifully short broadcast life. An interesting bit of trivia: David Andrews also had a small part in the film *Cherry 2000*.

WEIRD SCIENCE

(Original theatrical film, 1985; series on USA Network, 1994-present).
A cyborg *I Dream of Jeannie*, only this genie is nobody's fool. The original film, starring Anthony Michael Hall

and Ilan Mitchell-Smith as Gary and Wyatt, two unpopular superhacker teenage geeks, and Kelly Le Brock as "Lisa," the boys' computer-designed Venus, helped make director John Hughes king of the 1980s teen movie. Sure, there are some pretty gross sexist yuks to be found here, but much of the humor is based on the fact that two guys who have zapped this smart, savvy and intoxicating woman into existence have absolutely *no* idea what to do with her, and learn very quickly that chicks are not toys. Indeed, Lisa's mission is not to "service" Gary and Wyatt, but to get them into situations where they have to interact with other humans not as geeky boys, but as *men*. Why attachment to a "babe" is necessary for that to happen, we'll leave to you to figure out, but—in our book (and this is our book, after all)—"Lisa" sure beats Virtual Valerie (a popular piece of early simulated sex software) anyday, especially in her television incarnation as played by Vanessa Angel! Actually, and in a good way, she *sort of* reminds us of Carla Sinclair (see our interview with this *Net Chick* author and *bOING-bOING* editrix later in the book). As she becomes less sex-object and more guru, she's a pretty darn grrrl-positive fantasy character: the savvy female friend of all geekboys. Official Website: http://www.mca.com/tv/weirdscience/

"THE OFFSPRING," STAR TREK: THE NEXT GENERATION

(episode 1990; series 1987-94, in syndication forever)
Working in secret, the quirky and coolly endearing android intelligence that is Lieutenant Commander Data sets out to further his creator's work by duplicating his neural nets and making a "child," whom he names Lal (Hindi for "beloved"). No other android has ever done anything like this, so Starfleet is all in a twist. Crew members Troi and Guinan more or less agree to mentor the "girldroid" as she develops and learns, and Captain Picard won't let the meanie bigwigs from the Daystrom Institute take Lal back to their labs to monitor her development.

Soon Lal begins to outstrip Data's programming: She shocks everyone when she begins to use contractions and, in the midst of the fight over who will have "custody" of her, she begins to develop emotions (!). Her emotions overload her circuitry, and even though Data and the scientists from Daystrom team up to save her, she dies a strangely nineteenth-centuryish heroine's death in her father's arms, a death we are to understand is brought on not so much by "malfunction," but by fear, sadness, and a broken heart. Whoops . . . she became a bit *too* human there, captain. *Star Trek: The Next Generation* Website: http://cruciform.cid.com/ ~ werdna/sttng/

So why does any or all of this matter? Because if we—as women—are part of a new (cyber)reality, if we insist on a woman/machine interface which *empowers* women, then we need to think about why the dream of a docile bot-woman has been so attractive for so long. Given how women often show up in popular culture as idealized androids, it's hardly surprising that many feminists reject the woman/machine meld as negative, reductive and "unnatural." Mix in those "the feminine principle shall rise again" stories of woman-as-goddess displaced by the creep of crown- and state-enforced monotheism and the emergence of industrial society, and the whole anti-technology stance of some feminists makes perfect sense. What's most interesting about Jaime Sommers and Lal, however, is that they *die* when suspended in existing technopolitical frameworks that work oh-so-perfectly for their male counterparts. Their very *existence* is positive, however, for both characters suggest a future where the "feminine"-plus-machine equation represents amazing transformative cultural possibilities.

In her influential essay "A Cyborg Manifesto," Donna Haraway theorizes that

> we cannot go back, ideologically [to some myth of human "innocence"] or materially [to a preindustrial or predigital past]. It's not just that "god" is dead; so is the "goddess." Or both are revivified in worlds charged with microelectronic and biotechnological politics . . . Ideologies of sexual reproduction can no longer reasonably call on notions of sex and sex role as organic aspects in natural objects like organisms and families. (*Simians, Cyborgs and Women: The Reinvention of Nature.* Routledge, 1991, 162)

Uh, gee. That pretty much lays the gender-troubling implications of phenomena such as in vitro fertilization out on the table, no?! Think about this: As a rule, the affluent segments of our society who can partake of such "nature's helpers" prefer not to think of these issues in such unfuzzy (and a-theistic) terms. Similarly, it is more "comfortable" to conceptualize the Internet or cyberspace as a "highway" or "frontier," that is, in terms that reach back to some comforting, pointedly masculinist

LIVING DOLLS, EVIL FEMBOTS AND CYBORGS (OH YEAH!)

and mythically-loaded past rather than confronting full-on the ontological and social questions posed by the new, emerging "space."

Of course some people dismiss Donna Haraway as one of those "wacky feminists." Some of the "wacky feminists" *themselves* dismiss Haraway on the grounds that she ignores the material realities of the lives of "real" women. She answers those critics by arguing that "The feminist dream of a common language, like all dreams for a perfectly true language, of a perfectly faithful naming of experience is a totalizing and imperialist one" (173). Almost heretically, she claims that there is no "natural" political bond among all women, that the comforting myth of "sisterhood" is so much misguided hooey which ignores the artifice of gender itself, not to mention that of the rationalizations for the very "real" gendered oppression of this class of people called "women." *We* think that she—like many other fine feminist science fiction writers and on-the-edge socio-biologists—lays out some provocative descriptions, interpretations, speculations and questions about what it *means* to be a "real" woman in our post-mechanical age. Opines Haraway, "femininity" is a code like any other, for:

> By the late twentieth century, our time, a mythical time, we are all chimeras, theorized and fabricated hybrids of machine and organism; in short, we are cyborgs. The cyborg is our ontology; it gives us our politics. The cyborg is a condensed image of both imagination and material reality, the two joined centres structuring any possibility of historical transformation (150).

For reasons discussed at the very beginning of this piece, the cyborg, defined by Haraway simply as "a hybrid of machine and organism," is always already understood as female, or at least as "feminized." In the first of the seductive riddles that characterize her essay, Haraway depicts her as "a creature of social reality as well as a creature of fiction . . . that changes what counts as women's experience in the late twentieth century." She continues, "This is a struggle over life and death, but the boundary between science fiction and social reality is an optical illusion" (149). As she develops her complex manifesto, Haraway slowly fills in this sketch. In a particularly famous passage, she characterizes cyborgs as ubiquitous and invisible, as great guerilla fighters since—unlike "women descended from Eve" or "feminists"—they can't be pinned down by ideology and are, indeed, beyond demonization. Cyborgs, she suggests, are "resolutely committed to partiality, irony, intimacy and perversity . . . [are] oppositional, utopian, and completely without innocence." They " . . . are not reverent; they do not re-member the cosmos. They are wary of holism, but needy for connection—they seem to have a natural feel for united front politics, but without the vanguard party." (151) In short, according to Haraway's myth, "The cyborg is a kind of disassembled and reassembled, postmodern collective and personal self . . . the self feminists must code." (163)

Best of all, just like the Internet, Haraway's cyborg is "the illegitimate offspring of militarism and patriarchal capitalism, not to mention state socialism." She notes this fact as "the main trouble with cyborgs, of course," but seems to take a sly joy in pointing out that "illegitimate offspring are often exceedingly unfaithful to their origins [since] [t]heir fathers, after all, are inessential" (151). Just as we are trying to do in this section of this book, she emphasizes that cyborgian consciousness is an important, critical, mythmaking consciousness for people living in a world of bodies "textualized" by bio- and microelectronic technologies. In such a world, posits Haraway, "Feminist cyborg stories have the task of recoding communication and intelligence to subvert command and control" (175), for, in such a culture as ours, the potentials for patriarchal abuses of power are vast and deep.

See, when you get down to it, grrrlyness—especially Cybor-Grrrlyness—is a great example of one of those irreverent, playful "partial identities" Haraway talks about. That's hardly surprising, for varied articulations of this cyborgian anti-ideal—sort of a more hopeful, if hardly utopian, aspect of cyberpunkitude—flourish on the visionary edges where the free thinkers, hackers, phreaks, technopagans and cyberfolx frolic and fuss. Heck, it's almost a given to put the "grrrl" after "cyborg," calling up Haraway's own words: "I'd rather be a cyborg than a goddess!" So what understanding does Haraway share with this much broader community? A vision that insists "The machine is not an *it* to be animated, worshipped, and dominated." Rather, she writes, "The machine is us, our processes, an aspect of our embodiment. We can be responsible for machines, *they* do not dominate or threaten us. We are responsible for boundaries; we are they" (180). Somebody say "Amen." ;-)

Read the manifesto. You may also want to read more about Donna Haraway and cyborgs at the Storyspace Cluster at Brown University

(http://twine.stg.brown.edu/projects/hypertext/landow/SSPCluster/
Haraway.html).

Certain aspects of our popular culture and political landscape—
hysteria about "cyberporn" or "Internet addiction" and the goofy-sweet
belief that it's possible to regulate digital information—indicate that the
direction we're moving may be closer to some odd Orwellian *(1984)* or
Atwoodian *(The Handmaid's Tale)* vision than that suggested by Haraway. But at this point, things can still go "either" way, if you know
what we mean. Think about it. It *is* a big deal, a "which side are you
on" proposition. Get out there, be visible and represent yourself using
the technology to your own ends. *You* are the CyborGrrrl revolution!
With that in mind, we have to consider a few milestone television and
film representations of girls, women and the hardware they use. Oh, to
be a smart, geeky twelve-year-old girl *today*!

THE JETSONS

(NBC, 1962-1963; in syndication 1963-present)

All we needed to know about the amazing push-button future we
learned from Jane and Judy, right? Consume, girls! Consume! *Ugh.* Remember: In the future, girls won't dig anything that doesn't involve
shopping or boys. Get over it, please.

THE WOMEN ON ALL OF THE *STAR TREK* SERIES:
Star Trek (The Original Series), *Star Trek: The Next Generation*, *Star Trek: Deep Space Nine*, *Star Trek: Babylon 5* and *Star Trek: Voyager*

(all in syndication forever)

Communications Officer Uhura, Ensign Ro, Dr. Crusher, Guinan,
Counselor Troi, Major Kira, Lieutenant Dax and Captain
Janeway . . . kudos to all the women (and men) who have
(wo)manned the Starfleet decks! Such a vision of gender
equality and respect of cultural differences has existed nowhere else on television. And yay for Picard as an at least
nominally different kind of hero. And maybe we should
thank our lucky stars that if world civilization should be
plunged into a traumatic dark-age and the only surviving,
mythic texts were *Deep Space Nine* and *Voyager* videos, chicks
would basically run everything. (Heh, heh . . .) Did you know that the
annoying Wesley Crusher character on *ST:TNG* was originally supposed

to be a wicked-smart girlchild named Leslie? According to Larry Nemecek's *The Star Trek: The Next Generation Companion*, the writers were committed to the girl-character, but Gene Roddenberry nixed her at the last minute because "he thought there would be a wider range of stories available dealing with the character if he were a male instead of a female." Say what? Pay a call on The Star Fleet Ladies Auxiliary and Embroidery/Baking Society at http://www.eecis. udel.edu/ ~ masterma/ladies.html

WARGAMES
(1983)

A worst case scenario: Geek kid David Lightman (Matthew Broderick) hacks a U.S. Defense Department computer and trips an unstoppable countdown to World War III. Whoops. Will it be an accidental Armageddon? This father-son-machine movie demonized hacking and cracking, thus intensely glamorizing it for large segments of boy America. Close your eyes and try to remember the early 1980s: Rubik's Cube, Space Invaders, Dungeons & Dragons and "Do you want to play a game?" The geekiness validated by this movie is *the* subcultural ground from which the Internet grew so exponentially. And, sure, there were girls who were into this stuff, but for the most part, girls were girl-*friends*—just like Jennifer (Ally Sheedy), the smart girlfriend in this movie who spends the majority of her screen time standing around looking alternately anxious and confused.

COMMODORE COMPUTERS COMMERCIAL
(c. 1984)

Because Commodore targeted the family segment of the mid-1980s PC market, the company did some great parent-guilt commercials. Remember the disgraced son skulking home from college because (as the narrator tells us) he "lacked the computer skills to compete"? But the one we like is the one with a ten-year-old girl opening birthday presents. When she gets to the computer, the look of exuberant surprise on the kid's face is *so* excellent!

REAL GENIUS
(1985)

Directed by Martha Coolidge and starring a young Val Kilmer and a most geekin' pair of bunny slippers, this summer flick is a fun celebration of the spirits of hacking and geek culture, and an equally fun indictment of the military-research complex and the Strategic Defense Initiative (a.k.a. "Star Wars"). The wacky ensemble features Michelle Meyrink as Jordan, a compassionate-but-blunt, neurotic, extremely productive geekgirl genius who spends much of the movie on the periphery of "the plot" because she has so much of her *own* stuff to do. Patti D'Arbanville plays a woman on a quest to have close encounters (so to speak) with the ten smartest men in the world. An eminently rentable, stereotype-tweaking, not too hormonally-challenged comedy.

JUMPIN' JACK FLASH

(1986).

Whoopi Goldberg plays Terry Dolittle, a bank employee who finds herself sucked into high-level espionage after she decodes an anonymous e-mail message from a stranger. Like you'd ever discern *that* from the title. This movie might have done much better at the box office had it been released five years later. More thriller than comedy but Whoopi through-and-through; it makes a fun video double feature with *The Net*.

"THE UGLY DUCKLING," *MACGYVER*

(ABC, 1986; series 1985-91)

MacGyver (Richard Dean Anderson) helps whiz-kid hacker Kate Lafferty, a teenager with a wicked defensive attitude and major self-esteem problems. Kate (password: uglyduckling) has accidentally gotten on the wrong side of a plot to launch a stolen missile. The bad guys kidnap her, hold her hostage in a lab and force her to hack secret satellite info. Instead, Kate uses the computer system to cause a black-out and turn on the sprinklers, then escapes in the confusion. She and MacGyver eventually save the day, of course, and by the end of the episode, his pep talks have convinced Kate how cool she really is. See the Website at http://www.bgnett.no/ ~ botne/macgyver/macgyver.htm

CLARISSA EXPLAINS IT ALL

(Nickelodeon, 1991-1993; in perpetual reruns)

Of *course* Clarissa Darling (Melissa Joan Hart), the smart, hip teenage daughter of a wonderful nineties family is wired. *Duh.* Viewers regularly see her working at her computer, and her familiarity with programming, hardware and software is regularly alluded to in the breezily ironic and fantastic flow of the whole show. Clarissa is supposed to be the kind of chick who can pull off pretending to be Alicia Silverstone in IRC *and* design and plant an annoying-but-harmless virus in her obnoxious little brother's computer—all in one evening. She's a great mundane superheroine. If Lisa Simpson were real, she'd dig this show. http://www.ee.surrey.ac.uk/Contrib/Entertainment/Clarissa/

BLOSSOM

(NBC 1990-1995)

Like Clarissa, Blossom Russo (Mayim Bialik) has an intense sense of style and her very own computer sitting on her very own desk. Unlike Clarissa, after the first season of the series, the character (*and* the computer) was increasingly trivialized by the writers. For example, in one episode Blossom fantasizes that a video-phone connection with a big-name baseball star helps her decide how far she should go (second or third base) with a boyfriend. Oh, joy, but there you are: http://pmwww.cs.vu.nl/service/sitcoms/Blossom/

SINGLE WHITE FEMALE

(1992)

Bridget Fonda plays a chic, young programmer whose fabulous computer software package promises to completely revolutionize the fashion industry. Her life *should* be perfect, but during a temporary break up with her fabulous boyfriend, she acquires a seemingly-quiet-and-nice-but-actually-totally-psycho roommate (Jennifer Jason Leigh) who begins to ape her every fabulous move and who seems to want to take over her very fabulous soul. It's all very stylish. The scene in which our bound and gagged heroine manages to log on to Prodigy and summon help is an early nineties classic.

MURDER SHE WROTE

(CBS, 1984-1996)

She gave in and bought a computer sometime in the late 1980s, but legendary mystery novelist and lovably blunt busybody Jessica Fletcher (Angela Lansbury) found it frustrating and unfriendly and kept going back to her trusty, beloved typewriter. She finally made peace with the computer (and even bought a laptop!) when she moved to New York

City in the early 1990s. (Of *course* there was a murder tied in with the first computer class she took!) Jess uses her machine for writing, but we also see her using the Net for research and she has been involved in cases involving various sorts of computer crime. Independent, savvy and playful, Mrs. Fletcher is a great role model for older grrrls everywhere.

JURASSIC PARK

(1993)

Soon after their visit to Jurassic Park begins to head south, Malcom-the-chaos-theoretician (Jeff Goldblum) and Ellie-the-paleobiologist (Laura Dern) share the following ironic/prescriptive exchange:

> Malcolm: God creates dinosaurs. God destroys dinosaurs. God creates man. Man destroys God. Man creates dinosaurs.

> Ellie: Dinosaurs eat man. Woman inherits the Earth.

Almost, but not quite. Pre-woman simply saves the day. Everybody in that compound *would* have been lunch had it not been for Lex (Ariana Richards), a teenage computer geek who is repulsed by what her mad-scientist grandfather (Richard Attenborough) has done on the island. Earlier in the movie, her know-it-all little brother Tim (Joseph Mazello) teases her meanly about being a computer "nerd," but when the raptors (problem-solving dinos, remember!) have Lex, Tim, Ellie and Grant (Sam Neill) trapped in the control room, it's Lex who saves the day by rebooting the compound security system. This great look of calm relief comes over her face as she scans the screen and says confidently, "It's a UNIX system. I know this." *Yeah!*

THE X-FILES

(Fox, 1994–)

Even if we discount that little alien microchip she had removed from her neck, F.B.I. agent Dana Scully (Gillian Anderson) is wired. Without a doubt. She may not hang out on IRC or cruise Usenet as we suspect that her partner Mulder (David Duchovny) does, but she definitely knows her way around hardware, software and networks. It's her job. Not that we particularly *want* them to, but if  Mulder or Scully ever declared undying love for the other, it would have to happen via e-mail to be at all believable. And, on the darker side is

"2Shy," an episode with a fat-sucking "vampire" who seduces and kills big women he seeks out in IRC. A sort of stereotypically sensational and cautionary Net tale, but it has its moments. File under self-defense, everybody: Fat-sucking vampires *can* be killed by regular bullets.

THE NET
(1995)

Angela Bennett (Sandra Bullock), crack beta-tester and program systems analyst, resides in Venice, California, but lives online. She orders pizza and makes travel arrangements via the Web, flirts with guys in chat rooms, owns four Macs of different vintages, runs a "crackling fireplace" screensaver on her biggest monitor, and has never physically visited the San Francisco offices of her employers. The only people in L.A. who "know" her are her doomed shrink/lover and her Alzheimer's-stricken mother (who doesn't recognize her). This creates massive problems after a friend sends a disk and pointer to a site on the Web that conceals a secret gateway to nonpublic government and corporate databases. That friend is killed, and the bad guys begin to "erase" Angela bit-by-byte while—blissfully unaware—she vacations on a Mexican beach.

Yeah, the movie drags a bit, but the payoff is in the climactic scenes in which Angela takes charge and wrests back her identity, saving the nation in the process. A sobering, if sometimes heavy-handed, meditation on the vulnerability of "flesh" in this age of digital brains.

HACKERS
(1995)

Things sure have changed since *WarGames*. Dig this: Zero Cool (a.k.a. Dade), a righteous boyhacker invades the high-school turf of stylin' gothgrrrlhacker Acid Burn (a.k.a. Kate) who can sure throw some major alpha-chick attitude. They clash electronically, all the while doing that adolescent love-hate thing, but then band together with all their friends to unmask and defeat The Plague, an older, sell-out hacker-gone-bad, after he frames them in a hefty bit of industrial conspiracy. Yeah, some elements of the film are patently absurd, especially hardware-wise, but, hey, this is a teen flick, and they got the boy-plus-girl revolution thing right, along with lots of other stuff. Chill.

In *our* universe, Acid Burn would get her own sequel, preferably one in which we find out more about the character's relationship with her mother, a prolific author of those "women who love men who hate women who love men" books. Mom could see the light, and daughter and mother could team up to do battle with some evil plot lurking behind (no speculative joke) Martha Stewart's upcoming "affluent, cookie-cutter lifestyles online" venture. We can only dream.

TANK GIRL

(Comic art published in various periodicals and 1995 Movie)
Golly, but Tank Girl and Jet have panache, especially consid-ering that they're survivors of a comet-induced near-apoca-lypse. Tank Girl is fierce enough to take out all comers, espe-cially those who would mess with her little friend Samantha, and Jet can hack anything. Bored with the bland, institu-tional eggshell look of your hardware? Take a tip from Tank Girl and let it out, baby: Accessorize your machine to reflect your personality! (Just make sure to seal your drives, screen and vents with plastic and masking tape before you use any sort of paint or glue.) Who needs boys when you've got your grrrlfriends and a really sweet Ripper roo-guy? A real grrrl-cult comic and movie. It makes us insanely happy that Tank Girl was dreamed up by two guys, artist Jamie Hewlett and writer Alan Martin. Visit the unofficial *Tank Girl* Website: http://www.dcs.qmw.ac.uk/ ~ bob/stuff/tg/index.html

MICROSOFT COMMERCIAL

(1995-96)
You know the one we mean: Two thirteen-year-old friends are in one girl's bedroom talking girltalk, possibly working on a science project and playing around with *Encarta*, Microsoft's CD-ROM encyclopedia. Video clips of a frog catching a fly and a Venus Flytrap closing around a bug elicit giggles and groans. When someone knocks on the door, the girls—assuming that it must be a little brother—yell for whoever it is to "Go *away!*" Then the visiting girl has a thought: "Hey, what if that was your *older* brother?" As the commercial ends, a disembodied voice calls, "Ke-vin?" Our question is this: What do they *do* with Kevin after they lure him into their lair? Immobilize him, consume his life force, and throw his husk into the backyard? Yipes! Or do they play dumb and ask Kevin to *please, please, pretty please* help them figure out this CD-ROM

thingie, so the visiting girl can bat her eyelashes at him? Leave it to Microsoft to come up with this perfectly enigmatic technologically-empowered girl-as-*vagina-dentata* vignette!

Aside from the stubborn tendency for some writers to "soften" younger film and television geekgirls by showing them as at least *somewhat* stereotypically boy crazy, we can see some real progress here, right? We hope so.

Recently, artist-writer Garry Trudeau reincarnated Mike Doonesbury as a marketing guy at a New Edge software company. Ever the romantic, quintessential baby boomer, Mike has fallen in love with a Generation X-er coder (programmer) named Kim Lee. The strips from March and April 1996 where Mike brings Kim home to meet his daughter Alex are excellent! She wins the kid over by showing her the new beta version of a hot computer game, then Alex shows off her Website to Kim. In the next strip, as Kim is on the phone with Mike wondering how her interaction with his daughter had gone, we see Alex interrupt Mike to ask if she can bob her hair and wear it in her face like Kim does. Yes! Finally a young geekgirl with someone to look up to!

Of course, we can't fail to mention a recent *Cathy* strip showing Cathy logging on and looking up the IRS tax-tip Website, but ending up all frazzled after "wasting" an entire evening surfing "The Procrastination Superhighway." Sometimes don't you just want to slap Cathy?

When we look at all of these comic and dramatic images as part of a larger cultural narrative, we see women initially shut out of the action (*WarGames*), struggling with the dread social onus of girl-geekiness (*MacGyver*, *Real Genius*), then, finally, celebrating the empowering and creative elements of new info tech intergenerationally (*Murder She Wrote, Clarissa Explains It All to You, Hackers, The Net, Doonesbury*, et cetera). Could that make us anything other than happy? To some extent, popular art imitates life, and vice versa. Write your own scripts.

CYBERSEX

AND THE MODEM GRRRL

Okay, if you jumped right to this page to get to the goodies, you turn around and march right back to the beginning and read the FAQ! :-] Just kidding . . . well, kinda. Come on, grrrls, don't cha know already the Net is a great cesspool of depravity? That each and every cyber-corner is full of drooling, leering trolls just waiting to lure innocent prepubescents into dark alleyways? Well, that's what we were told at the door. But we checked it out, and it's okay to come on in. For the most part, it's safe.

See, that's part of the fun of the Internet: There is sex-stuff out there—we won't kid you, we won't lie, and we won't cover it up. But we don't *have* to, since the nature of the Net itself seems to keep the public spaces clear of sex-spam, yet leave plenty of space for erotic explorations and the occasional bawdy interaction between lovers, friends and strangers alike. Frankly, we're *glad* to find another forum for the (re)creation of erotic interaction. We think the Internet—heck, pretty much any human-to-human computer-interfaced interaction—

Take Back *alt.feminism*

One of the places a lot of you are going to check out as soon as you figure out how to read Usenet news is the *alt.feminism* newsgroup. Just so you won't be surprised, you should know that very few women bother to post to *alt.feminism* because it is so over-run with trolly, whiny, hostile-defensive men. If the group wasn't so pathetic-serious and scary, it'd almost be funny, a sort of very predictable satire of anti-feminism. We each made a few posts to the group, then pretty much washed our hands of it. We even made a grudging, uneasy peace with *alt.feminism* as our mainline into the most ourageous, slick/smarmy and subtle flavors of misogyny our culture has to offer. Hey, after all, forewarned *is* forearmed, right?

During our lurkings in the occupied territory that is *alt.feminism* (and, to slightly lesser degrees, *soc.feminism, soc.women,* and *alt.music.alterntive. female*), we have developed only the highest admiration for the minority of brave, stalwart, patient procession of women and thoughtful men who have stuck it out in this atmosphere for some substantial period of time, actually trying to *discuss* issues. Props to them and to the moderators of *soc.feminism!* Theirs has been a lonely, near-thankless mission since the typical male *alt.feminism* posters are given to inappropriate crossposting, personal attacks, lengthly, ill-in-formed, point-by-point dissections of how all social institutions, especially the legal system, are so *unfair* to men, and how women are manipulative *bitches.* Illuminating it's not. Tedious it is. For all these reasons and more, it's time to call in the cavalry.

Yeah, grrrls, we say it's time to take back *alt.feminism.* Hone your wits, assess the situation, pick your opening, then join the charge, keyboards blazing, sucking up flames like love: a righteous, wily, CyborGrrrl warrior-babe representing the interests of your people and sector. Our goal isn't and shouldn't be to silence anyone. Let them say whatever they want, and burn themselves with their own flames. Together we can re-orient *alt.feminism* and re-make it however *we* want. We don't have to put up with their bullying or allow them to hold the newsgroup hostage to their discourse. They seem to think they can wear us down with their whiny drone. Don't misunderstand: We hardly expect all women to agree with one another, but it sure would be nice to have *women* driving the conversation in these groups. Five or ten minutes per day from each of us: That's all it will take. Let's have a revolution. Let's make a statement. And start some real discussions.

offers fabulously innovative ways for thinking sex, writing sex, doing sex, talking sex, and having sex. And because it's as *anonymous-as-ya-want-it-to-be*, the Net is one of the few really *safe* places where people can play with what turns them on (especially if what turns them on is somehow considered deviant or immoral), try on different erotic identities (and discard them if the fit isn't right), and become wonderfully and warmly comfortable with their erotic desires before venturing out into the big, bad world where some adults play mean and people sometimes get hurt. Take, for example, young adults who are feeling just this side of uncomfortable with their assumed straightness, but who aren't ready to run right out and become an instant butch-bottom at a gay bar. The Net? No problem . . . it's even kind of fun.

A graduate research project of Laurel's confirmed our thoughts.

She interviewed (mostly college age) gays, lesbians, bisexuals, and transsexuals who were using the Internet as a space to explore their sexuality, build (and rebuild) their identities and flirt with text-based erotic intimacy (yeah, yeah, cybersex . . . sharing real-time erotic fantasies or "if I were there I would's" with someone while chatting). Most of these young people were very glad (and totally aware) that they had this mostly anonymous, virtual and, above all, *safe* space in which to explore and play, relate to one another, and form an identity as a young gay man, lesbian or whatever . . . *without* (for the most part) the dangers of coming out in the real world (those usually came later, but af-

ter the baby-dyke or queer-boy was comfortable with having an alternative identity). In fact, the Net sort of gives anyone the potential experience of being gay or lesbian . . . even if one simply *isn't*.

We also think the Net is a great little invention for furthering intimacy . . . gay, lesbian, straight or otherwise. The sixties mantra of "Turn on, tune in, and drop out" implied a "don't think about it, don't talk about it, don't muse over it, just do it" mentality. Unfortunately, the loss of talking, thinking, hinting and alluding to sex made us forget something: Talking about sex is *sexy*. Keep in mind that for centuries, writing provocative and suggestive notes to your future-lover and sealing them with hot, dripping wax was considered a highly erotic form of foreplay. Today, writing electronic love-letters to your distant (or not so distant) lover can be a turn-on, and cybersex is a big, old erotic rush when it's done well. It puts silky, throaty words back into our breathless mouths, and affirms to our lovers and ourselves that we like sensuality, that we are desirable, that we want to do these things with each other and that we have the power of words to voice our desires. Writing "I want to tickle your earlobe with my tongue, and breathe softly on the nape of your neck" (*shiver*) calls those words into action, reifies that intimacy with language, gives proof to our desires and gives us the freedom to create our own erotic fantasies. And writing the same thing to a stranger met in IRC channel #netsex allows any grrrl to live her fantasy of anonymous, hot, pulsing sex with a stranger (if, indeed, she has that fantasy; Nancy Friday bets she does!), without the danger, fuss or fear of rejection based on physical measures of attractiveness. In the cyberscape, if you can describe the most beautiful, erotic, sexy, sensual, hardcore lil' big-grrrl to ever walk the virtual earth, you can *be* her and leave those sex-starved boyz trembling in your wake. If you can describe yourself as a virtual dominatrix in black leather and a kitten mask purring and growwwllling *lick my boots* to your submissive partner, you can go ahead and be that, too. Our point is, cybersex can be hot. It's up to you to make it that way.

BUT WHAT ABOUT THE *CHILDREN?* FIE, CYBERPORN!

And where there's sex, you know censorship can't be far behind. Lots of Very Important White Boys Who Run Things have a whole bunch of people convinced thzat the Web (well, really the whole Internet) ought to be regulated for content. These good ole' boys have it in their minds that they're saving us from stumbling across smut on every third site we browse. *Humph!* We don't think there *should* be a ban on smut on the Internet. In fact, we're against any regulation of content on the Net, especially sexual/sensual content. The history of smut has shown that, unless we are totally willing to give up our right to privacy, well-financed pornographers and dedicated amateurs alike can route around any roadblock in any distribution system. That is especially true when the medium is a digital one; the flip side is that it is equally easy for the innocent surfer to slide right by sites and groups they might find objectionable. The new round of Web-surfing software to hit the shelves (SurfWatch, Skyway and Net Nanny, to name a few) conveniently and quietly erases any site with "objectionable" content (and the definition of objectionable content is usually left up to the surfer) from the user's screen. You don't wanna see it, you don't gotta see it; it's as simple as that. In cyberspace, no one has to hear anyone scream. Or moan in lust.

For the most part, the anti-porn frenzy uses kids as the potential victims of cyberporn. Some children *have* been the online victims of particularly trolly adults who attempt in various ways to exploit them. However, the danger is found not in the information on Websites or in newsgroups but in the inappropriateness of people. For parents who find certain Websites inappropriate for children, there are many self-screening Web browsers which allow parents to "block" objectionable sites. Unfortunately, far too many parents delude themselves by thinking that their children and teenagers are nonsexual and apolitical beings who need to be protected from sex in all its forms and flavors. Of course, *those* kids are going to sneak a look at alt.sex.stories or http://www.penthouse.com/ as soon as Mom or Dad leaves them alone with a modem. Kids are curious and, however uncomfortable it might make adults, they need that information whether or not we think they should have it. In that same vein, children need to know how to protect themselves sexually, both online and in face-to-face situations. When a cyberchild is of appropriate age, it would not be at all untoward for a parent to sit down with him or her and talk about sex, how it gets represented in our culture and the media, and how to own sexuality and not be owned by it (and hence by all companies and individuals who "sell sex").

THE SEXUAL REVOLUTION . . . IN CYBERSPACE

The move into cyberspace and our changing relationship with communication technologies has already radically changed the way many netheads think about bodies and sexuality. This sexual revolution in cyberspace has fostered a new appreciation of the incredible erotic powers of the disembodied and imaginatively re-embodied cerebral cortex. The old in-out, in-out, lick-lick, rub-rub will be around as long as humans are humans, but as lots of tantric practitioners (and long-distance cyberlovers who may never have met face-to-face) can tell you, that's not all there is to "sex." As one of our guy-heroes, Timothy Leary, says,

> No one is implying that the basic skin-tissue hardware is in any way outmoded. Nothing can replace the kissing, cuddling, licking, nuzzling, nibbling, smelling, murmuring, sucking, joking, smoking, honey-moaning, fondling, biting, entering, and receiving of the tender exchange of love's soft bruises. But, however enjoyable, our bodily contacts exist for us only as registered in our brains. We sense the touch and taste and perfume and the membrane softness of our lovers only in clusters of electric signals picked up by our neurons and programmed by our mindware. (*Chaos and Cyber Culture*, 148)

We are totally with him there. If the greatest sex organ is the brain, then the best sex toy ever invented is the Internet.

If we really had it together as sexual beings, we would be taking advantage of the accessibility of these fun, new, erotic spaces—like the Usenet News alt.sex hierarchy—to *discuss* sex. Alt.sex shouldn't just be a forum in which mostly heterosexual, horndog men crank out mega-megabytes per day describing, enumerating and fretting, about how, and how often, and what or who they've done, what's normal and what's not, but should be a forum where we discuss why we do what we do. Why we like what we like. And why we're all so damn uptight about it. Hey, nice dream, isn't it? The discourse on alt.sex—perpetually one of the top-three highest-traffic Usenet groups—seems to replicate the current state of what little public conversation there is about sex, sex, *sex*. The idea that we ought to ban or censor such talk in what amounts to less than 1 percent of Internet traffic is preposterous! We are on the verge of discovering that intimate interaction doesn't rely on the real-time, face-to-face meetings of the physical world. We're beginning to (re)discover that erotic, fun, intimate and (con)sensual adult interaction can, does and probably should (at least in part) take place via this new virtual medium we call the Net. And we're beginning to— sometimes in very awkward ways—deal with the open spaces of the cyberscape and how and why and when others (children, particularly) should begin to learn about these things.

WATCH OUT FOR TROLLS!

However, let us backtrack a few sentences and point something out. Did you catch that "what amounts to less than 1 percent of the Internet?" back a few lines? *But wait,* you say, *I saw that* Time *article about smut on the Net and it said . . .* Whoa, grrrl, hold on there. Let us tell you what can go down out there in the cyberscape. Number one on your list of Things to Watch Out For are trolls. Also known as trollz, these spineless little creatures act out in inappropriate ways on Usenet groups, listservs and the Web for the express purpose of starting flame wars, harassing netizens from all walks of life, creating useless, even damaging controversy, and generally drawing attention to themselves. First in line for the Troll of the Nineties Award is Mr. Marty Rimm, perpetrator of the cyberporn controversy and all-around opportunist. In 1995, Rimm (then an undergraduate at Carnegie Mellon University) published "Marketing Pornography on the Information Superhighway: A Study of

917,410 Descriptions, Short Stories and Animations Downloaded 8.5 Million Times by Consumers in Over 2000 Cities in Forty Countries, Provinces and Territories" in the *Georgetown Law Journal.* *Time* magazine featured "Cyberporn" as its July 3, 1995, cover story, with Rimm's study as the basis for the media hysteria (fueled by Senator James Exon's (D-NE) furor and the (then) proposed Communications Decency Act). Rimm's research, however, did not concern the Internet at all; 99.7 percent of the images he surveyed were found on adult-oriented BBSs . . . the vast majority of which are not accessible via the Internet and which require proof of legal age and a credit card. *Ooops.* Having misinterpreted Rimm's intentionally misleading study, *Time* published a grossly erroneous statistic claiming that 83.5 percent of downloadable images on the Net were pornographic. All of the usual suspects—from the Christian Coalition's Ralph Reed to anti-porn lawyer Catharine MacKinnon—popped up to condemn the Internet community and in so doing perpetuated the myth of the Net as a hypersexed, masculine space with pix of "nekkid lil' boys" and underage girls engaged in the full spectrum of sexual and violent acts.

In this climate of hysteria, overnight the word was that the Net was not a safe place for *anyone,* especially children or teenagers. But of course, a little delving into actual Internet statistics showed that only about 0.35 percent (yes, that's about one-third of one percent!) of Internet traffic was pornographic, coming mostly from Usenet newsgroups like alt.binaries.pictures.erotica, where pictures are posted as coded files, not readable messages. In other words, for little Dick or Jane to view one of those pictures he or she would have to learn to download the many sections one photo is broken into, and *then* decode them using special software. Yeah, right.

In addition to carefully crafting the attention-grabbing article from bogus research, Rimm had also authored and self-published a book called *The Pornographer's Handbook: How to Exploit Women, Dupe Men, and Make Lots of Money.* Rimm offered his services to adult BBS sysops, giving them instructions on tricks of the trade—for example, which shots of blow-jobs were most popular among adult BBSers. What an enterprising young man!

It seems clear that Mr. Rimm deserves our vote for Troll of the Nineties Award. And we're not alone. Let's just say that the verb "to rimm" has now entered the vocabulary of the Net-savvy set. It means "to publish sensational and unsubstantiated facts without the benefit of a peer review and with the sole intent of demonizing the Internet." We'd add to that definition—as Paul Harvey might say—the *rest* of the story. "To rimm" is also to "engineer a controversy about matters of gender and sex online from which the perpetrator plans to capitalize and turn a huge profit."

ALL THOSE WEB BABES! THANK YOU, TOUPSIE, WHEREVER YOU ARE!

Unfortunately Marty Rimm isn't our only troll *de jour.* Nominee number two, Mr. Rob Toups, Jr., has the dubious distinction of being the first troll to successfully perpetrate a rimm job and have the media fawn all over him for it. Heck, he even managed to parlay it into a Web developer position at a major magazine! Why was Toupsie (as he likes to be called) successful whereas Marty Rimm found himself universally vilified? Well, let's just say that his approach seemed much more friendly.

Rather than dropping the dime on digital porn to fluff up the market, Toupsie manufactured a firestorm among women with Websites, then played the "What, me sexist?" card when some of them complained. Rob Toups's Babes on the Web site isn't one of those T&A Websites that Net Nanny and Senator Exon are so fond of *(not)*, but a list of women from many walks of life who maintain personal (and some institutional) pages on the WWW. *Cool,* you're thinking, *What's wrong with that? It's great to have as many lists of women's sites as possible, right?* We agree, but here's the catch. Toupsie will only add a woman's Website to his list if the site includes a photo of herself: a photo for Toupsie to rate. Yes, next to each photo and accompanying link, the woman is rated on The Toupsie Scale. The ratings range from *Babe-O-Rama* (four Toupsies) to *Dog-O-Matic* (one Toupsie). Is Toupsie ranking these women according to physical attributes? Well, yeah.

Of course, he says that's not the case. And *sometimes* it's clear he's rating the Babes on HTML skill and style as much as anything else. Now Babes on the Web is mostly composed of links to Websites contributed by women—which is great—but the original Website was just a bunch of chick pages Toupsie plucked from the Web without the authors' knowledge. And even a "Four Toupsie" page becomes a "Zero Toupsie" page should the Babe for any reason remove her photo from the site. What's up with that?

Here's what makes Toupsie a malicious geek, though: He gets it. Check out the form letter he mailed to his critics, (mostly) women he classifies on Babes on the Web as "anti-BOTW Wackos." (And although it's generally bad form to reprint private e-mail sent to you by a correspondent, this letter was posted in mid-1995 on several Website and Usenet groups, so we consider it fair game.)

You might want to list these Magazines and Periodicals that have/are promoted/promoting my page:

Internet World
WebWeek
NetDay
Der Spigel [*sic*]
.net Britian [*sic*]
WIRED
WIRED UK
Houston Chronicle
USA Today
L.A. Times
Esquire
Boston Phoenix
Cyberwire Dispatch
Link Magazine

and many more are in the works.

As I said in my first mass mailing to the critics, thanks for all the noise, all your bitching has only allowed me to obtain the press coverage I wanted and the massive support I desired.

The problem is that I am now the darling of the net and not some evil being. I have managed the coverage regarding my site and focused it to the point of view I wanted. Thats [*sic*] what a wonderful Journalism education can do for you. If you understand how the media works, you can assist the media in working for you. So far it has been perfect. Since May 5, 1995, I have had over 300,000 seperate [*sic*] IPs visit 'BABES ON THE WEB' and roughly 1,500 email messages running 95% positive. The repeat visits put the hit rate at over 750,000. Over 150 women since June 3rd have sent in their URLs. I am larger than *any* feminist list of women on the web. Just while typing

this, two women from Sweden have checked out my 'butt nekkid
bod' in WIRED UK and have sent in their URLs. I am having to
defer journalists so I can keep control over the coverage and
prolong it as long as possible. I should be able to string it
out for another two or three months.

Have a nice day...I know I will, I am moving to NYC,
Tuesday, to work in the heart of SOHO designing Web pages for a
Major National Magazine with a million subscribers for bucku
dinero. I will give you a hint. It's listed above.

Cheers..

Gak. Now, does that make you want to puke or go wash yourself or
what? Babes, you have been *played.* Yup, Toupsie managed a first-class
rimm job. And since he courted his fifteen minutes of fame so assidu-
ously, we think his name deserves to live in infamy. To that end, we've
immortalized his trolliness for a particular brand of rimm job. Hence-
forth, "toupsie" shall be understood to mean 1) v. "to exploit women's
Net spaces or creations in a stealth anti-feminist manner for the express
purpose of drawing criticism from so-called feminazis and, hence, media attention to oneself as a victim of feminists." 2) n. a creature who
engages in such pursuits, e.g., "alt.feminism sure has been full of
toupsies lately."

Fortunately, a lot of other people have responded to Toupsie-gate
online. These pages illustrate rule *numero uno* of the Net: If somebody
cheeses you off, pluck some electrons from your quiver and have at
them. We dig these pages that respond so very eloquently to such a
troll, so check them out.

ELLEN SPERTUS'S THOUGHTS ON WEB PAGES LISTING WOMEN
Thoughtful response to Toupsie *and* the listing of women on the Web in a general
sense.
http://www.ai-mit.edu/people/ellens/Gender/webwomen.html

BABES OF THE WEB II
Ms. Blake Krizeberg turns the tables on the boyz. Hey, it's a dirty job, but
somebody had to do it! ⟨---grin---⟩ No "ratings," of course.
http://ucsub.colorado.edu/~krizeber/new/babes.html

REAL WOMEN ON THE WEB
A site featuring biographical portraits of cool, historically important women.
http://www.intac.com/kgs/babes

GUYS ARE PIGS
A male feminist view of the matter. Go, Killroy!

http://www-leland.stanford.edu/~dove/killroy1.html

WONDERFUL WEB WOMEN BY DAVID DENNIS

No "ratings" or massive ego here, just thoughtful, respectful commentary and
links to pages of women DD finds wonderful, neat-o or intriguing in some way.
You'll be pleasantly surprised. He also comments on Babes on the Web.
http://www.amazing.com/david/women.html

We told you it wasn't a pretty site in some of the shadowy corners out
there. Yes, Virginia, there are trolls on the Internet, and they are an
active, menacing, icky part of all that goes down in the wired world.
But we actually prefer to look at the up-side; the more all you wonderful wired women get out there and do your grrrlie thing, the fewer the
trolls who will have the guts to open their virtual mouths in and around
spaces we've staked out as our own.

These spaces on the Net might include (but are not limited to!)
erotic-exotic, sensual-sexy type havens where others dare not roam:
IRC channels in which we engage in fabulously, funny, flirty, foxy netsex
with long-term lovers and strangers; Usenet newsgroups where we post
our fantasies, tell stories that turn us on, ask questions about our bodies and our desires, and converse with other women (and men) about
sexuality and eroticism, and Websites where our sexuality and our desires and our erotic selves are paramount and not squelched. And, of
course, don't forget to send some sexy, growly, naughty e-mail to a
loved one. Just pretend it's written on luxurious, vanilla scented paper
with a flourishing pen, and then sealed with wax, and enclosed with a
pressed flower or two. And let the wires do the delivering.

The Story of Hardcore Feminism, or, How I Crashed www.bgsu.edu in One Fell Blow . . .

I figured out how to access the Web, and decided immediately I had to have my own homepage. It wasn't enough. I decided I had to start putting my "projects" up on the Web. After all, my account through the university was supposed to be for research and educational purposes, right? So I took a recent presentation I'd done on women and online pornography, collected some porn by sulking around in the dark corners of the Net, made it all "feminist erotica" with my newfound Paintshop skills, and put up Hardcore Feminism: CyberGrrrl Porn (http://www.bgsu.edu/~lgilber/femex/femex.htm).

I was an instant Web hit.

Unfortunately, so was the server, which at that time was gasping and wheezing for breath every time some unsuspecting off-campus surfer stumbled into its aching hard drives. It seems that every time some poor schlock out there in the void plugged "porn" or "sex" into pretty much any decent Web searcher, my pages came running right out to meet them. Of course, Hardcore Feminism wasn't *porn*, it was more *about* porn, with some pretty weird pictures thrown in. But Mr. Joe Blow didn't know that, and went skipping off to the poor *www.bgsu.edu* server without a care in the world.

After about three weeks, I couldn't log into my server account to change pages or update pictures. Weird.

On the fourth week, I got a piece of e-mail from a nice, knowledgeable, and friendly—but at that moment pissed off—computer science student:

```
>TO: Laurel
>FROM: Jeremy
>DATE: 22 February 1995 22:04:31
>SUBJECT: The problem you've caused on bgsu.edu
>
>As of two nights ago, the WWW server your pages were on had
>gotten over ten thousand hits in less than a week. In the hour
>before the server went down, your pages alone got about two
>thousand. Because of your pages, none of the pages at BGSU are
>available right now.
>Right now the server is back up and running but only barely.
>PLEASE remove your pages or do something else with them so
>we don't have this problem again.
>
>Jeremy
```

Jeremy was quite helpful and eventually the rest of the students subtly demanded more resources, and a bigger and better server was put in. I changed the title of the   →

pages to "Femex," which wouldn't come up in any search for "porn" or "sex," and the pages went back up. There they stay, an illegitimate tentacle of my lonely and forgotten dissertation, waiting for attention.

The moral of the story remains, however. Pretty much anything on the World Wide Web or in Gopher-space that has anything obvious to do with SEX will be easy to find, may very well crash a server and become quite unpopular with a service provider, and be whisked off of the cyberscape faster than you can yell "*Susie Bright!*" Rest assured, however, something else will come along to take its place . . . and the whole cycle will begin again.

Glad to report, however, my Hardcore Feminism pages are doing okay. Pst. Don't let the computer science department know I told you about 'em.

Paving, Weaving, Surfing and Consensually Hallucinating the Cyberspace Frontier

A meme is "a unit of cultural transmission, or a unit of imitation. Examples of memes are tunes, ideas, catchphrases, clothes fashions, ways of making pots or building arches. Just as genes propagate themselves in the gene pool by leaping from body to body via sperm or eggs, so memes propagate in the meme pool by leaping from brain to brain via a process which can only be called imitation . . . [M]emes should be regarded as living structures, not just metaphorically, but technically. When you plant a fertile meme in my mind, you literally parasitize my brain, turning it into a vehicle for that meme's propagation in just the way that a virus may parasitize the genetic mechanisms of a host cell."

—Richard Dawkins in *The Selfish Gene*

The imaginary is that which tends to become real.

—Andre Breton

[Women] are confronted virtually with the problem of reinventing the world of knowledge, of thought of symbols and images.

It seems that everyone has heard about "the information superhighway" by now. Even people who have never touched a mouse or trackball yammer about "surfing the Net." Conversation about the Internet is dense with fresh memes and metaphors designed to help us map this new space and make it familiar and natural, hence making it easier to "sell" people on it. Some of these are reductive and grounding (the information superhighway), while some, like "CyborGrrrl," try to be provocative and visionary.

Memes and metaphors are neither innocent nor stable; they have histories and are invested with accumulations of cultural meanings. Internet enthusiasts often go on about cyberspace as "a whole new world." Our question is whose world? A lot of the Net memes and metaphors circulating out there are grounded in myths, cultural activities and fads that traditionally have included women only as marginal or suspect participants, for example, surfing, hitchhiking and even "driving the car." Some people may think we're way too nitpicky here, but we know better: Language makes reality. The "manly" words and metaphors we use for the Net—the highway and frontier—are very telling.

GAiA's WAKiN' UP!

In pre-modern times, many civilizations held sacred the unity of Mother Earth and Father Sky. Mother Earth, sometimes known as Gaia, wasn't particularly happy with the way the kids were running around causing trouble and messing things up, so (as many stressed-out mothers often do) she decided to take a nap, a cosmic Calgon moment, a little time for herself. Following a nice cosmic massage from Father Sky, she drifted into a deep, rejuvenating slumber. According to legend, she's either still snoozing away or has been suffocated by the King's men, but according to other, less well known myths, Gaia's conscious brainwaves are beginning to spike all over the place, stimulated by the electronic web being woven around her motherly shape. As each new human being logs on, another neural connection is formed. Eventually, Gaia's eyelashes will flutter, she will sigh, and begin to stretch. Is that the point at which we know the World Wide Web is complete? Then, what next?

At this relatively early stage of the Net's explosion in the popular consciousness, we believe it's vital to remember that reality—virtual or not—is socially constructed and that girls and women have a major stake in the ongoing process of defining and building new realities. For example, many women on the Net have seized on the "web" and "webweaver" memes, finding their traditional associations with so-called feminine values of holism and continuity to be both personally and politically empowering. Like the "webweaver" metaphor, each of the metaphors we pummel and pick apart here is fascinating in its own way—each one focuses in on a different facet of the Net's oh-so-complex character.

ARACHNE'S REVENGE

Tuff and fair Athena, goddess of wisdom, was an establishment chick and a real daddy's girl: That is, she was born from Zeus's forehead after he had literally eaten her mother, Metis, goddess of prudence. Athena, who hung out a lot with Nike, the spirit of victory, led armies in just battles, but was also very skilled in both the fine and the useful arts. A talented weaver and potter, Athena was not above standing behind and instructing mere mortal practitioners of these arts as long as they were appropriately grateful and respected her as a goddess. One of her pupils, Arachne, was a country girl who was amazingly skilled at the loom. People from all over came to admire her weavings, and Arachne got a big head and began to brag that she was a better weaver than even Athena. Now, as you would expect, it didn't take long for this to get back to Athena. She dressed up as an old woman and headed out to see what the obstreperous girl was up to. Just who did Arachne think she was anyway?

Athena started out nice enough: "Your work is indeed beautiful, Arachne," she said, "but why can't you just be content to be the best among mortals? Why dis Athena?" Arachne sniffed at that, bragging, "I could take Athena in *any* one-on-one loom match!" This pushed Athena over the edge. "Right here, right now, you vain little twerp!" she cried, tearing off her disguise and accepting Arachne's challenge. And so they set to work.

Athena wove a most beautiful and perfect tapestry. The colors of her depiction of the Olympian gods in all their glory and majesty were rich and fine, and not a thread or knot was out of place. When Arachne finished her tapestry, even Athena had to admit that the girl's technique was flawless, but she flew into a most un-goddess-like rage when she stepped back and discovered that Arachne had woven an irreverent scene making fun of Zeus and his wives. Athena immediately ripped the tapestry to shreds and then smacked Arachne with the shuttle from her own loom. Upon being struck, Arachne felt herself begin to shrink and change shape, and felt her nimble fingers change into spindly arms. Athena had turned her into a spider! "Now you can spin thread and weave your empty, stupid webs forever," Athena cried. Then, thinking somewhere in the back of her mind how proud her daddy would be, Athena turned and left. If she and her kind had to sometimes use extreme measures to remind the mortals who was who, so be it.

Now millennia older, her hubris (as well as that of Athena) tempered, might the World Wide Web be Arachne's feminist revenge?

CONSENSUAL HALLUCINATION

Metaphor
Cyberspace as "consensual hallucination"

Origin
William Gibson's cyberpunk novel *Neuromancer*, 1984.
Legions of netheads and cyberpunks influenced by Gibson's work/thought.
Legions of netheads and cyberpunks influenced by Dr. Timothy Leary

Orientation
Gibson: dystopian, cautionary
Net: utopian, yet gritty, cynical and analytical

The Internet is . . .
Gibson: The Matrix, a nightmarish Cartesian eventuality dominated by transnational corporate and organized-crime conglomerates. A virtual reality.
Net: Nothing compared to what it's gonna be, man.
  or
  Already sold-out by the greedheads

Relevant quote(s)
"Metaprogramming is becoming aware that you have been programmed already . . . It is taking charge of and RE-programming yourself. A most excellent experience." — LeriWeb
"For the first time ever," Art said, "it's possible for people to die of bad memes . . . " — Pat Cadigan, *Synners*

Anagram(s)
"Caucasian? He isn't null, loon!"

McLuhan-o-meter
Gibson: Panoptically cool and murderous.
Net: open, self-organizing, mutating.

Computers are . . .
Mind vehicles, projectors

Humans are . . .
Rigidly "classed" meat. Expendable. Resisters. Boring.

How to navigate cyberspace
Jack directly into your brain, morph, and go, go, go.

Cultural associations
Blade Runner and other dark, futuristic pieces.
Neuromancer was the primary meme-bearer for the cyberpunk movement.
The Doors of Perception, Aldous Huxley
"Serious" independent psychedelic experimentation of the mid-1960s.
Chaos theory

Icons and heroes/heroines
The cyberdeck, hackers, deck cowboys, neural implants, the Sprawl, Frank Zappa, St. Jude (see interview in this volume), *Mondo 2000* (c. 1991).

Nostalgic for . . .
American noir
The Electric Kool-Aid Test
The Year 2000 A.D.

Women . . .
Girls will be boys, and boys will be girls. Bio- and digi-enhanced, of course. Part of the glam, punk, new wave heritage of cyberpunk.

Outlaw women . . .
Are likely to have retractable, razor-sharp steel disks embedded in their fingers and are not to be messed with.

CyborGrrrls might . . .
Read some feminist science fiction.
Write stories about rad cybervigilantegrrrls who infiltrate and stage a coup in a gated and heavily defended Sprawl community known as New Stepford. Post them to alt.cyberpunk.stories.
Undertake secret experiments in aesthetic mindwarping.

URLs
The Sprawl Website http://sensemedic.net/sprawl/
The Mirrorshades Conference on the WELL (Hosts include WELL technomaven Linda Castellani.)
  http://www.well.com/conf/mirrorshades
The LeriWeb page, http://nexchi.org/leri/
The Pat Cadigan Webpage, http://www.wmin.ac.uk/
  %7Efowlerc/patcadigan.html

THE ELECTRONIC FRONTIER

Metaphor
Cyberspace as "electronic frontier"

Origin
John Perry Barlow, cofounder of The Electronic Frontier Foundation, former Wyoming rancher and Grateful Dead lyricist, c. 1990

Orientation
Democratic/progressive libertarian

The Internet is . . .
The postmodern Garden of Eden. The promise of the American frontier experience revisited. Communities working and making decisions together. Virtually unlimited opportunity.

Relevant quote(s)
"We won't get fooled again."
"Don't fence me in."
"Up against the wall!"

Anagram(s)
"Reconcile *notre* rift."
"Reconcile, fritter on."
"Electronic fern riot."

McLuhan-o-meter
Subject to greenhouse EFFect

Computers are . . .
horses, 4WD vehicles, Colt .45s, spaceships

Humans are . . .
Iconoclastic, rugged individuals

How to navigate cyberspace
With your back to the wall, one eye on the door, the other on the Constitution. Emphasis on homesteading.

Cultural associations
Monroe Doctrine. The mythic Old West of novels and movies.
The frontier as a cultural safety valve allowing men to escape the "feminizing" effects of Eastern Civilization.
The oligarchic West eventually ruled by utility, mining and railroad interests. Imperialist genocide.
Wyoming giving women the vote way before any other state. JFK's "New Frontier."
Until recently, the frontier *demographic* of the Net (high male:female ratio).

Icons and heroes/heroines
Thomas Jefferson, John Wayne, Billy the Kid, Robert Redford, *Smokey and the Bandit*, Hunter S. Thompson

Nostalgic for . . .
Disney's Daniel Boone, Marshall Dillon of *Gunsmoke*.

Women . . .
Fiction: whores or squaws (savagery); virgins or schoolmarms (civilization).
Reality: women from a variety of backgrounds making do, working hard, and building new lives under demanding circumstances.

Outlaw women . . .
Cracked whips, broke horses, were trick shots, went in drag and did what they wanted to do.

CyborGrrrls might . . .
Rent *Johnny Guitar*. Jot down fashion and attitude tips. Rent *Heaven's Gate*. Read Jane Tompkin's 1992 book *West of Everything*. Pay close attention.
Get smart about the Constitution in cyberspace, and then call up a few radio talk-shows or write a letter to the editor. Be an activist.
Be inspired by the suffragists like Carrie Chapman Catt who worked her butt off in West during the early twentieth century.

URLs
"Stopping the Information Railroad" by John Perry Barlow
http://gnn.com/gnn/bus/ora/features/barlow/index.html
Virtual Communities: Homesteading on the Electronic Frontier
http://www.well.com/user/hlr/vcbook/index.html

PAVING, WEAVING, SURFING AND CONSENSUALLY HALLUCINATING . . .

INFORMATION SUPERHIGHWAY

Metaphor
Information superhighway/ Infobahn/I-Way

Origin
U.S. Vice President Al Gore and high-up policy wonks, c. 1992. Originally referred to plans for a massive universal connectivity infrastructure similar to the Interstate Defense Highway project of the 1950s. Has since taken on a life of its own in popular media and advertising.

Orientation
Democratic, free-market capitalist with contradictorily censorious moralist undertones, e.g., the Telecommunications Decency Act

The Internet is . . .
A new basic utility. The future of information and entertainment media, business and personal communication, and participatory democracy.

A huge, elaborate Hot Wheels set. Interchanges and drive-through windows servicing a steady in-out stream of data-packed, high-performance sport cars, utility vehicles, minivans and turbocharged Big Wheels.

Relevant quote(s)
"The Interstate Highway Act literally brought Americans closer together. We were connected city to city, town to town, family to family, as we had never been before. That law did more to bring Americans together than any other law this century, and that same spirit of connection and communication is the driving force behind the Telecommunications Act of 1996."
— President Bill Clinton,
signing the TCA into law, February 8, 1996

Anagram(s)
"Oh, wormy infuriating phrase!"
"New Utopia? Horrifying sham!"

McLuhan-o-meter
Hot and sticky like freshly spread asphalt. Full of potholes.

Computers are . . .
Your choice of make, model and year. *The* new choice for those into the conspicuous consumption of planned obsolescence.

Humans are . . .
Consumers, tourists, citizens.

How to navigate cyberspace
Drive defensively. Watch out for trolls, spam, cyberpornographers, stalkers, hackers, viruses. The highway patrol is your friend.

Cultural associations
"Mr. Toad's Wild Ride," Route 66, Howard Johnson's and other roadside attractions of mid-century car-culture.
Woody Guthrie, *On The Road*, The Interstate Defense Highway Project, *The Vanishing Point*.
BMW commercials.
The deaths of communities and cultures passed by or destroyed by the Interstate. The boring, standardized, strip-mall/fast-food sameness of Interstate travel.

Icons and heroes/heroines
Speed Racer, Richard Petty, toll-booths, traffic tickets, cruise control, the daily commute, traffic jams, AAA Trip-Tiks.

Nostalgic for . . .
Optimistic affluence of the days of big tail-fins and cheap gas.

Women . . .
More welcome in the back seat than in the driver's seat; subject to jokes about "women drivers"; condescended to by car salesmen; harassed by truck-drivers, and targeted by serial killers. Mainly for reasons of personal safety, the "open road"/roadtrip Zen option is closed to women.

Outlaw women . . .
Challenge boyz to drag races.
Conceal weapons in the glove box.

CyborGrrrls might . . .
Imagine their own e-vehicles, and describe them in a .sig, plan or somewhere on their Web page.
Virtually ram other drivers who annoy them. Instead of flame wars, engage in demolition derbies.
Talk to people about how to work toward the infrastructural goal of universal access, and explain to people how the Net really works.

URLs
Toward a Global Information Infrastructure (U.S. Information Agency)
http://198.80.36.82/11s/usa/media/global/
"The 50, 26, 20 . . . Corporations That Own Our Media" by Ben Bagdikian (FAIR)
http://www.econet.apc.org/fair/extra/best-of-extra/corporate-ownership.html

ENCYCLOPEDIA GALACTICA

Metaphor
Encyclopedia Galactica

Origin
Douglas Adams's *Hitchhiker's Guide to the Galaxy* series
Ed Krol, *Hitchhiker's Guide to the Internet*

Orientation
Ironic, playful, chaotic, anarchistic.

The Internet is . . .
A cross-referenced compendium of intelligence about the cosmos. Very verbose, not always to the point and full of holes, but extremely useful. You can never tell what you'll need to know, after all.
Perpetually under construction and revision.

Relevant quote(s)
"Don't panic."—Douglas Adams

Anagram(s)
"Galatea: clay picnic coed"
"A goal: edit cyclic panacea"

McLuhan-o-meter
Coolish

Computers are . . .
Temperamental friends and servants, e.g., Marvin, the perpetually depressed robot of Adams's novels.

Humans are . . .
Just another species transparently interfaced with cybernetic intelligences.

How to navigate cyberspace . . .
As a matter of course. As you will.

Cultural associations
Monty Python, *Lost in Space*, Indiana Jones movies, Diderot, *Let's Go* guides, *The Heart of Darkness*, *Bill and Ted's Excellent Adventure*, *The Whole Earth Catalog*.

Icons and heroes/heroines
The babel fish, the oddest thing in the universe. When placed in a host ear, the babelfish is a universal translator. By removing all barriers to communication between cultures and races, it has caused "more and bloodier wars than anything else in the history of creation." —Douglas Adams
The infinite improbability drive.

Nostalgic for . . .
Everything. The always already. A workable definition of the word "culture."

Women
"When I tried hitchhiking after reading Kerouac's *On The Road*, I got picked up at gunpoint and had to give someone a hand-job. . . . . There's no *On the Road* for *us*. I looked at Kerouac's work, and from a feminist viewpoint felt it was a lie. Yet I feel that as women, we're naturally Dharma Bums—we just get paid less!" — Karen Finley interview in *Angry Women* (RE/Search)
On the lighter, fictional side, we also have Sissy Hanshaw, the born-to-hitchhike heroine of Tom Robbins's *Even Cowgirls Get the Blues*.

Outlaw women . . .
Run off with two-headed, rock-star-politician pilots from another planet and become pilots of the hottest spaceships in the universe.

CyborGrrrls might . . .
Examine their hands to see if they have hitchhiker's thumbs.
Write some entries for Project Galactic Guide (*http://vela.acs.oakland.edu/pub/galactic-guide*). They're very low on women and grrrly perspectives.

URLs
XVR27's super collection of *Hitchhiker's Guide to the Galaxy* links http://www.en.com/users/xvr27/otherguide2a.html
Ed Krol's *A Hitchhiker's Guide to the Internet.* E-text available at http://www.softlab.ntua.gr/internet/hitchhikers-guide/thgtti.html

Metaphor
The Net

Origin
Recalls TV networks and channel-surfing. The Internet as
a networked ocean of hypertextual, narrow-band
information channels.

Orientation
Equal parts grudging socialism, libertarian chic and
mainstream techno-mysticism.

The Internet is . . .
Epcot via AT&T.

Relevant quote(s)
"Catch a wave, and you're sitting on top of the world." —
The Beach Boys
"You will." —AT&T advertisements

Anagram(s)
"He tent."

McLuhan-o-meter
k00L, cool, kewl

Computers are . . .
Surfboards.

Humans are . . .
Increasingly virtualized consumers in a new global
economy. Creatures of the moment.

How to navigate cyberspace . . .
By catching and riding wave after wave after passing
wave. Intuitively and by aping what the kool kidz say is
kool.

Cultural associations
Surfing as first countercultural obsession of children of
WWII generation. Part of mythos of "innocent" America
of traditionally defined gender and other social roles.
So. Cal, where the American surfing mythos took off,
was also where the Net was born.
Mystical side to surfing: being one with ocean, waves and
tide; understanding/living by those cycles; being in
tune with the flow and power. This was packaged and
sold in the 1980s as the basis for New Agey management techniques.

Can also be extremely individualistic and/or violent, e.g.,
1980s surfpunk.

Icons and heroes/heroines
Moondoggie (Jeff), Gidget's college/surfer boyfriend
Jeff Spicoli, *Fast Times at Ridgemont High*
Dylan, *Beverly Hills 90210*
The Hawaiian Tropic Bikini Girls

Nostalgic for . . .
Most of the same things as the Info Superhighway
metaphor. Only accessorized with a balding hipster
ponytail or pierced ear.

Women
Beach bunnies who go for tandem rides on boys'
surfboards or ride belly-boards.
Gidget, the fictional character created in 1957 by
Frederick Kohner, spawned a series of novels, movies
and TV shows and became the symbol of and
inspiration for the surf craze of the early 1960s. Excerpt
from the novel: "I was sixteen last month. I'm really
quite cute. I've real blonde hair and wear it in a
horsetail. . . . I've got a couple of real sexy-looking
bathing suits that're pretty low-cut and have a skin-
tight fit. When Jeff saw me the first time I was wearing
the pink one and that's why he called me Pinky—real
corny."
Though a women's pro circuit exists, in the guy surfer
fraternity, there's *still* a prejudice against women who
surf, but it is much less intense than it used to be.

Outlaw women . . .
Wax up, paddle out and shred. Develop their own
trademark style.

CyborGrrrls might . . .
Dial up, log on and shred. Develop their own trademark
style.

URLs
The Hawaii Women's Sports Homepage
http://www.soc.hawaaii.edu/con/com634/home/sports/
sp_home.html

Metaphor
The World Wide Web

Origin
Human fascination with the beauty of natural mathematical logic. A natural metaphor for interactive, multimedia, hypertextual systems. Web filaments may be woven into a utilitarian document or artwork or used as a mode of transport.

Orientation
Emphasizes interconnections between ideas, people, cultures, institutions; pluralistic, holistic, environmentalist.

The Internet is . . .
A digital ecosystem of mental and spiritual projections; a web of webs. The web model is widely considered the basis for future of the Internet.

Relevant quote(s)
"'Networking' is both a feminist practice and a multinational corporate strategy — weaving is for oppositional cyborgs." — Donna Haraway
"Truth is cheap, but information costs." — Pat Cadigan

Anagram(s)
"Behold dew we writ!"
"The wild breed. Wow!"

McLuhan-o-meter
98.6° F

Computers are . . .
Webshooters.

Humans are . . .
Texts. Electronically interfaced relational beings connected empathetically by digital linkages: cyborg thinkers/lovers/resisters.

How to navigate cyberspace . . .
Relationally. By shooting a filament to a point on the Web, and then drifting over on the digital breeze.

Cultural associations
Traditional Native American origin stories about Grandmother Spider spinning the universe out of Chaos. Greek myth of Arachne. *Charlotte's Web*. Spiderman (sensitive-guy mutant superhero). "The Itsy Bitsy Spider."
IDIC: Infinite Diversity, Infinite Combinations. Continuance, memory, contingency.

A more human-friendly way of visioning grids of power/discourse.
The history of exploitation of women workers in the textile industry.

Icons and heroes/heroines
Grandmother Spider (cf Gaia)
Nineteenth-century New England "mill girls," young, single women who worked commercial looms for long hours at low pay to support themselves and other family members, and who created proto-feminist subcultures in places like Lowell, Massachusetts.
Arachne and Athena

Nostalgic for . . .
The Goddess.

Women
"*Webster* **n** [(fr. OE webbestre: female weaver—Webster's): "A weaver . . . as the designation of a woman"—O.E.D.] : A woman whose occupation is to Weave, Esp. a Weaver of Words and Word-Webs. N.B.: The word Webster was Dis-covered by Judy Grahn, who has written: "Webster is a word that formerly meant 'female weaver,' the 'ster' ending indicating a female ancestor, or female possession of the word. The word-weavers of recent centuries have given us the oration of Daniel Webster, and the dictionary listings of Merriam-Webster stem from English family names that once descended through the female line. Some great-great-grandmother gave them her last name, Webster, she-who-weaves." —*Websters' First New Intergalactic Wickedary of the English Language*, conjured by Mary Daly in cahoots with Jane Caputi

Outlaw women . . .
Believe in themselves and their art and abilities. Go one-on-one with the gods in weaving contests. Often face censorship attempts and/or persecution.

CyborGrrrls might . . .
Think of hypertext mark-up language (html) as a weaver's shuttle that can be slung around like battering ram *or* be used as delicately as lace-tatting needles.
Encourage other women online to "make/express," not just "use/consume."

URLs
Susan Teel's ode to women web weavers http://www.alaska.net:80/~mteel/susan/web.html
Web-sters Net-work
http://lucien.SIMS.berkeley.EDU/women_in_it.html

PAVING, WEAVING, SURFING AND CONSENSUALLY HALLUCINATING . . .

HAPPINESS IS A

WARM, NOIZY INTERNET

Do you remember those darn AT&T "You Will" commercials? Weren't they just so *smug?* And if that weren't enough, they tried to offset the totalitarian vision of super-techno-ease for the very upper classes—and the absence of "the rest of us"—by employing actors with non-threatening demeanors to perform the voice-overs. For us, just about the most amusing thing in the film version of William Gibson's *Johnny Mnemonic* (a movie/adaptation we liked on lots of levels, contrary to most of the critics) is the way AT&T's product placement strategy backfired and became part of the darkly ironic culturescape of the piece when overloaded cyber-courier Johnny dials his duplicitous boss on a public AT&T *(you will)* video phone.

Plop rearview tiaras on our heads and call us Little Ms. Paranoids, but we get little chills up our spines when corporations stop courting customers and start issuing orders. That's why Crystal cursed aloud and almost fell out of her chair when she inevitably ended up zapping over to the Netscape "Cool Site of the Day" Website and encountered these words:

> Someday, we'll all agree what's cool on the Net. In the mean-
> time, the Netscape cool team will continue to bring you a list
> of select sites that catch our eye, make us laugh, help us work,
> quench our thirst . . . you get the idea.

Now, Netscape is a generally cool . . . um . . . innovative company right
out there on the cutting edge of browser software and maintains really
good relationships with users and customers, but *whoa*—"Someday,
we'll all agree what's cool on the Net"? Exactly who the heck is this
royal we?

It doesn't end—or begin—with Netscape. The first—and still one
of the most popular—lists of Net "coolness" is Glenn Davis's "Cool Site
of the Day" at InfiNet (http://cool.infi.net/), which continues to log
tens of thousands of hits per day. *Cool* (meaning desirable, fun-n-new,
particularly engaging or unthreateningly countercultural) has already
been so commodified by beer companies and MTV, that—like (almost)
all of us trained to be vacuous citizen-consumers—Netheads salivate
almost reflexively at being given an opportunity to do, see or interface
with something cool, so much so that lame and unironic "cool site of
the day (night, week, month, et cetera)" sites have proliferated all over
the Web. Some sites wear the mark of coolness like medals. During
most browsing sessions, you will see at least one site bragging "This
site was named Cool Site of the Day by X on [date]." We are somewhat
surprised that there has not been a "cool site" payola scandal of some
sort!

Some other cool folx on the Net take a more sanguine, give-it-up-
to-Allah, pomo approach to the whole cool thing. Consider the
doublespeak epigram of Brandon Lay's Cool Place: "Unique is not original, just different. Nothing is original. So, unique is cool. Original is a
Miracle." Others encourage folks to culture jam Net cool. For example,
HotWired's Cate Cochoran (http://www.hotwired.com/staff/cate/hype/
hype.html) encourages *everyone* to display those prized cool site and
"Top 5% of the Web" icons on their sites. Now that's cool for real.

See, grrrls and other culture jammer types (see http://www.
adbusters.org/adbusters) know the contemporary popular logic of
"cool" is very much invested in a detached, objectifying—did we hear
someone say "male"?—cultural gaze. Cool is blasé, detached. It wears

sunglasses so it can seduce without having to engage or react. It is a self-protective, predatory pose that makes its superficiality and seeming emotionlessness into a virtue to be fleshed out by your deepest desires. Cool isn't into discussion. Grrrls know: Cool usually has meant dishonest and exploitative. Cool uses up and walks away. Cool is not into commitment, stewardship or work toward resolution of conflicts. Cool is into *cool*. On the Net, this emphasis on coolness works to create an atmosphere in which established and oppressive ways of being/seeing/doing/defining are allowed to code and shape this new space.

Now, given the approximate 65:35 ratio of men to women using the Internet, and given the much higher ratio (perhaps as high as 7:1 or 9:1) of men to women who are, for various structural and economic reasons, active players on the Net, it shouldn't be at all surprising that cheesy pornography and "babe" sites, and lots of other things Beavis and Butthead would understand as cool abound *as* cool and now almost define the "personal" side of the 'Net. ("Heh-heh, heh-heh, *cool!*" as Beavis might say.) To get melodramatic for a moment, this is exactly why it is important that women begin to fight, frolic and homestead in the cyberscape in greater and more involved numbers. We've got to get in there and enunciate and agitate and argue for what *we* think is important, fascinating, weird, whatever.

Recall for a moment your Marshall McLuhan, and consider, too, this big irony: The Internet is *not* a "cool" medium, nor is it a "hot" medium. Although McLuhan often seemed to contradict himself in typing media as hot and cool—his classifcations of newspapers and television are more than a little obtuse—he generally defined a hot medium as "one that extends one single sense in 'high definition' . . . [in] the state of being well-filled with data" and is therefore low in audience/user participation, and a cool medium as one that is "low definition, because so little [information] is given and so much has to be filled in" by audience members or users (*Understanding Media*, 1964). Hot media include radio, film and lectures; cool media include telephones, television (in most references) and discussion. Hence, if we carry McLuhan's typology into the online multimedia moment, then, like Baby Bear's porridge, the Net as a whole should be "just right." And the just-rightness of the Net is what has just about everyone from peons like us to the plotters and schemers at the shrinking number of media corporations all atwitter! The rub is that lots of people with extensive experience making money in "hot" media and who have $$$$ signs in their eyes are selling a "hot" vision of the Internet as "cool" and defining "cool" as "hot"! For example, America Online tries to make it seem cool to pay big money for heavy, regular interaction with "hot" features on their "hot" and easy-to-use service: areas sponsored by MTV and Microsoft, online celebrity appearances, online versions of mainstream magazines, and image and software libraries. *Wired* even credits this mix-up right to the horse's mouth! In the January 1996 issue, *Wired* featured McLuhan as centerfold/coverboy/channeled entity come back from the dead to pronounce "The Web is cool." *Humph.* Let's all recall yet again the Netscape chiller: "Someday, we'll all agree . . .".

We like to think of the corpus/climate of the cyberscape as perpetually 98.6° F and *noizy*, as variously warm, fussy, sublime, mutating and endlessly contestable. In simplest terms, because it puts the "me" in media, the Internet escapes McLuhan's definitional boundaries. That's what's "cool" about it—that a huge number of utterances from a vast number of sources become accessible at heretofore unthinkable rates along heretofore unthinkable routes. The Internet is a grid-flow of electrons freaking out, a bunch of machines talking to one another, but the machines are talking at the behest of participants (not just "users" or "viewers" or "listeners"), of people participating in e-mail discussion groups, of people chatting/sharing/pranking/debating/fighting on Usenet, of people building Websites that reflect their lives/passions/ work/obsessions, of people searching libraries and downloading software, of people hanging out or putting on plays on an IRC channel. To risk alienating some of you by copping a term from Jacques Derrida, one of our fave Frenchy philosophers, the Net is a "postal" system; *desire* circulates via those fiber-optic bundles and is inextricably mixed-in with "information" and recombinant information from vastly heterogeneous sources. That is, grrrls, the Net is both cool and *funky*.

The Internet is all about active relationships between and among people, texts and ideas. Following the lead of Donna Haraway, we envision the Net *herself* as an extremely unfaithful bastard girl-child of the U.S. Cold War military-industrial complex, who, seduced by a rising tide of visionaries (many of whom grooved on the Net's next-sibling: synthetic psychedelics), forsook her roots as a post-apocalyptic fail-safe system and set about evolving into a living, pulsing ecosystem of her own, where the diversity and noizy proliferation of everything is, perhaps, the *only* rule. When you consider this, any notion of the Internet as cool (or "hot" as cool) becomes ridiculous, if not outright pernicious, and that's why we ridicule it here! Yep, the Net is Topsy and Pandora and Medusa and Janis Joplin all rolled into one and, boy, is she laughing at the Netscape "cool team"! Coolness, as currently *commodified* on the Net, equals the slow suffocation of this fabulously chaotic system. A vision of a Net future in which we will all someday agree on what is cool, in which some consortium of Perseuses will chain our grrrl Net face down and gang-bang her into becoming their concubine, is simply rather revolting.

Don't buy (into) Net cool. *Make* Net cool, baby.

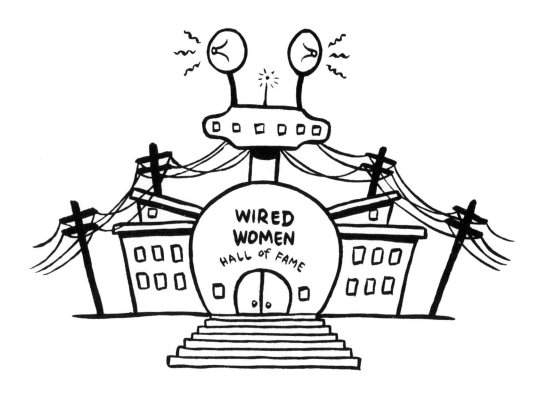

Wired Women Hall of Fame

ST. JUDE, PROVOKE US!

Name: Judith (Jude) Milhon
Alias: St. Jude
Age: 50, heh.
Geographical location: Berkeley, California

Introduce her? Why, she's *merely* a grrrl hero, a legend in her own time. What's to introduce? An original, hardcore geekgirl with a chewy caramel center, and (IOHO) the very soul of *Mondo 2000* back in the early 1990s when *Mondo* really mattered, she's always where the action is. Revel in her revelations and wit. More important, listen to her, you little larvae! Set your transponders to receive her signals; then after you finish here, head on over to http://www.next.com.au/ spyfood/geekgirl/001stick/jude/jude.html. Mama Mutant is a wise, experienced, insanely playful hacker of everything, and, baby, does she have stories and visions to share. She's currently at work on a project called *Grrrlz Need Modems.* Of course.

Profession: current and past lives?

Writer, editor, humorist, hero, co-author (with R. U. Sirius and Bart Nagel) of *Cyberpunk Handbook [The Real Cyberpunk Fakebook]* (Random House, 1995) and (with R. U. Sirius and The Internet 21) *How to Mutate and Take Over the World: An Exploded Post-Novel* (Ballantine, 1996).

Internet projects and communities with which you are or have been involved?

Community Memory Project, *Mondo 2000,* the *How to Mutate* project, which collected collaborators to a postnovel online—"the Internet 21."

Other personal info you want to share?

I'm fairly normal—working-class background, autodidact, politico, civil rights activist in the South, polygamist, bisexual, braggart, petty criminal...yeah, back in the sixties we all had convictions, but I've got 'em listed on a rapsheet. Come on baby, light my FOIA.

What were you doing with computers during what was for many of us the dark ages of home computing (the game and word-processing phase)? Did you have any inkling that the Net was going to happen and be such a huge cultural phenomenon?

The Net...o yas, yas...that was the vision we had, only we figured it would spread to become *Berkeley wide!* I was with Community Memory Project, which was trying to extend computer power to the people, back when home computers were science fiction, in the early seventies. Lee Felsenstein and others had scavenged some Big Scrap Iron (a 940 mainframe, like a roomful of refrigerators) and set up a computer room in an old warehouse, Project One. This was a political project infiltrated by Marxist sociologist programmers who wrote papers on us (I was code-named Rosa Luxemburg), an enterprise whose secretary was *Processed World's* Chris Carlson (leader-for-life of the Nasty Secretaries League), a project wracked by political despair and weekly infighting and lots of personal rancor. We tried to build a local net that would be Bay Area wide, creating an online community through shared postings (keyword-retrievable, not like Usenet)—personals ads and other want-ads, and poetry and commentary—which would link people in this area into an online community. We hoped the idea would catch on in

other cities, and someday we'd all link up together, and form one
huge metacommunity...

What do you think of the current metaphors for the Net (info sooperhighway, the cyberspace frontier et cetera)? What do you call the Net?

How about...the nosphere, yow! Or the mycelium? Mycelium is the
underground net that occasionally pushes mushrooms up into the
overground.

What's the current status of *Mondo 2000?* We think it's unfortunate (to put it mildly) that *Mondo*-consciousness is being steadily overtaken and supplanted by *Wired*-consciousness. What sort of shift in cyberconsciousness does this represent, and what are its implications?

You mean *Mondo* as anarchic, happy, free-spirited voice of the
future and all that? Actually *Mondo* was a monarchy, ruled by a
couple of queens, and the anarchists had to run for the hills some
time ago—about when the zine stopped coming out regularly, fancy
that. Organized anarchists can do anything, btw...except, I sup-
pose, rule the world. And, well, *Wired*—a zine based on a corporate
business plan—is not your happiest standard-bearer for a happier
future, but here it comes...

How old were you when you started messing around with computers?

I was twenty-seven. My boyfriend at Antioch sent me a letter
setting out a Turing machine problem. I had politics like a case of
herpes back then...incurable and recurrent, and I couldn't think
about anything else...but I couldn't stop thinking about the
problem, solved it, fired a letter back. Whereupon he—Efrem Lipkin,
my longtime companion—insisted I was born to program.

Yeah? Yeah? And?

I started out by teaching myself FORTRAN—went to the library in
Richmond, Virginia (where I was in recovery from the civil rights
movement) and checked out that square green book *Teach Yourself
FORTRAN* and sure enough! Soon I got a job where I could *look* at
computers, operating a machine that converted merchandise tags into
punch cards in Miller's department store. (This is real geezing,
here.) After six months of this, my boyfiend (ha) convinced me to
go to New York City and find a job as a junior programmer. *O
joy...!* I was the *only* programmer (the other one had quit) so I had
to teach myself IBM 1440 assembler, sink or swim. I managed to

swim. Six months later I got a high-paying job with a systems design house, again because of my boyfiend. If this sounds like I was lame and shy...I was.

Did you ever have to deal with any sort of techno-sexism in labs, computer stores or wherever?

In my first job, o yes. The Catholic boss at Horn & Hardart kept me in my place (I was uppity) with female jokes that also bonded him with his male staff. He made me serve coffee at a meeting. Once. I brought coffees in on my leather clipboard and spilled them—maybe I got a little on his handcrafted suit (he'd unbuttoned his sleeve-buttons for us once—look, serfs, here's how you tell it's custom-made!) Ooops—I was gruff—oops, sorry...not used to playing hostess. A couple weeks later I was in the job that doubled my pay. It was a programmer's market back then.

When I got into the higher levels, in those days there was a lot of reverse sexism. I was always getting the equivalent of "you're a credit to your race." The guys were delighted to have a sex-integrated shop. They chatted me up some, in a shy sort of way, and oogled me when I wore minis...but I've always enjoyed that sort of thing. I like male nerds, I like dressing up and I understand the wired-in visual-display response of male primates. (We are primates. When a male baboon sees a swollen blue bottom, he swells up also. When a male programmer sees a miniskirt, he gets it up...if he's het. If he's not, he can quibble with you on the style. It's a game we can all enjoy.)

Do you think you had a different approach to computers than your male classmates or co-workers?

I think it was a class difference. See, I used computers—being a programmer—to crawl out of my political-burnout working-class life and into those woolly dresses and alligator pumps that meant you got money. But sex differences...? Most high-level male programmers are what you'd call female-stereotype people—they're socially shy, their friends tend to be female and their minds are intuitive and artistic. I often feel very butch in their company—I'm a jock in comparison.

What did you do with computers before you went online?

I was a classical programmer...I composed algorithms, I wrote code, I debugged. I used to say I wanted to be a writer, but writing *computer* language, you know when something's buggy. I compared programming to writing sonnets: It's demanding and difficult, and you know when you screw up. *heh*...now I can stand to write *prose*, in English!

When did you discover the Internet? Why did you first go online?

Well, I'm a freak. E-mail was a unique opportunity to exercise my style of weirdness. In the early eighties I read *Tale of Genji* and immediately felt I'd be at home in agoraphobic Heian-era Japan. A thousand years ago you'd write delicate verse letters to your friends in exquisite calligraphy on paper appropriate to the content, wrap it in silk, perhaps tuck a leaf or a bud into the binding cord and have a pageboy deliver it. But I tried to do it online: I'd conduct e-mail haiku correspondence with my friends, all obliquity and restraint and stuph...

What really blew your mind about the Internet and convinced or inspired you to get involved in this revolution?

There was a *there* there, *and* I could stand to live in it. I was a terrible agoraphobe. I was crippled up by depression—hail, *Zoloft*! I spent years doing nothing much till R. U. Sirius dumped the *Mondo* stuff on me. When I started editing *Mondo 2000* it was a paper zine— snail mail manuscripts. I hate to do data entry—retyping the submissions—I hate mailing things, I hate reading things on dead trees and I was chicken about meeting people f2f. So: THE NET!! I badgered writers to send stuff in living electrons. Via e-mail, the medium of instant gratification...but I'd accept snailed disks. (Then I only had to fight the aberrant formats—a regular contributing physicist tried to send me WordStar files on rectangular diskettes.)

How did you go about becoming a fully functioning netizen? What resources and people were useful to you?

O, I just jumped into the WELL.

So far, what has been your best Net experience? Your worst?

Best: I've hacked access to an Oxford English Dictionary. (Hey, this is a deep thrill, and it took some doing.) I'm still looking for a dependable route in to Medline...maybe I shouldn't say that. And I don't think I've had *any* traumatic experiences. Tedious, frustrating, trying to find access to this and that, but in offensive situations I have the edge—stand back! I've got a sense of humor, and I know how to use it. And being online gives me the

emotional detachment to deal with anything that comes up. Yes: It's
only words. ONLY WORDS. No muscles = no real threat. Most women are
better with words than most men, and isn't it nice to wield *that*
edge?

Online sexism, a problem or not? Your most heinous or unsettling experience? Your best experience as a woman online? What's the best way to deal with sexist trolls/flamers and unwanted sexual attention?

Hmmm...well, I was in pleasant conversation in a chat room with a
guy who suddenly lowered his pants and requested I service him.
Fascinating. I Southern-belled him—no, not the corporation, the
gender mode—o dear me, I'm afraid I'm not interested in *that* sort
of thing, my goodness look at the time! This tactic worked okay.
It's a campy take on the Miss Manners mode—which would be setting
limits tactfully, with no female affectations to provoke more
infringements. Don't diss Miss Manners. She takes a strategic
approach to human interactions and manipulates them intelligently.
Miss Manners is *hackerly*, you might say. That's the attitude that
women might best use against sexist and unwanted sexual stuff
online.

   I met a fourteen-year-old riot-nrrrdgrrrl, Terran, in D.C.—
actually, she shoved a pie into R. U. Sirius's face on our book
tour (and pouffed some pie on my nose) because *Cyberpunk Fakebook*
is outing the cyberpunk shtick she happily mystifies the world
with. She's like the grrrl I invented five years ago, o joy, but
real. She's been compiling a guide for dealing with what she calls
cyberstalkers. I haven't seen it, but she told me it's putdowns and
off-turnings...oneliners to detumesce the devil himself.

What is your take on the ways gender gets played out, expressed, discussed online? What are your experiences of online spaces made by and/or maintained for women? How is interaction in these spaces different from that taking place in mixed forums or "guy" sites?

Hmmmm. You have to realize that I'm fairly manly myself. I'm old
enough to have grown up thinking that manly was the only way to be,
if you were going to get anywhere. And not just manly, but
warriorlike. Fave Nietzsche quote: "A malcontent is one of those
old-style fighting men: He has no love of civilization, because he
thinks the object of civilization is to make all the good things of
life—honors, plunder, beautiful women—accessible also to cowards."
(This is ironic, okay???)

   I was so proud when my daughter turned out to be a six-foot, blonde Amazon. BIG POWERFUL VOOMAN. We're both still trying to bring each other up—maturity *HOOHooooh!*—of course.

Why do you think it's important for girls and women to get online and participate in the imagination and realization of what we here at *SurferGrrls* call "the cyberscape"? What hopes do you have for the future and impact of feminism(s) online?

That is the big question. I think cyberspace is the place. It's boot camp for grrrlz. It's where you can practice your chops until you can take on the so-called real world. And no, I'm not proposing that girls should grow up to be men—I'm hoping they'll grow up to be free women. I don't think we know yet what free women are like. Maybe we can find out.

What is your next project?

I'm going to write a book called *Grrrlz Need Modems,* on exactly what I was just talking about.

What is your utopian fantasy (or worst nightmare) of the impact the Internet will have on culture and society as we move into the next millennium?

Funny that cyberpunk has been labeled dystopian. In fact, it's the mode for the only utopian ideas we can possibly formulate. Real education at last...real understanding among different cultures...so many opportunities for the human imagination in aid of human possibility. The Net allows us to get to the root, in effect, of human culture...to become culture hackers. Okay, here's my definition of the hack: the ingenious circumvention of imposed limits. Now we can become culture hackers. We've got a chance to do in software what the hardware—the realpolitik of economics and geography—has always kept us from achieving: a human future that we can stand to live in.

AUTHOR, EDITOR AND CHICK

EXTRAORDINAIRE

Name: Carla Sinclair

Age: ;-)

Geographical location: West Hollywood, California

Machines: Centris 610, PowerBook 165 and GranGaggia cappuccino maker

Probably best known for her work as editor of the "world's greatest neurozine," *bOING bOING* (see it at http://www.zeitgeist.net/Public/Boing-boing/), Carla Sinclair actually has a number of fingers in the wired pie. With a circulation of fifteen thousand readers and soon to celebrate its seventh birthday, *bOING bOING* is enough of a brain-child for any techno-mom to be proud of. But wait! Carla's got two more projects out there to help you get a grip on what goes down in the world of weird, wild and wacky neurozine culture. Last fall, two books hit shelves—thanks to Carla: *Net Chick* (Holt, 1995) and *The Happy Mutant Handbook: Mischievous Fun for Higher Primates* (Riverhead Books, 1995), co-authored with Mark Frauenfelder and Gareth Branwyn. Know what? There's even more. Carla's often spotted hanging on the WELL (that oh-so-hooked-in BBS-turned-ISP) and featured in *Wired, Future Sex* and *The Net* magazines. She's also rumored to be haunting around Cyborganic, a young upstart of an Internet presence at http://www.cyborganic.com/People/carla/. Whew.

We snagged Carla long enough via e-mail to ask her opinion on a few topics we considered relevant for any femme-Net Presence. Here's a sampling of what she had to say.

How old were you when you first started messing with computers?
Around twenty, when I realized it was much easier to type a school paper on a PC than deal with a typewriter or handwrite it.

Have you ever dealt with any sort of sexism in your online/computer life?
You know, I really haven't. But then I haven't really experienced much sexism in any other aspect of my life, either.

But the media sometimes portrays the Net as this totally dangerous and awful space for women, and tries to convince us to make it "safe" for women and children. What do you have to say to the media?
Only the cornballs of the media who have probably never spent more than a few nanoseconds on the Net—besides maybe e-mail—would claim that the Net is a dangerous and awful place for women. I don't really understand where those kinds of statements come from. *Where* is it "dangerous" for women on the Net? And if something is danger-ous for women, wouldn't it be dangerous for men as well? And *how* can it be dangerous? Is something going to leap out of the keyboard and swallow up the damsel in distress? It's hard for me to even respond to such ludicrousness. I hope that women don't buy into these kinds of fallacies about the Net, because if they think of themselves as victims, then they'll become a victim. They'll say they were harassed online, and that it has traumatized them, or something silly like that, when in reality they've just experienced a flame, which everyone—girl, boy, ape—will experience online at one time or another. So what? I'm not saying there aren't crude jerks out there in cyberspace who don't sexually come on to others, because you definitely will see those types of humans on the Net from time to time, but you'll see them just as often in bars, classrooms and supermarkets. Deal with it.

What did you do with computers, early on?
I started off just using them to write school papers. But then I

very quickly learned about BBSs and then the WELL, and that's when my adrenaline went haywire. ;-) A lot of the people on the WELL were really helpful.

Some people might feel the WELL—because it's been around since the early days of cyberculture—is a scary and "hardcore" place, especially for women, who might not be into cyberpunk culture as much as men. Comment?

Well, I'm female, at least that's what they tell me, and I love cyberpunk culture. And the WELL is filled with all sorts of people, some extremely nice, and others a little more persnickity. But one thing most of them have in common is that they're smart and opinionated, yet they respect other people's ideas and viewpoints. Although many a flame war has taken place on the WELL, I don't find it a "nasty" group at all. Just a hotbed of intellect, creativity and fresh perspectives.

When did you first discover the Internet?

Right about the time I was starting *bOING bOING*. Around 1989. When I realized what a gem of a resource the Net was for the newest, edgiest and most radical information out there, I became hooked.

How did *bOING bOING* get started?

Well, Mark [Frauenfelder, also of *Wired*] and I started it about six years ago as a hobby. We had no idea it would get as big as it is. We had been reading *Factsheet Five*, which reviews thousands of zines in each issue, and after reading tons of zines over a few years, we finally thought, "Hey, we can do this!" So we did. Now I wear all kinds of hats, from editor on down to secretary. We can't afford to hire too many people, so we each take on about six different positions. Eventually, I'd like to sell half the magazine to a real business-type person—but I don't even have the time to put a business plan together!

Oh. And, just for the record, describe your book *Net Chick*. ;-)

Net Chick covers online grrrl-culture and is filled with interviews and profiles of women who have helped shape the wired world such as Lisa Palac of *Future Sex* and *Cyborgasm*, hacker St. Jude of *Mondo 2000*, and Rosie Cross from the fab Website *Geekgirl*. *Net Chick* is also loaded with reviews of sites, tips, and how-tos.

◊

AUTHOR, EDITOR AND CHICK EXTRAORDINAIRE

What's been the response so far?

Really great! I just sold the book to Japanese publishers, and I've gotten wonderful reviews so far. And tons of e-mail from readers—a surprising amount from guys—come in every day. That's what's so great about e-mail. If I just had a snail-mail address I bet I wouldn't hear from so many people at all, but with e-mail being so easy and instant, I hear from all sorts of readers from all over the world!

Obviously, a plethora of fun chick-sites are out there, but there's also a need for books like *Net Chick* and *SurferGrrrls.* Who is the target audience of your book? Why do you think there's this popular notion that no chicks are online, when they are?

I honestly think the media just doesn't know any better. Poor things. I'm sure once *Net Chick* and *SurferGrrrls* and other hip-to-grrrls publications come out, we'll get a glut of news stories about online chick culture from excited journalists who think they're the first to discover such a scene.

But then there's the whole macho-nerdboy mentality: These are the geeks still living in the 1960s punch-card days, who will probably never understand the estrogenic side of the Net. And frankly, who cares? Let them be ignorant bores! We know better.

To change the subject some, Jayne Loader, a multimedia artist and developer, has gone on record as saying "if video games are masculine, the Internet is feminine." How do you react to the gendering of the Net? Do you think it's feminine? Why or why not?

I'm not sure if I like gendering the Net, since I think, like all mediums, it possesses both feminine *and* masculine aspects. But I do think the Net is feminine in the way that it's hypercommunicative. It's a place where people can express themselves through their words, art and even voice (audio) to the whole world. And millions of people can respond. Since expression and communication are considered to be feminine traits, you could say the Net is very powerful for women. *But*...let's not forget the (flame)warlike and visual aspects of the Net, which are considered to be masculine traits. I would say the Net is actually a yin-yang-balanced chaos, if you will.

How do you feel about the metaphors being used for the Internet? Like, the Net is a frontier, which implies that it needs to be tamed, and so on?

I don't think using "the frontier" as metaphor to describe cyberspace implies that it's got to be more civilized before "the women and children can be let in." In fact, I think it's a pretty good metaphor, since—as with all new frontiers—the Net is pretty anarchistic at the moment. If some women feel they can only handle civilized territories, then they better stick to their knitting and off line PTA meetings. But in general I suspect that most women will find the Net a liberating space where they can take advantage of business opportunities, communicate with others on a grand scale and stimulate their brains with just about any subject they can imagine.

Do you see any indication that women are becoming more wired?

Oh, yeah. There's been a huge change in the Net scene the last couple of years. I've even noticed a rush of new grrrly Web sites within the last six months! *[of 1995]* I'm talking about online magazines for chicks, Websites that talk about women's issues, lots of new fashion sites...Finally! I think it has to do with the graphical nature and easy access to the Web. More and more women and men are getting online for these reasons. Once women realize what a wonderfully communicative tool the Internet is, they're hooked.

And so, Ms. Sinclair, what's next?

I've got a few projects brewing. Not sure which one to focus on yet. But I want to do something completely different from *Net Chick* to keep my brain cells alive.

Any encouraging words for chicks getting into the Net?

Once women and girls plug in their modems and experience for themselves what the Net has to offer—access to mainstream and alternative information, worldwide communication, merchandise and a way to express oneself to literally millions of people—they won't *need* encouragement! They'll shove the boys over and make room for themselves!

Scoot Over, Ms. Thang,

NetDiva's Here!

Name: Eno Jackson
Age: 29
Geographical location: Brooklyn, New York

Isis is a Website that, should you be the first person in your little Net circle to chance upon it, you immediately add it to your bookmarks and then zap the URL out to your best friends. And you do that not because it makes you look cool or feel hip, but because a site drew you in, enticed you up and down, satisfied you, taught you something or pointed you somewhere you didn't realize you needed to go, and compelled you to send the author a love letter virtually begging for more. What this sort of respect/response illustrates, ladies, is the difference between keeping a Website and curating a Website, and Eno "NetDiva" Jackson (found at http://www.netdiva.com/) is a curator of the highest degree. Eno also runs her own Internet consulting firm, NetDiva Communications.

Profession?

Internet communications consultant, at present.

Internet projects or communities with which you are or have been involved?

I curate the Isis pages on art and culture of women of African descent.

Other personal info you'd like to share:

I am from the greatest city in the world, New York. I have a degree in women's studies from Barnard College and an MBA from MIT.

How old were you when you started messing around with computers?

I was about eighteen years old.

In what sort of setting?

I had an internship my last semester of high school at a management agency for classical musicians. They had this computer, an IBM PC type, that used 8-inch floppy disks—really a dinosaur! They were really nice and let me fool around with it as much as I wanted. Later, I went to Barnard College, which had just installed a state-of-the-art computer lab (with PC ATs and XTs...come on, it was 1984), and I spent a lot of time using the computers. I had also taken a college class when I was in high school and a weekend workshop at Hunter College.

Did you ever have to deal with any sort of techno-sexism in labs, computer stores or wherever?

I remember in junior high school the computer lab was strictly baby-testosterone central. I wasn't tremendously interested, though.

Barnard was an all-women's college, and sexism was not a problem there. Also, I was doing this strictly as an off-hours hobby—I had no intentions of adopting computers as a career or being a computer science major. Those types all looked very haggard and sleep-deprived! To me, this was just for fun.

When I got to graduate school, that was another story. Some people really had a hard time believing that I knew as much about computer systems as I did. I worked as a lab assistant in my last year of business school, and even some of my fellow women students did not believe I actually had that job unless I was literally wearing a name tag that said Eno Jackson, Lab Assistant.

Do you think you had a different approach to computers than your male classmates or co-workers did?

I don't know, really. I don't think that my approach is different from those men who have backgrounds like mine—people who are self-taught, with liberal arts backgrounds, whatever. One of my best Net pals is a guy, a system administrator who has a degree in English—I think we deal with information technology in very similar ways.

What did you do with computers before you went online?

I usually ended up helping people with software, doing set up and install, et cetera. In 1990 I decided to go back to school (to Hunter College) and I got my own PC. Having a computer of my own was really the turning point.

When did you discover the Internet? Why did you first go online?

When I was at Hunter I got an e-mail account. I started using e-mail, and then I found out about Net tools like telnet and gopher. I also had gotten an account on Prodigy and logged a zillion hours online...

What really blew your mind about the Internet and convinced or inspired you to get involved in this "revolution"?

When I started using telnet and gopher to log on to remote information systems. One day I had logged on to Hunter and went to a system at Columbia and used it as a point to get to the tech info server at MIT and got from there to a university in Great Britain. It was mind-boggling! Here I was sitting at a computer in my mom's house in Brooklyn, and I was getting weather and current events in London, for the cost of a phone call to 68th Street in Manhattan.

How did you go about becoming a fully functioning netizen? What resources and people were useful to you?

I just spent hours and hours and hours logged on. I got information from the user help department at school. The most important book I got was the *Whole Internet Users Guide and Catalog* by Ed Krol.

So far, what has been your best Net experience?

This is e-mail I got recently about Isis:

> "I just visited your Website...fantastic!!!! It's exactly what was needed...and the additional links...great! The solidarity and immediate presence was breathtaking.I felt so incredibly connected and embraced. Thank you."

My best experience has been working with the Isis pages. It has really connected me with people I would never meet otherwise. I get e-mail from all over the world about it; a few days ago some man in Australia sent me e-mail about a Billie Holliday Website in Holland. Most of the e-mail I get is from other African-American women who write to tell me that they like the page, like the excerpt above.

What is your take on the ways gender and race get played out, expressed, discussed, skirted, ignored online?

I think that race and gender have been dealt with very differently online. In the case of gender, you have people pretending to be the opposite gender, or no gender, or whatever. When it comes to race, I think that Black people have gone to great lengths to assert identity and presence. Look at the homepages for the soc.culture.african. american Usenet group, for example.

What are your experiences of online spaces made by and/or maintained for women?

I have not really spent a lot of time in the spaces for women online. Most of them seem very white, however, with not a lot of women of color participating. Try looking through Femina, the database at Cybergrrl, for example, searching for Black or African American! Last time I checked, there was not a lot there...

I think there are really big differences for Black women and white women in online communications, the same way that there are differences in print media. If you look at *Essence* magazine versus *Vogue*, you will see very big differences in the politicization of content, the way in which men are dealt with, et cetera, in terms of what they would like in an online service.

Popular "wisdom" is that African Americans think that the Internet is a "white thing" or that the Internet is a final step toward "Big Brother." What do you think is going on with that?

I think it means a lot of things, a group of very complex issues all interactive at the same time.

A lot of these "analysts" don't understand the incredible depth of suspicion and mistrust that many African Americans have toward white institutions and power structures and the people in them. (After all, if we had been a little more suspicious from the beginning, we wouldn't be here, right?) I think there is also a certain amount of shock that Black people would have a concept of "white things" that are for white people. In this case it happened to be the Internet, but it could just as well have been psychotherapy, keg parties or suntan lotion, also frequently regarded as "white things."

Many people are also just afraid. They see a communications medium that goes through an indeterminate number of unknown channels and over which they have absolutely no control, and they are terrified of the potential it may have as a tool for control and manipulation of our communities.

For others, though, saying that the Internet is a "white thing" is expressing the fact that there has not been a lot of content devoted to people of color. Much of the information I collected, especially when I first started the Isis pages, was actually made available on gopher servers, that had been around for a while, rather then HTML pages. There were a lot of people out there in the media dancing fandangos in the street over the Web's incredible depth and breadth of information, and cultural content. Yet, and still, I see so much about my community and its culture which is nowhere near the Web.

Last, there are a lot of African Americans who are very active on online services and the Internet. Take a look at the commercial online services, such as Prodigy and AOL's NetNoir. There are dozens, probably hundreds, of pages out there by people of African descent on and about their communities. In concentrating on those people who want to avoid cyberspace as a "white thing," people are broadswiping those people who are very much a part of cyberspace.

The Internet is a powerful tool for communication and organizing. As electronic networking becomes more accessible and widespread, what political and social impact do you think the Net will have on the cultures of the African Diaspora as we move into the next millennium?
It is a tremendous tool for us in communicating with each other. For example, the Black Women in the Academy conference at MIT had over two thousand women attending and made a big splash. Think of how much bigger an impact it would have had if there was a Website, updated live and internationally available!

And another thing, people who are not part of those communities will have more access to information about them. People frequently have this attitude of "if I don't know about it, it doesn't exist" when it comes to our communities and their achievements. If they are forced to acknowledge things that are going on because they are on the Internet, it's a good thing.

Online sexism, problem or not? Ditto racism.

Yes. Racism for me more than sexism. People who have big problems
of their own with African-American people frequently take it upon
themselves to use Usenet groups to have an audience for their
hatred. Just look at the soc.culture.african.american newsgroup
after the OJ Simpson verdict, or the hate mail that was targeted to
people through that hacked University of Michigan account last
year.

What's the best way to deal with sexist trolls or flamers and unwanted sexual attention online?

If you can, ignore them. What they really want is for someone to
respond to them. If you are good at being incredibly vicious,
though, that may be okay, too.

Why do you think it's important for girls and women to get online and participate in the imagination and realization of what we call "the cyberscape"? What hopes do you have for the future and impact of feminism(s) online?

Cyberspace is the next frontier of communication and information
and the media. The people who have input (and control) over the
content and construction of cyberspace will have input and control
over how people find out about, view, think and perceive themselves
and the rest of the world—in the same way that broadcast media do
now.

How was the idea for Isis born?

I went to MIT, a very white, male environment. It was an environment where the people and icons that were an integral part of my
daily life did not exist. I was coming from NYC where I had spent
my life surrounded with this intense cultural sophistication and
immersion in the culture of Black people in general and women in
particular.

So I would spend a lot of time on the Internet looking for
stuff about Black women, and there was almost none to be found. If
there was any, it wasn't indexed and organized someplace central. I
realized that if I couldn't find anything, other people couldn't,
and there was a serious need for information about Black women.
Especially on the international scale that the Internet represents.
Information that presents us in, I don't want to say a positive,
light, but a light that is more realistic than the constant "Black
women are enmeshed in pathology but can't really help it, poor

dears."

I also wanted to focus on culture as whole, not just entertainment. People sometimes get the idea that singing and wiggling derrières are the extent of our achievements. There is a little bit more to it than that. So I set up the Isis site, and whenever I felt like it, I could be reassured that breadth of expression still existed. I recently went through a lot of drama redoing Isis for serious Netscape—setting up different sections, doing heavy content and layout. It was almost like I was possessed. At three in the morning on Sunday I was glued to my computer, and I thought to myself, "Why?" And I realized it was because this site wasn't just about me. I was actually publishing something, something about Black women that was going to be internationally available and used (rightly or wrongly) to evaluate us and what we are. It was like writing a book.

How did you go about setting up your site?

I taught myself HTML and used a server at school [MIT]. Since then I have gotten my own virtual Website at Netdiva, and Isis is now located there—through an Internet access provider. It will stay there pretty much in perpetuity.

What is your utopian fantasy (or worst nightmare) of the impact the Internet will have on culture and society as we move into the next millennium?

Worst? I heard Tim Berners-Lee, the founder of the Web, talk about the Web becoming something like Nazi Germany, but because it has no geographical or physical boundaries, no one can go to war with it to get rid of it. That sounds-worst case to me.

Best? Everybody has ISDN to their homes and a Sun or SGI [Silicon Graphics Inc.] station to run Web browsers on. People who have previously been subject to the whims and ignorance of the mainstream media (people of color, especially) are now able to talk about themselves and their own communities in their own words and under their own control.

How do you feel about the ways in which the Internet has been sold and explained to the public? Would you do it differently?

It is really annoying. I think that at first people just tried to capitalize on the Internet as a fad, but now cyberspace has really become a part of the functioning culture of the United States, and it is here to stay. I don't like how people who are really a part of the Net are being cast as bizarre nerds who can't get dates—or should I say bizarre men who can't get dates. The Internet is used by a totally broad spectrum of people all over the world who are not child pornographers or murderers cruising for lonely and helpless victims. There are lots of perfectly normal people who have made computer-mediated communication a part of their lives.

Any final tips and words of encouragement for our readers?
Cyberspace is great.

Anyone can learn how to use the tools of the Internet. Don't be afraid of technology: be proactive, and take the time to learn how to use it.

A FILMMAKER'S ADVENTURES

IN MULTIMEDIA LAND

Name: Jayne Loader
Age: May have been born to run, but wasn't born yesterday.
Geographical location: Waxahachie, Texas (trés unchic!)

We first encountered Jayne Loader in the flesh when she was a keynote speaker at "The Atomic Age Opens," a July 1995 conference sponsored by the Bowling Green State University Department of Popular Culture and the Popular Culture Library to commemorate/ interrogate the golden anniversary of the dawn of Dr. Strangelove-ness. Ms. Loader presented her CD-ROM *Public Shelter* (check it out online at http://www.publicshelter.com/), a sort of "follow-up" project to her documentary *The Atomic Cafe,* and like most of the rest of the audience, we were mesmerized. Mesmerized? Heck! Her rifts on multimedia and the Net were setting us off like bottle rockets and we were madly scribbling notes about her presentation and notes to one another!

When the lights came up she was literally rushed like a rock star, and guess who was there first to offer congrats and pluck that first business card from her fingers even before she had time to come out of her lecture-daze? And hey, you gotta know that we don't move that fast for just anybody. Then again, we're content grrrls, too.

Jayne is all intellectual, political and aesthetic continuity, "rigor" and playfulness shot through with vision, creativity and business sense. As we all know, there never seems to be enough of that particular combo to go around, and never in the history of media has it been so sorely needed as now. In January 1996, Jayne inaugurated "The World Wide Wench," a bi-weekly hypertext column, on the www.publicshelter.com site. Very groovy.

Your profession?

Multimedia developer, filmmaker, writer.

Internet projects which you are or have been involved with?

My Website for *Public Shelter* is my only Internet project. It's a place where people can sample our disc, post their own comments, add cool links and even enter contests. We're starting to get a lot of strange and wonderful content from Net surfers who are finding atomic memorabilia in their attics and local bookstores, scanning it and mailing it to us—Boy Scout "atomic merit badges," civil defense pamphlets, whatever. Hopefully, as Internet technology advances, we'll be able to create rooms within the Shelter where people can hang out and chat, a gallery where artists can show their work, and a library where people can read.

Other than that, I have no community spirit whatsoever. My main interest in the Internet thus far has been to gather information. Mostly, I just spend hours and hours cruising government laboratories and weapons manufacturers—the harder to find and get into, the better—downloading massive amounts of junk, and, late at night, lurking on Usenet. Oh, and I've been doing online chats as a guest on Prodigy and the like to promote my new CD-ROM. It is true, however, that all us smartass leftie Texas types do yammer to each other night and day on this lil' ol' mailing list called Bobwahred, sugarpie.

Other personal info you want to share?

I won a cooking contest once.

Tell us a little bit about your background as a filmmaker and activist.

I was an American Studies major in college (Reed) and wrote my
thesis on documentary photography in the
1930s. I was also very involved in Marxist-
feminist theory and in the history of women in
the Communist party. When I failed to get that
big fellowship to graduate school, I took the
path of least resistance and followed my rich
boyfriend down to California, became a Beverly
Hills housewife, audited film theory courses
at UCLA, and got involved with an old Communist filmmaker named Tom Brandon who was

active in the Film and Photo League in the 1930s and later made a
fortune distributing German and Russian films in the United States
on 16mm. Tom hired me as a researcher/ghostwriter/publicist and
became kind of a mentor. He was particularly interested in smart
young women (including Barbara Kopple and Connie Fields, who also
became filmmakers). I worked for him all through graduate school
(Michigan) where I studied film theory, structuralism, semiotics,
and critical theory, and later, after I dropped out, in New York.
Through Tom, I met everybody in the left-wing film community,
including Peter Biskind. Peter gave me writing assignments for
Seven Days, which was the first time anybody ever paid me for my
writing. I had always wanted to write fiction, and since I had
money for the first time in my life because of *The Atomic Cafe* I
decided to find out if I had any writing talent. I wrote two
books...neither of which sold particularly well despite or because
of the great reviews. So then I put together a film project about
animals—why we eat them, why we wear them, why we make them sit on
the beach, drugged, surrounded by bimbos, with Bud cans tied to
their little paws.

Why, and how, did you make the decision to make the big leap into multimedia and onto the Internet?

At the same time my animal project crashed and burned, the building
we were living in changed hands and the neighborhood (the Lower
East Side) started to get crazier. We had a fantastic loft with a
three-thousand-square-foot roof garden where we grew corn and
tomatoes, but the woman who owned our building was trying to empty
it of tenants—there was no heat, no hot water. She left the door
unlocked so criminals would come in. Classic slumlord tactics. I
was so stressed I couldn't work. Since we couldn't afford a loft in
a better neighborhood, I convinced my husband to move me to the

small town in Texas where I grew up. If you've ever seen *The Trip to Bountiful* or *Places in the Heart*, you've seen Waxahachie. You literally do not have to lock your doors here, the air is clean, it's incredibly beautiful. I have twelve huge trees, a pond, squirrels, possums, raccoons, skunks, butterflies and birds. Coming here was like getting in a time machine and going back to 1920.

Unfortunately, political attitudes down here also stopped evolving about 1920. White people live on the West Side, Black people live on the East Side, and when you cross that line, walking west to east, the sidewalks stop. Also the streetlights. We were told during the Texas governor's race that if we put a sign for Gov. Ann Richards on our lawn, somebody might burn down our house. So there was virtually no one here I could talk to. That's when I started spending all of my time on the Net.

Of course, once you take that first step, anybody with half a brain can see the possibilities.

Getting involved in multimedia was a very different story.

In 1993, I discovered multimedia as a form and very quickly realized that virtually all products were being produced by and for men. The weird thing is, no one in multimedia thinks there's anything wrong with this.

This friend of mine—rather, former friend of mine—asked me to help him develop a children's game. It was about a boy, his grandfather and their animal friends. Not only were all the human characters male, but all the animal characters were male as well. When I pointed this out and suggested some changes, he got outraged.

Women were getting left out of the loop yet again. It was almost like they were finally forced to let women (and African Americans) into a few jobs in the film industry, but now all of the guys from film were moving into multimedia and saying, okay, you girls can have this, but this new thing, it's *ours*. No Grrrls Allowed!

If women exist at all in CD-ROMs, they're presented as threatening sex objects to be blasted or princesses to be rescued. (Even the PC games that give you a choice of avatars limit your choices to these: white man, Black man, brown man and Asian man.) Recently I read this in a review: "As a companion, choose between Ginger Lynn and Tia Carrere, but your choice of love object doesn't effect the outcome of the game." Just like life, right?

I tried to do a CD-ROM about a year ago that attempted to address the absence, or denigration, of women and girls in multimedia. I wasn't able to sell it because, surprise, it was designed

for women and girls. It was at this point that I decided to form my
own company.

**Besides the fact that it's absolutely jam-packed with content and sup-
ported on the World Wide Web, what sets *Public Shelter* apart from most
historical or social science CD-ROMs we've seen is the careful, pointed
art-direction. Instead of a designed data bank (a model popular among
nonfiction CD-ROMs), you contextualize information in a self-consciously
filmic experience/environment. Have you had problems approaching the
CD-ROM market from a director's perspective? Why do you think that is,
and why do you think it's important that a vision of multimedia product
and WWW design as a director's medium emerge?**

What I've found is that most CD-ROMs have no directors, period.
They have producers, writers, animators and programmers. But no
directors. Why is this significant? Because in filmmaking, the
director is a hired gun, employed by the producer, true, but with a
certain amount of independence and autonomy, both contractually and
traditionally. It's the job of the director to bring together all
of the elements and ideas and people on a film, to make sure they
mesh, to apply the stamp of her personality to the whole. It's also
the director's job to mediate between the money people and the
crafts and technical people. So, by excising the director, what you
end up with is a marriage of commerce and technology, unmediated by
(for want of a better word) art. In multimedia, all power resides
in the producer, whose *raison d'être* is money. Producers love this
new system, because it gives them more control. (Of course there
are exceptions to this rule. Respected artists in other media—the
Residents, Peter Gabriel, Laurie Anderson—are given a certain
amount of freedom to create their own visions in the CD-ROM format.
But there is an almost total division between "art" and "entertainment.")

Multimedia is where the film industry was about the time we
released *The Atomic Cafe.* No one understood that you could make a
non fiction product that was also "creative." (For the most part,
they still don't understand this!) This is why most educational CD-
ROMs are incredibly boring. They're boring for the same reason most
documentary films are boring. The Voice-of-God narration, ubiquitous in bad documentaries, is replaced by the Script-of-God in bad
CD-ROMs, which give the illusion of objectivity and pretend to tell
the "truth." The question is, of course, whose truth? T. W. Adorno
would have a ball analyzing text-based CD-ROMs. History is simpli-
fied. Point of view is obscured. Political decisions are natural-
ized. The history of people on the margins—women, the working

classes, the nonwhite—is completely written out of the story. The user is infantilized. And don't you love that word "user"? It's like you're mainlining the over processed information they feed you: the one-page biographies, the sepia photographs, the videos in fifteen-second increments. God forbid that the user should think for herself or make her own connections within the material.

You've said something to the effect that "video games are masculine; the Internet is feminine." Would you care to elaborate on that a little?

Some feminist theorists have argued that the computer is an extension of the male brain—that men are binary (either/or) while women are analog (both/and). I don't agree with this "biology is destiny" crap—if most women haven't yet mastered computers, it's because nobody's convinced them they should bother, not because their brains are different—but I do believe computer games are metaphors for male life under advanced capitalism. Think about it: You get to kick people in the face, abuse animals, rescue bimbos, collect power objects (property) and bucks (bucks). Like a bio-pic of Donald Trump.

We modeled *Public Shelter*, our first CD-ROM, on the World Wide Web. Not the Web as it is now, but the Web as it will be in the future, the way we want it to be, when the images and videos load and play instantly. Because if games are male, the Internet is female. You get to move from place to place without killing anyone or collecting anything (except ideas). You meet new people and talk to them if you're in the mood, be an observer (lurk) if you're not. Shop if you want to, or just peruse thousands of catalogues! Watch videos, view art or photos, listen to different kinds of music (as opposed to being driven on relentlessly by bad Kraftwerk). Go down different paths, make linx, find hidden connections, customize your trip. The Internet is fluid, non hierarchical, analog not digital, both/and instead of either/or. Mary Daly couldn't have invented a more flexible Open CyberCity for women. And that's what the Net means to me. Amen.

What does the "grrrl" in your nickname "content grrrl" mean?

One day, I was in a meeting with eight or ten guys in their early twenties who were working with me on *Public Shelter*, and I noticed that all any of them cared about was hardware, software and technical issues. I was the only one who cared about content. It didn't matter to them what they were designing, animating or programming, as long as it went fast. It could have been Marx, Hitler, chopped liver, whatever. I pointed this out to my programmer, who is twenty three, and he started calling me Content Girl. I changed it to Content Grrrl, because "grrrls" have attitude; "girls" don't.

How old were you when you started messing around with computers?

I got my first computer when I started to write my first book, in the early '80s. It was a Kaypro, the first portable. I dragged it all over the world, to film festivals and artists' colonies. It weighed something like twenty five pounds.

Are you a Mac person or a PC person?

I'm PC. Would have been Mac, probably, but I couldn't afford one.

Do you think you have a different approach to computers than the guys you work with?

The men I work with are all fascinated with the hardware. They have to have more and more of it, whatever is newest and fastest, the way guys in the sixties were about their stereos.

I see a computer as a machine, like a car. You don't have to know how to fix a car, or even exactly how a car works, in order to drive one. If it breaks, you have somebody else fix it. The point is, does it get you from New York to Cleveland, or doesn't it? My programmer, the legendary Thomas Hughes, sees the computer as an extension of his body. He goes into withdrawal when he is separated from it. That's why it's primarily men who are pushing to make the William Gibson science-fiction universe—where the computer actually plugs into your brain—a reality.

So far, what has been your best Net experience? Your worst?

My best Net experience was when a guy I had only known for about three weeks via e-mail offered to loan me two thousand dollars, so I could master my disc. That was truly amazing. Hope I can pay him back some day! (Just kidding, Gene. Your check is in the mail.)

The worst experience was when we experimented with doing a mailing to a list we had downloaded which we thought was full of people who would be interested in our disc. We sent out eight thousand pieces of mail and got something like a thousand flames— all from men, of course.

Online sexism, problem or not? Your most heinous or unsettling experience? Your best experience as a woman online?

I think online sexism is a problem though I've actually only experienced the benign versions—like, men begin to "talk" to you about a subject (say, bull terriers) and the next thing you know they are telling you about the group sex they had with two lesbians the night before.

My most unsettling experience was more a problem with racism...I posted a picture of my sister-in-law and her family on my Website. She owns a small children's book distribution company that specializes in books for multiracial families and has been handling mail orders for our CD-ROM. Margot's married to a black man and has three gorgeous multiracial children. The day after I posted the picture, I got a 30K racist diatribe in my mailbox. Majorly creepy.

What is your take on the ways gender gets played out, expressed and discussed online? What are your experiences of online women's spaces?

I think women are much kinder than men online, which reflects our real-life roles in the world. I've never been flamed by a woman. If I send an unwanted e-mail to a woman, the response is "please take me off your list" while a man is likely to send me a 3 MB file along with a message that says "I HOPE YOUR ACCOUNT CRASHES AND BURNS!!!!!", "FUCK OFF AND DIE", or "YOU ARE NOT OBSERVING NETIQUETTE!" Stuff like that.

Men and women have different styles of communicating on the Net that seem to mirror the way they communicate in real life to a certain extent, but then veer off into all sorts of new strange directions. For example, the question of netiquette is really interesting. Men, having been in cyberspace first, seem to care more about netiquette than women do. They want to make sure every-body follows these rules even if they had no part in writing them. Women seem to still care about, uh, etiquette. My programmer is twenty three, eats with his elbows on the table, sticks his bread in the butter instead of using a knife, hates to bathe and change clothes—you get the picture by now, I'm sure—and if I sweetly suggest I'd prefer a little bit more in the way of old-fashioned etiquette in my house, he thinks I am a total idiot. But he cares passionately about netiquette, and we often discuss its intricacies and how it differs from what's commonly accepted as good behavior in the real world. Personally, I've never met a single woman who really cared whether or not advertising should or should not be allowed online or got irate if someone sent an ad to her mailbox.

My own guess: if women had written netiquette, the rule on advertising would have been "no advertising on evenings and week-ends" or "no advertising more than 5 lines long", or "no ads that are not clearly marked 'advertisement' in the subject line. If women had written netiquette, there would be rules against being gratuitously rude, rules about sending personal e-mail to a woman every time she posts in Usenet—no matter what the subject—and turning the subject to sex, and rules about writing splatterporn stories about real women, using their real names and posting them on alt.sex.stories. None of this is covered in netiquette.

I've never spent time in women's online spaces (like Women's Wire) because all the ones I know about cost money and I don't believe in paying anything beyond $19.95 a month for full twenty four hour-a-day Internet access. I was on a "women's only" mailing list for about two seconds. I got so angry at one message from a computer consultant recommending that a newbie woman get on either Women's Wire or AOL that I had to get off. I think women should get out into the "real" Internet and just bite the bullet and learn those pesky UNIX commands rather than restricting themselves to those kind of places which offer "Internet Lite." How can you learn what the Net is unless you spend eight, ten, or twelve hours a day online? How can you afford to do that on Women's Wire or AOL?

Why do you think it's important for girls and women to get online and participate in the imagination and realization of "the cyberscape"? What hopes do you have for the future and impact of feminism(s) online?

If women do not get online, they will be left behind and written out of history. And if women's political groups don't digitize their information, it will be lost, because some of us now don't bother to go to libraries, and scanning in paper documents that come in the mail and OCRing them is a big drag. When I did the *Public Shelter* CD-ROM, only one peace group in the entire world had all of its photos, position papers and historical documents online for me to download and use. That was Greenpeace. Consequently, other peace groups, including women's peace groups (like Women's Strike for Peace and Women's International League for Peace and Freedom) are not represented on the disc, while Greenpeace is all over the place. I spoke at a peace conference in Texas a couple of weeks ago, and the organizer (a woman) didn't know the difference between a CD-ROM and a video. It was very discouraging.

Plans for the future?

I'm just beginning to work on a project called Liberty Net with my producer Eric Schwaab and Frank Hernandez. Liberty Net will provide access to computers and online resources to women, minorities and low-income people in Texas. My primary interest is in developing content, but to access the content, people have to have the hardware, right? So Liberty Net will provide that. We'll try to get computers into churches, community centers, public schools, libraries, Boys and Girls Clubs and the homes of at-risk children. Frank has this brilliant idea about putting computers in prisons and in the homes of the families of prisoners so that families can stay in touch. This will benefit the prisoners, but it will really benefit the children of the prisoners, who are for the most part low-income kids who would never have a chance to have computers in their homes without a program like this one. And of course it will benefit the prisoners' spouses (mostly wives) too. (We figure the state of Texas will go for this program big time, because most of the drugs and contraband come into the prisons via contact visits with families.) Also, volunteers could tutor prisoners via chatlines without having to go into the prisons physically. This is important because since prisons have become so dangerous, nobody who doesn't have to go there wants to, so volunteerism is way, way down.

What is your utopian fantasy (or worst nightmare) of the impact the Internet will have on culture and society as we move into the next millennium?

I don't like the fact that when you cruise the WWW, somebody is assembling a portrait of who you are and what you like so they can market consumer goods to you more effectively. That's one reason I will never use e-cash or give my credit card numbers out over the Net. (Big Brother did arrive in 1984, IMHO. We were just all too coked up to notice ;) More digitization of information means a greater likelihood that such information will be used for social control. We know that if Liberty Net takes off in the prison system, it is bound to be used for censorship. But we think the benefit to the families of having computers in their homes outweighs the prisoners' loss of privacy.

It bothers me that every time there is a new technological development on the Net, somebody figures out how to use it to purvey pornography. Of course, in that sense, the Net is no different than every other new technology throughout history—still cameras, movie cameras, the printing press, oil painting. Still, I hate to see CUSeeMe being used to turn computer terminals into Times Square peep show booths. I think making pornography even easier to get than it was before is negative, because the more pornography men consume, the more they want and the less likely they are to be satisfied with "real" women (and especially grrrls) who do not look or behave like the girls in pornography. But then again the alternative—censorship—is worse.

My programmer had a chance to have a date with a real live girl a couple of weeks ago. Instead, he stayed home showing one of his guy friends a program he'd written that goes into all the alt.sex.binaries groups on Usenet and downloads all of the pix to his account. It even has a function that censors all the gayboy porn, so his hetero eyes don't have to be exposed to it (but not the lesbian porn—of course not).

Any final tips and words of encouragement for our readers?
Being Net savvy is not brain surgery. If I can do it, anybody can.

DAMN IT, JANET, GREAT JOB!

Name: Janet Planet
Age: forty somethin'
Geographical location: Southern California
Machine: Pentium 90 PC

Very few people really know anything about African music. And when you stop to think and listen, you realize that this is *truly* the origin of popular American music; first there's the Latin music from Cuba, which is really driven by the African rhythms brought by the slaves. Then there's jazz, blues, rock'n'roll, rap, hip-hop, and this new music people are calling ambient and trip-hop where I've heard some sampled African music. People don't often understand this music's true roots; I'm hoping my page might help expose African music to a wider audience. At the very least, it's a place where music lovers, composers, disc jockeys, producers—and anyone else—can come to learn something.

—Janet Planet

J ust when we thought very little out there in the electronic datasphere could surprise us anymore, along comes YAWS (Yet Another Website) that really knocks our socks off.

Music from Africa and the African Diaspora (http://matisse.net/~jplanet/home.htm) really pushes to the limit the possibilities for women webweavers. This page includes a giant, alphabetized list of information, links and sound samples of music from Africa and the African Diaspora. Janet Planet uses her addiction to the Net combined with her webweaving talent to offer an entertaining and valuable resource for anyone interested in African music and its influence on all forms of modern music. More important—for our purposes—she's used the World Wide Web to put her useful, fun and expansive project out there for the world to see. It's this accomplishment that puts Ms. Planet in our Wired Women Hall of Fame; she is a perfect example of what can be accomplished by cybergrrrls everywhere who want to present their passion—whatever it might be—to the world.

When did you get involved with computers and the Net?
I got my first computer—an Amiga—in 1988, and I joined the WELL (Whole Earth 'Lectronic Link) around 1989. In the spring of 1995 I got a PC and full Internet access via PPP. I originally got a computer because I'm a writer.

Is your involvement with the Internet and the Web a part-time thing?
I'm trying to make it a full-time occupation. Right now, I'm writing a business plan for my African music pages; I'd like to make it a nonprofit corporation and then seek sponsorship for pages. It's a huge project, and I need to find a way to pay for the time I spend on it. I also design Web pages for various clients.

How did you learn about the Net and/or Web?
A good (UNIX god) friend of mine kept begging me to get on the Web. It combined so many of my own personal interests (writing, art, graphics, design), he knew I would love it—and he was right. I was immediately fascinated by the possibilities.

How did you start the pages on African music?
I initially started working on my African music pages as a vehicle to learn how to write HTML. I bought Laura Lemay's excellent book (*Teach Yourself Web Publishing with HTML in a Week*, Sams Press,

1995) and just started writing HTML in my text editor. My friend urged me to learn the code and not depend on the editing software.

Why pages on African music?
When I first got on the Web, I surfed around for quite a while. I was looking for links about African music—something I've been involved in for a long time. I found a few places, but there was really very little information, and I felt there was a need to have the music I love so much represented. There are only two or so comprehensive books written on the topic, so it's hard to find background information on any of these artists.

Describe the African Diaspora music pages?
I'm working on these pages I call the *Encyclopedia of African Music: Music from Africa and the African Diaspora.* It's a comprehensive site featuring artist bios, photos, graphics, discographies and sound samples as well as lots of related African links for and about the birthplace of modern popular music.

So what's so great about the Net?
What's wonderful about the Internet is that you are accepted (or not) based upon the quality of your work, your mind and your creativity. Outer physical distractions cease to exist. Who you are (and what you choose to show of yourself) is what counts. Also, what's important about the Web is its graphical manner. You can have fun learning about something, you can explore anything your imagination can come up with. It's not like sitting down and memorizing a bunch of numbers or facts, you can just kind of absorb the information. To see pictures, hear sounds, see movies, tell someone how you feel—it has an amazing impact.

The Web is fast changing our world. You can talk to your many friends or relatives anywhere in the world in real time via telnet or any of the many Web-chat sites (BTW, a great music site that has a great chat area is Firefly, where I was just asked to host their African music venue—it's http://www.agents-inc.com/), do just about anything your heart desires. Of course, you end up forfeiting your privacy in many cases, which is why I use the nom de plume Janet Planet, but it's worth it in the end. I've met some fascinating people online, reacquainted with a few old friends—the Internet is like a giant umbilical cord connecting you with your life as you know it, and your life as it can be.

START THEM WEBGRRRLS YOUNG

Name: Heather Susan Reddy
Age: 15
Geographical location: Michigan
Machine: PC clone/hybrid

Sometimes when you're out there surfing around, it seems like the only women—even the only people—shaping this new electronic cyberscape are over twenty or twenty-five. However, every so often, there is a young grrrl out there, a chick with attitude and access to an ISP, making waves with her keyboard. (Be assured: Their numbers are swelling!)

Heather Susan Reddy is one such fifteen-year-old, with a homepage full of good HTML code, sweet graphics, some really nice info and links important to every angst-ridden teen. (http://www.pmc.grand-rapids.mi.us/lucretia/) Also known as "namerank serialnumber," "lucretia" and "He at her," young Ms. Reddy shows the promise of the next generation of wired women.

So, what's your life like? What do you do?

I'm a full-time high school student. I publish a zine, write for the Web and local underground publications—rarely for money—write volumes of poetry (pseudo-erotic absurdity/free verse/pathetic-angsty-pop-culture-inspired babbling), attend concerts, music festivals, art fairs, haunt coffee houses more than could possibly be healthy, play the guitar, garden and see almost every "art" film that makes its way to our small theatres. Occasionally, I sit down.

Describe your very cool homepage ...

Adrienne Clermont

My homepage . . . I have a useless self-advertisement, an artistic picture of myself, some Sylvia Plath poetry (yum!), links to a college I'd like to attend and a few other links to pages with info on my favorite writers (I think Sartre, Robert Pirsig and Plato are there....J. D. Salinger, Allen Ginsberg and William Gibson are up and coming...).

How did you get into computers?

Elizabeth Muzzo

I had technologically minded parents, and I can never recall not having a computer, however mediocre it might have been. I started with a Commodore-64 and an online service that later became America Online called Q-Link. I started by obtaining games from them, but soon fate—and a misplaced click—led me to the people connection, and my addiction to communication began. As for the technical aspects of computers, I've never gained many skills, or interest for that matter. I use the computer essentially as the means, not the ends. I can operate a computer better than most of the population, but that's because I've had to acquire just enough skills to manipulate it for my purposes.

How did you get into the Internet?

I'd operated almost exclusively from private online services that my parents sponsored, until 1993, when I started accessing local bulletin boards and made a great deal of local friends off them. Aside from using e-mail to communicate with friends I'd met on online services and sporadically posting to Usenet for a few years, I regarded the Net as a fearsome thing. This changed last fall when a local BBS got full Internet access, and I was astounded at the wealth of information available. Internet Relay Chat proved to be an addiction, followed by MOOs, then aimless Websurfing...and the like. As a child and adolescent, I've always been regarded as, at best, "gifted," and, at worst, socially inept. I've always felt "not of this world," or marching to the beat of a different drummer and unwilling to throw myself into the mediocre masses. The release from these tensions on the Net has been immeasurable. Conversing on IRC, you are bound to encounter someone of a like mind and can shed your inhibitions while talking to them. Posting to newsgroups allows a sort of venting and internal dialogue that is so lacking in our society, and maintaining a variety of e-mail pen-pal-ships allows for connection with people who give a damn. Using the Web as a showcase for my work gives me an opportunity for feedback and refining it. Despite the fact that the Net often inspires a feeling of reclusiveness, it's been my salvation, an alternative to a reality that isn't always all that attractive.

Girls Need Homepages!

Contrary to popular belief, there *is* a kid culture in cyberspace, and it is growing all the time. If you follow the links from Adrienne's and Elizabeth's pages (see their addresses below), you'll find all sorts of cyberplaygrounds, educational resources, edutainment for kids, kid-only chat rooms and e-mail lists. You'll also notice lots of other kids out there with their own homepages on the World Wide Web, often created with help from an older mentor. Of course, we think all of this is fabulous and is the best solution to the very serious question of how to "protect" kids in cyberspace. Personal homepages serve the needs of both parent and kid: They provide a "safe," adult-vetted launchpad from which the kid can explore the Net, and they are a great way for kids to be creative, share their interests and discover who they want to become. Given the continued gender disparity in computer education, introducing your daughter, little sister or a young friend to cyberspace and/or helping her build a page of her very own is a mega-super good deed. You'll help her find her voice, and your interest in her and other people's interest in her page will do amazing things for her self-esteem.

CHEZ ADRIENNE
Homepage of Adrienne Clermont, a pretty darn nifty Ithaca, New York, ten-year-old who wants to be a writer when she grows up. Initially mentored by her dad, she is now a fully competent webmistress who can sling HTML with the best of 'em. Fun original stuff and links about everything from magic and Lois and Clark to woodpeckers.
http://teddy.law.cornell.edu:8080/chezadri.htm

ELIZABETH'S SNOW WHITE PAGE
With help from her big brothers, eleven-year-old Elizabeth Muzzo, who has Down Syndrome, cerebral palsy, bad asthma and one big Snow White obsession, shares her view of the world from her hot pink and black wheelchair. Here's what the Net means to her:

> Sometimes before I go to bed, my Dad lets me "surf" the Internet all by myself! This is really fun. I get to find out a whole lot about everyone out there in "WEBLAND." I've already met a lot of friends from different colleges, schools and even different countries. I really like to "surf" — it lets me be free, and I can go anywhere I want! Without my wheelchair or walker.

You go, girl!
http://www.ecn.bgu.edu/users/gjmuzzo/lizzie1.htm

What do you want to do with computers and/or the Internet?

Eventually, I'd like to have a publishing site on the Web for writers to showcase their work. I'd like to put up my zine, *Heather's Head*, on the Web. One of my primary goals is to create a forum for women and grrrls who are intimidated by the ways of the Net. While passive activities—like Web browsing—seem almost gender-equal, interactive activities—Usenet, IRC, MUDs—are populated by raucous males eager to harass anyone without a phallus. Many of the women I know on the Net are dykes and punks—in short, outcasts—while mainstream men flood every corner. The world of the future will probably be heavily dependent on the Net, and it's essential to women's futures that they get with the Net to avoid earning fifty cents on a cyber-literate man's dollar.

What resources and/or people have been really helpful to you?

Helpful in what fashion? I've started relationships via MUDs, IRC and America Online chat rooms. One pen-pal-ship has lasted for three years. When I went through my teenage crisis, people on the alt.suicide.holiday newsgroup and in IRC saved my life. I'm better at expressing my feelings in writing, so people on the Net are more in tune to what's going on inside my head. The World Wide Web has been a vital information source—and a time killer. I've always had an insatiable thirst for pointless research. It caters to my short attention span. I've used it to begin to apply to colleges as well.

What's been your best Net experience?

Attending gatherings with my sysop. Gathering nightly on IRC with close friends to discuss brisk iced tea and punk rock. Being written to by insane people who enjoy my homepage. Reading *Sandman* on the Web.

Do you think that women and grrrls are getting more into computers?

Passively, definitely. But many lack the technical expertise necessary to do anything but point 'n click. There seems to be an increasing lesbian community on IRC, and women who attend universities often use IRC as well. But aside from the inevitable Generation X-ers, women seem absent, and that troubles me. There are a great deal of feminist/grrrl resources available on the Web, but women seem hesitant to explore it because of social conditioning— you know, these are men's toys and should be used for men's ends. Some women have an initially bad experience with harassment when they speak up on the Net, and they retreat to passive exploring. We need to begin taking it like *women!!* ;-)

START THEM WEBGRRRLS YOUNG

WIRING WEST COAST WOMEN

Name: Amy Goodloe
Age: 28
Geographical location: San Francisco Bay Area
Machine: PowerBook 520c

If *SurferGrrrls* featured an inspirational centerfold to tear out and hang over your computer, Amy Goodloe just might be it. And not just because of that very beautiful Celtic and rose tattoo framing her bellybutton (the truly curious can check out the photo on her wonderfully well-designed Website, http://www.best.com/ ~ agoodloe/ home.html). Nope, the real reason we love her is because within a year of first being blown away by the potential of the Net, this not-so-mild-mannered graduate student in English moved from Syracuse, New York, to the Bay Area and started her own business. "Amy's Obsession," as she calls it on her Web page, is Women Online, a consulting and referral service, for women who want help with their Macintoshes and/or the Net.

But Amy is not simply in the hunt for all that money to be made off the information revolution. Nope, another reason we admire her is because she's figured out how to blend her business with personal and political commitments. From her space on the Bay Area Internet service provider best.com, she runs and facilitates eight women-only electronic mailing lists: Internet-women-help, Internet-women-info, mac-women, women-on-line-news, lesac-Net [for lesbian academics], ba-cyberdykes [a Bay Area chat list], odd-girls and lesbian-studies. When Amy went online as an out lesbian and queer scholar, she was distressed by the paucity of specifically lesbian resources on the Net and decided to do something about it. She registered the domain name lesbian.org and operates the lesbian lists she moderates under that name (e.g., odd-girls@lesbian.org), and she donates space on her Website and her services as a Web page designer to several lesbian organizations. As of this writing, she's got 20 megabytes of space open on her site, so get in touch! Amy's also working with the Virtual Sisterhood group to create a comprehensive index of women's resources on the World Wide Web, and she is active on the Spiderwoman e-list (a community of women Web designers and HTML authors). She also maintains a homepage for her cute lil' girl beagle, Wimsey. When does this woman sleep?!

So. How old were you when you first started messing around with computers?

My first experience with computers was in a programming class in high school, in 1983, but I didn't start using them regularly until 1986, when I got a dual-floppy DOS machine. I got my first computer to use while in college, primarily for writing papers. My first experience with a Mac, in 1988, was for desktop publishing. I became a total Mac convert and enthusiast in 1992.

What were your early computer experiences like? Did you have to deal with any explicit or implicit sexism in labs, computer stores, wherever? If so, how did you deal with it?

Not really. My high school was pretty progressive for a southern private school and almost as many women as men took computer programming classes. I went to a women's college [Agnes Scott in Decatur, Georgia], so of course all the students who used computers and the computer lab were women, and by the time I got to graduate school *everyone was* using computers for basic word processing and online communications. I find that most women pick it up easily and intuitively, especially if they're working with a Mac.

What do you do with your computer?
Until I got a Mac I mostly did word processing and some very simple desktop publishing; I also used local BBSs and the university's online system. When I got my first Mac, three years ago, I started doing with it what I still do: organize/plan my life, keep track of my finances, do research via online services, do *lots* of word processing and desktop publishing, play around with graphics programs, and of course now, design Web pages and play with my PPP account.

Do you have any academic or technical training in computer science?
Nope. My training is all in English, English education and Medieval and Renaissance Studies. I've never taken a formal class on anything relating to computers, although I did take a graduate class in Instructional Technology.

When did you discover the Internet and why did you go online?
I had access to the Internet in graduate school, starting in 1991, but I didn't really get into it until I got an America Online account in June 1994. After about a month, I had learned just about everything there was to learn about AOL, so I got a shell account at a local university where I was taking a class and proceeded to master the online world via UNIX. I got my first PPP account in January 1995, and it took me about two days to figure out how to do everything I could with that. All along I'd been offering free or really cheap tutoring to people who were having trouble with the various online services and accounts, and that's what gave me the idea to turn the tutoring into a business.

What blew your mind about the Internet and convinced you to really get involved in this "revolution"?
I was hooked as soon as I'd spent about five hours on AOL. The thing that really appealed to me was that I could exercise my verbal skills in defense of something I really believed in (lesbian and gay rights) *and* have an effect on hundreds of people, as I did by posting in various forums on AOL. I also quickly got into e-mail lists and immediately saw the amazing potential of that kind of "online community," especially for academics, so I started a list of my own, for lesbian academics, in August 1994. By December I was

running four women-only e-mail lists, and I currently run eight.

To get back to what blew my mind: the ability to communicate with so many different people, so quickly and to share ideas, resources or opinions. That kind of interaction can't happen in any other forum, certainly not with that speed.

How did you go about becoming a fully functioning netizen? What people or resources were most important or useful for you?

I think I'd figured out netiquette by my second week on AOL. I didn't get any help from people, other than from those who had made resources available on how to use various online tools, and the only resource I found helpful at first was AOL's easy search function. Now I use all the major Internet magazines—*NetGuide, Wired, Internet World, .Net*—to keep me up to date on new technology and resources, and I have a small library of books on the Internet, although I hardly ever use them unless I have to answer a particularly difficult question for a client. I do recommend Adam Engst's *Internet Starter Kit for Macintosh* to clients because it's one of the only comprehensive Internet books for Mac users around.

Online sexism—problem or not? Your experiences?

I just don't see it. But then, I don't frequent forums where straight men are likely to be present, so that could have something to do with it. Whenever I announce a change in one of my women-only mailing lists, I do get some men writing me to protest what they see as "reverse sexism," but I also get just as many men writing in support. Also, out of the ten to fifteen notes I get a day in response to my Web site, about two to three of them will be from men who aren't flat-out sexist but whose comments don't exactly betray a progressive or feminist slant of mind. A couple of those notes will be mildly homophobic, but then I also get quite a few notes from men who identify as "straight, white, conservatives" who are very supportive of what I do and very complimentary of my Website.

You're obviously very committed to empowering women through personal computing technology and the Internet. What are the underpinnings of this commitment?

I'm a committed feminist and have been for a long time, so that feeds my desire to see that women have equal access to the technology that will shape the future. I also prefer interaction with women socially and professionally, and particularly online, so I

would like to see as many women as possible online. The benefits—
social, economic, professional, emotional—are vast, and the
negatives, the "supposed sexism" online, are largely the product of
male-produced myth. The online world is a level playing field, and
any assertion that women ought to be "afraid" of the sexism they'll
find there is simply an attempt to disguise this fact—because of
course those in power don't want to give it up!

How was the idea for Women Online born? How did you go about setting up your business? How're you doing? What are your plans and dreams for the future?

I modeled Women Online after some of the tutoring services I've
worked for, fine-tuned it for my own needs, applied for a small
business license in February 1994—and off I went!! We're currently
taking about six or seven new clients a week, and I have about five
regular, highly skilled trainers who take most of the jobs—so we're
doing pretty well, and growing all the time. I only take the jobs
that my trainers can't fill, which are usually the HTML training/
Web page design or Mac troubleshooting jobs. My plans for the
future are to continue growing at this rate, to offer Windows
training as complete as our Macintosh training, and to offer
regular classes for women (I don't have a space for this—yet!) I'd
also like us to take on as clients more small businesses and
nonprofits, especially women-owned and women-oriented businesses
and organizations. And I'd like to be instrumental in getting more
lesbians and lesbian organizations online.

Some people claim that the beauty of the Internet is it allows us to slip the surly bonds of embodiment and discuss matters of "gender" and "sex" objectively and truthfully. That is, by disembodying ourselves, we can produce knowledge of how to become more properly embodied in real life. Many even say that discussions of online sexism and the creation of women-only spaces on the Net undermine the liberatory potentials of cyberspace. Your practices at Women Online run counter to these arguments, so what would be your response to someone who, for example, accused you of actually hobbling women by ghettoizing them as a group in need of special technical and Net support, and women's communities on the Net?? Like, "C'mon, Amy! You're the *real* sexist here?" That sort of thing.

First of all, I would say that the Net does not in fact allow us to
slip the bonds of embodiment because we still communicate in
language, and it's language that constructs reality. The distrac-

tion of the body is momentarily suspended, but that is also true for any form of written communication, not just for the Net. I would also say, regarding my "women only" business, that it is first and foremost a practical issue. We offer private, individualized tutoring in people's homes, and I think just about everyone today realizes that it simply isn't safe for a woman to go to a "strange" man's home alone. It is also an issue of empowerment: Currently most computer and online consultants are male, which just underscores the myth that men dominate this medium, but by being able to provide a number of highly qualified women consultants to clients, Women Online proves this to be false. That is in fact one of the things I like most, both about Women Online and about my four women-only computer-related e-mail lists—that women who are experts in these fields get the chance to share their knowledge and expertise with other women.

I should also add that in terms of Women Online, I do have one male trainer and may take on a second, and I do have several trainers who are willing to take on male clients, so we don't "discriminate" in terms of our clientele. But the number-one reason women call the service is not because they think we'll have "special methods" for helping women, as if women needed a special kind of training in technology, but because they want to support women in the field by hiring women trainers. And the second reason is the practical one: They'd rather have an unknown woman coming to their homes than an unknown man.

And, finally, I don't expect some men to ever understand why women (or lesbians in particular, for that matter) would want their own "space," either on the Net or in "real time," because those people are usually speaking from a position of power, the position of the oppressor, and they have no concept of the ways that solidarity with one's own "group" can be empowering and affirming. They have always had their own "separatist communities"—the "white, straight boys clubs" that are still around today and still effectively prevent many oppressed groups from gaining access to power. I have ceased defending women's right to their own "space" (that's like debating racism with a Klansman) and instead focus my energies on providing that space and facilitating the exchange of knowledge among women, because knowledge is power.

[*Note:* Here's how Amy frames the women-only issue in her (open-to-all) Website: "All my lists have a strict women-only policy. The lists serve as forums where women can feel comfortable getting advice with various subjects and where they can exercise their technological skill in helping each other solve problems. Some of

the lists enable women to network with other women to increase
their visibility in areas traditionally dominated by men, and
others provide forums for discussing academic issues, research or
everyday life."]

**Jayne Loader, writer-director of the documentary *The Atomic Cafe* and the
companion CD-ROM, *Public Shelter,* is on record with this statement: "If
video games are masculine, the Internet is feminine." What do you think
about that? If you think there's some validity to what she's saying, what
do you think may be the cultural implications as we move more deeply
into an informational world of online hypertext/multimedia?**

I think the terms "masculine" and "feminine" are constructs that
have little bearing on the physical world in which we live—they are
in fact terms designed to create and enforce a binary gender system
where one does not naturally exist. What gets associated with the
term "masculine" are those qualities that ensure access to power—
conveniently enough for those men who are supposedly "masculine,"
eh?—and what is deemed "feminine" is usually the absence or
opposite of those masculine qualities, which, in theory, is supposed to mean that women are not suited for positions of power. So
to call any kind of technology masculine or feminine not only
perpetuates the use of terminology that constructs a false reality,
but also suggests, however subtly, that there is more power associated with one than the other.

   I really can't imagine what is meant by the Internet being
"feminine," and my immediate reaction is that this can only per-
petuate false stereotypes about what men and women "are really
like," rather than working toward deconstructing those stereotypes.
I think the Internet is, in fact, a good example of a space where we
can actively deconstruct popular preconceptions about what men and
women "are really like," because you don't have to spend too long in
any forum to realize that people of any gender are capable of the
same hateful and the same wonderful kinds of behavior. And then
there's the issue of people "passing" as the opposite gender, which
sort of blurs the lines even further.

   Hmmm. Did I answer the question? I guess I instinctively react
with suspicion and a touch of dismay when people categorize things in
terms of "feminine" and "masculine," because I don't believe we have
sufficiently rescued these words from their patriarchal connotations.

**What's your take on the ways sexualities are played out, expressed,
discussed online? What is your experience of, say, lesbian cyberspace? Is**

there such a thing as lesbian cyberspace? If so, what is its ecology?

It might take me a book to answer this one...I do know many, many
people find the Net a great way to explore their emerging homo-
sexual or bisexual identities, and for many this is the first place
they "meet" others with similar experiences and/or similar feelings
about themselves. In short, the Net has helped many people come out
of the closet, both to themselves and to others. The potential for
lesbian community online, for example, is great—as is demonstrated
by the number of lesbian lists there are. Women from isolated,
religious-right-dominated parts of the country (or the world) are
able to interact with us liberal queers in San Francisco and to see
what gay life is like for different people in different parts of
the world. That goes a long way toward educating people about
themselves, others and queerness in general.

**Now, an academic question. How do you see the Internet impacting the
humanities and social sciences?**

Oh yikes. Got another hour?? <grin> I think one of the most incredible uses of the Internet, of e-mail in particular, is in the
formation of "virtual academic communities" via mailing lists. I am
currently on four academic lists, WMST-L, QSTUDY-L, lesbian-studies
and lesac-Net (the last two being among the lists I run), and I
think this concept is most vividly demonstrated on QSTUDY-L and
sometimes on lesbian-studies. Of the 450 or so subscribers to that
list, about 10 to 20 percent are well-known scholars in the field
of queer studies, and another 20 to 30 percent are up and coming in
the field. The rest of us are either graduate students or faculty
members, with a few nonacademics and undergrads in the mix, so that
the range of conversation on any given topic is incredible. Nowhere
else would 450 people from such widely different backgrounds be
able to participate in these kinds of discussions, often with the
best known minds in the field debating those who would otherwise
remain "unknowns."

Final thoughts?

My favorite things about the Net (and what I find most empowering)
are e-mail lists and the Web. I think the Web has incredible
potential as a medium for exchanging information, providing an
outlet for creativity, and leveling the playing field in terms of
race, class, gender and sexuality. It has that *potential*, but until
access to the technology becomes as widespread and affordable as
television, that potential will not be fully realized.

I'm Not a Seeress...But I

Play One on the Internet

Name: Tana B. (If you finger my account, the last name "Boticelli" appears. That's all I tell.)

Age: 36

Geographical location: Santa Cruz County, California

If you were to do a search for "babes" on the Net, you just might find Toupsie out there (see our CyborgCulture section for *that* story), but you might also find Tana B.'s pages (http://we.got.net/ ~ tanab/), the oh-so-excellent curator of our own Babes of the Web, a rating of the babeliness of various boyz and their pages. We give her three snaps up for admitting that John Perry

Barlow is "babely on many levels ..." We *sooo* agree. Included along with all these boy-toys are various pages for "Unearthing Treasures for

Aphrodite," and "Reclaiming the Erotic" (going along with what Audre Lorde had in mind), a lot of great links and general all-around useful and aesthetic layout. Tana B.—also known as Diotima; keep reading to see why she picked her nick—is an inspiration to us because she's a relative newbie, and yet has jumped into the muck with both feet and offered forth some really interesting and useful stuff to dot the cyberscape.

Profession—current and past lives?

1) Waitress (ages 18 to 25)
2) Jack of all graphics: calligrapher, paste-up/layout, editor/ proofreader. (ages 17 to present)
3) *Real* graphics designer (computer!): 1988 to present
4) Writer: comedy, children's books, poetry, erotica, e-mail and irreverent responses to questionnaires

Internet projects and communities with which you are or have been involved?

I'm so new [as of October 1995] that I am still just finding my groove. I have a solid dozen individuals with whom I exchange regular e-mail, and a lot of that is site recommendation. I am close to Ms. Blake Kritzberg, of the Babes of the Web II page (http://ucsub.colorado.edu/~kritzber/new/babes.html), and that "work" (play!) is a substantial part of my community. I have actually met her and a number of the "Babes" we feature on our pages. Thus the Internet comes to life!

Any other personal info you want to share?

I am really a writer trapped in the body of a graphic designer. Kind of like a Siamese twin who got absorbed. I have a very famous sister, a stand-up comic with a top ten TV show on ABC. I have written for her, heard my jokes performed on the Letterman show and even been *paid* for this. Meanwhile, being a geek pays the bills. And let's don't forget the one hour and forty-five minutes of fame that have come my way from my little Web page!

How old were you when you started messing around with computers?

Twenty-nine and pregnant in Boulder, Colorado. The university had a free public computer lab filled with Macintoshes. I went there because I got some small freelance work on a book and began to acquire Macintosh skills then. I just wandered in whenever I wanted because it was free.

I'M NOT A SEERESS...BUT I PLAY ONE ON THE INTERNET

Did you ever have to deal with any sort of techno-sexism in labs, computer stores or wherever?

If I did, I didn't notice it. It's my experience of the Macintosh community that people bend over backwards to help any newbie, regardless of gender. I've done the same. It's a very supportive group, and if I received any erroneous assumptions, it was that I knew more than I did. These people (men and women alike) would start firing techno-speak at me (SCSI, initialize, force-quit, et cetera) until I'd have to wave my hands and say "Stop! You're going too fast!"

Do you think you had a different approach to computers than your male classmates or co-workers?

Hmmm. I don't think so. Perhaps it's because the Macintosh interface is so intuitive and artistic, I have always regarded the community as people who share my values. Oh sure, there are always some dry engineer-types with gray desktops on a color screen...but that's bound to happen, if only because of statistics.

What did you do with computers before you went online?

My education in Macintosh dovetailed nicely with my previous graphic arts background. I started learning PageMaker and some art programs. I cross-fertilized myself, learned quickly and eventually achieved a plateau, a level at which I remained comfortable until I encountered the Internet. I have often said that the Gregorian monks would have sold their souls to the Devil to have had the ability to force-justify with a keystroke.

When did you discover the Internet? Why did you first go online?

I am embarrassed to admit that I had AOL for four months before a concerned friend easily convinced me to dump it and use her "$20/ All You Can Eat" provider. I went to the WWW in June 1995 and feel sorry for people with AOL (if only because of the usurious rates, if not the pabulum-filled, middle-America interface and homogenized/unrealistic worldview). Why did I go on? Because it's the ultimate community, the ultimate global brain and a mostly wonderful, incredibly broad avenue of self-expression and collective knowledge. My kinda place!

What really blew your mind about the Internet and convinced you to get involved in this "revolution"?

In a nutshell, to be able to do a "Net Search" on anything about which I was curious, and have there be not one but ten or a hundred bunnies in the magician's hat. *Yowsah!*

How did you go about becoming a fully functioning netizen? What resources and people were useful to you?

My friend, Kristin, who got me off AOL, was instrumental. Let's call her "Prometheus." Once online, I discovered Ms. Blake Kritzberg's Babes of the Web II page. One stroll through her brilliant and bountiful outpouring of intelligence and creativity, and something clicked in me. I fired off some e-mail and introduced my humble self (I never thought she would write back!). She certainly did write back, measure for measure, and thus began a treasured friendship. She and one other person, Paul Vachier (one of our "Babes" and our friend) encouraged and goaded me, insisting that I produce my own Web page. They kept saying it was easy, and Paul even offered the lure of HTML work paying good money if I could acquire the skills.

I started by looking at people's source code (not unlike peeking into their bathroom cabinets) and finally, at Paul's suggestion, bought Laura Lemay's book, *Teach Yourself Web Publishing in a Week with HTML.* I did three days' worth of a seven-day course, grokked the rest and started to assemble my own page. I had already accumulated backgrounds and scanned some photos. I'd say the assembling took two weeks of spare time...and a lot of that was sifting through all the pretty backgrounds and writing the copy for my pages. It was delightful fun. Then I didn't know how to post it. Enter Knox Bronson, an online buddy (author of *Flapping,* the world's first online novel, also a Babe). He was the one who sent me a screenshot of his desktop, information about using Fetch to post files to his directory, along with meticulous instructions.

The lightbulb went on over my head again. I called my guys at Got.Net, and within two hours, my page was up. Moreover, as Jay, the tech support guy for Got.Net, simultaneously viewed my page as he helped me load it (we were talking on the phone), he said, "This is your first page? I think I can promise you some work!" That was a luxurious feeling for a newbie to have!

So far, what has been your best Net experience? Your worst?

My continuing best experience is how many interesting and wonderful people, all over the world, I am meeting. Having the focus of "unearthing treasures" (be they Babes or great links) has enabled me to hand the world my Web page with the confidence of a waitress who knows the menu will delight you, no matter what you order. Well, unless you wanted that Aryan Hate Page soufflé or the Republicans Rule ragout. *Excusez-moi*, but the chef cannot do those things here.

Additionally, last weekend, I finally met my cybersistah, Blake Kritzberg, and we had a fabulous time! She flew to San Francisco, and we had brunch with one Babe and dinner with another, and filled up the meanwhile with accosting and waylaying Babes on the street, asking them if we could photograph them for journalistic posterity. Opening gambit: "Have you heard of the Internet? We own it. Can we photograph you for our Web page?"

Worst experience? My friends have had some doozies, but I haven't had anything bad. Perhaps it is merely the many quiet moments, when I view thousands of homepages that reflect the stultifying lack of freedom in people's self-expression. To see the results of a lack of imagination is, to me, far more insidious than an encounter with a single asshole with an ax to grind.

Online sexism—problem or not? Your most heinous or unsettling experience? Your best experience as a woman online? What's the best way to deal with sexist trolls/flamers and unwanted sexual attention?

Sexism hasn't been any more of a problem than in the "real" world. If anything, it's easier for me to deal with because I rarely lose my aplomb in e-mail. In cyberspace, nobody can see you blush, infuriated. Perhaps it could be argued that what Blake and I do is sexist...finding Babes (though I do have a few double-X chromosomed Babes). But I feel pretty centered in myself, and it doesn't feel like what I am doing is wrong. I have yet to meet a guy who isn't flattered or thrilled at being highlighted as a "Babe."

I would have to say, in the greatest honesty, that if there is one consistent comment in my fan mail, or in personal correspondence with a great many people, it's that "Women are rocking the Internet!" This is constant.

My best experience as a woman online is that I have the happy satisfaction of receiving mail from men and women, appreciating my writing and my style. I seem to be traveling a blessed path, in that I have not offended anyone so badly that they can't hear what I am saying anymore. Thus I can slip in the candy-coated consciousness pills. I love men and women, and I want ever-better relations for all people. I want more kindness and laughter. And I am getting it because I insist on it!

What is your take on the ways gender gets played out, expressed, discussed online? What are your experiences of online spaces made by and/or maintained for women? How is interaction in these spaces different from that taking place in mixed forums or "guy sites"?

Well, women are who we are in the analog world, of course. We are generally networkers and friend-makers and realize the importance of relationships as they strengthen and enhance our lives, personally and presumably professionally. Moreover, I see a lot more colorful wit and self-expression on the WWW in women's pages. I think that we "dress" our pages in the same way we are allowed to dress (and men mostly aren't) in the "real" world.

I don't have any experience of guy sites. Except Rob Toups's Babes of the Web...which bothers me only in one tiny way. And that, of course, is that he deigns to "rate" the women he finds. Or their Websites. But I prefer to think that his showcasing women's homepages is something we can use to our advantage. It's not like we had to take our shirts off to get the job. I don't lose a lot of sleep over this stuff. I make the best of what I have and focus my energy on creating more of what serves. In other words, "add your light to the sum of light."

Why do you think it's important for girls and women to get online and participate in what we call "the cyberscape"? What hopes do you have for the future and impact of feminism(s) online?

The Net is like a global brain. Information needs to be presented in appealing ways, in digestible ways, for it to impact the planet positively. If I can take my strength and ideals, the wisdom I have acquired from my years as a soul-searcher and a planetary adventurer-student, and make them "taste" good, then maybe it'll be like getting someone to eat a sugar-coated vitamin pill. If our pages can bring the feminine experience, rather than merely an ideological assemblage of rhetoric, to the world, then we have the chance to make changes! I would like to see more of the feminine cooperative mindset reflected; it's good for all those "good ol' boys"—especially if it's done in a way that is positive and respectful.

How was the Diotima born?

Blake Kritzberg christened me that, after I sent her an e-mail with four Babes in it. Rather than admit my ignorance of the classics, I did a Net Search and found the "Diotima: Studies of Women and Gender in the Ancient World" homepage. Diotima discoursed with Socrates on the mysteries of love. She was brilliant. And that

planted the seed in my mind, that my homepage would take a classical theme...Mount Olympus, gods/goddesses and Muses. That theme
provided me with the fabric you presently see at my site: plenty of
Aphrodites and temples. I have a "Diotima's Dharma" page at my
site. Check it out; it has some quotes from the other Diotima's
page, from Plato's Symposium. Of course, I love that Blake gave me
this alter-ego. It's fun! Originally, my page said, "I'm Not a
Goddess, But I Play One on the Internet," but I modified that out
of respect for the truth.

What is the philosophy behind your project/business?

"Add your light to the sum of light" —Billy Kwan, *The Year of
Living Dangerously*

That sums it up. I find that highlighting what is positive
works better for me than trying to correct what is negative. Which
doesn't mean I can't proofread (oh, that I could shut that ability
off sometimes)...merely that it works far better to be an example
of what can be, rather than to waste too much energy making bad
examples of others. Otherwise the world becomes too polarized. I
have found that I can relate to almost anyone, on some level. In
some cases, the way to relate is to draw in; in others, it's to
make strong walls. Either way a relationship is formed. I'm not a
warrior, only occasionally. I respect the fighters; it's just not
my way.

What is your utopian fantasy (or worst nightmare) of the impact the Internet will have on culture and society as we move into the next millennium?

I really don't have one. I would like to think that people would
use the Internet as I am: to create real relationships that enter
our lives physically, so that we might turn more people on to
greater numbers of good things. The alternative, that more and more
people get sucked into limbo (like, MUDS and role-playing games
that don't appear to contribute much to the work that needs to be
done on this planet), is oppressive. I like the idea that the
Internet can enhance my life, not the idea that I become the tool
of the mindless. (—shiver!—)

How do you feel about the ways in which the Internet has been sold and explained to the public? Would you do it differently?

Gee. I told a Nigerian cab driver that it was like cable TV, and I
have my own station. That seemed to work for him. I hate all the

hype about money and the commercial aspects of it, but I guess that's the way the world is.

How have you approached initiating your daughters into Net culture?

My girls are fourteen, eleven and seven. All of them are aware of the honors of my WWW page. All of them are aware of the skills needed to operate a Macintosh. Somewhere between those two terrains lies a vast expanse of land that is being revealed to them one step at a time. I have taken them surfing, but with Bianca and her trolls out there (and I like them fine), I can't really just let the girls hook up to the Internet at their whim. But they shall, oh, they shall!

They are all adept at using the various programs they like and are even capable of printing a multi fold greeting card and using the spell checker.

My daughters are all impressed that I can make good money sitting at home. I recently got a coveted contractor's position with a design firm in town who is *paying* me to learn Photoshop and Director! Yes, I am getting paid to learn to animate. And the girls know my rate of pay, which I think inspires them.

Any final tips and words of encouragement for our readers?

Variety is the spice of life. I dumped my whole spice rack into my Web page, and I have found that it sets it apart from the majority of pages. As one piece of fan mail put it: "In a net full of dead fish, it's nice to find a pearl." Look for the rare—in yourselves and the WWW—and showcase it. A link to Dilbert won't do it. Nor will references to Star Trek. What the world needs are individuals brave enough to reveal themselves and say "YES!"

I was looking at Toupsie's page once, and went to a random site of a Four T Babe. I am not going to defend him, because the rating system stinks any way I slice it (who the hell does he think he is?). *But:* the page I visited had a woman that, by no stretch of RT's imagination would have been considered a Four Toupsies. She was zaftig, bespectacled, and I can't imagine that he thought she classically beautiful. However, she warranted a 4-T rating. I believe it was her great HTML he was praising, as her page was beautifully designed. And mind you, there was no evidence of political affinities or cowboy boots, both of which I would have suspected. Just one little "for what it's worth" story. It puzzled me, and it puzzles me now.

THEY'RE RAD, THEY'RE POPPY,

THEY CHANNEL THE SPIRIT

OF OLD SASSY

Beaming out from L.A., Clea and Keva and all the kids at tumyeto.com really live the whole boy + girl revolution thing. From the Poot boutique to the beauteous e-zine *Foxy*, everything in their world is simultaneously punky and cuddly. Skatepunks/grrrls will love this stuff. So will folks looking for examples of bright and funky page design.

Name: Clea Hantman
Age: 28
Geographical location: San Diego, California

Profession?
Currently editorial director of said Website; previously editor of various mags and all-around cheesy freelance writer.

Internet projects and/or communities with which you are or have been involved?

This be the first!

Other personal info you want to share?

I'm short. Just thought you should know.

How old were you when you started messing around with computers?

College age, and only to write papers and such. Then I bought my
own and started messing around with various programs. Saw a job I
wanted in the newspaper where you needed to have experience in
Quark so I borrowed it, played for an evening and got the job: the
beginning of my brilliant career...

Did you ever have to deal with any sort of techno-sexism in labs, computer stores or wherever?

Not nearly as much as car-salesman sexism, but certainly the stores
are a little less friendly and explanative, but not so bad that I
am forced to explode into fiery red and blue flames. Like I do at
the car dealership.

Do you think your approach to computers is different from that of your male colleagues?

I have a different approach to computers than most I've come
across, but I don't know if the divisive lines are gender-based.
See, I just look at them totally creatively, a fab tool like any
other art tool, and I'm not just talking "art programs" but with
everything, even the Web. I try to think FUN. I just try not to
picture computers in any sorta mathematical context, and they
remain my friends.

What did you do with computers before you went online?

Just wrote for the most part. I worked for a newspaper, and I did
layout as well as write. Basic.

When did you discover the Internet? Why did you first go online?

I read lots. Friends started talking a bit about it. Then a job
offer came up, but I needed to know about the Web. So I went down
to the relatively friendly neighborhood computer store and bought a
modem (novel idea!) and hooked into AOL at first for free. But soon
I realized AOL was bogus and went through a local provider. I'm
talkin' like four days later. Within a week I was familiar with a
lot of what was online, and I got the job (MY CURRENT ONE!). They
taught me how to do the (very easy) HTML programs, they taught me

how to scan, and now, six months later, I can create a whole site from thin air. Woo. I love learning!

What really blew your mind about the Internet and convinced you to get involved in this "revolution"?

Well, I love learning. (Hah.) And I love this instantaneous response thing. I had been writing for mags for years, but you'd do a story and three months later it would finally be in print, and then it took another two months before you ever saw any response from readers. Well, here I get letters EVERY DARN DAY telling me what's good about what I do and what's bad, what's inspiring and what's lame, and I love it. For me, that's the best part. But then again, I have a massive ego.

How did you go about becoming a fully functioning netizen? What resources and people were useful to you?

At home, I pretty much did it myself with a generic how-to book in hand, but I did call on one geek friend of mine for phone advice. At work, we have a nice set up, not perfect but damn fine. This Website is totally sponsored at this point by Tum Yeto, the parent company to Foundation Super Co. and Poot. So there is a little dough. Not heaps, but a bit. The guys (and, yes, they are guys) who do the r&d for the company, and who do the regular uploads and all that, taught me how to basically do everything myself. But then they were a bit bummed I think when I picked it up so fast and didn't NEED them any longer. Hah. Actually, now there is only need for one other person doing computer stuff, and he's a great guy. If I ever have questions, Rob's there to explain to me HOW TO, rather than just DO IT for me. And that's the best.

So far, what has been your best Net experience? Your worst?

Best: Very cheesy, but I wrote this stupid little note on one of my columns that said I was frustrated with it and essentially: "oh man, does anyone ever read this crap, I'm sick of this, if anybody out there is reading and cares, tell me or I'm throwing in the towel" and well, I got TONS of mail back saying NO, DONT DO IT! it was fab. (my sensitive but ever-blossoming ego was terribly thankful.)

Worst: I was kinda net-stalked. This guy was kinda casually stalking me 'round town—asking questions about me, randomly following me, trying to "know" my friends, coming into my shop (I own a store—hey, a POP culture store as we call it, but I digress)

Magazines and Zines

Of course there are folks out there who worry about the lack of editorial "authority" controlling online publications, but we think that's one of the grooviest things about the whole "do-your-own" zine revolution. And that's why we haven't separated out the fun DIY zines from the "serious" stuff with money behind it. Ha ha!

ZINE NET
You can check out anytime you like, but you will never leave. Have a couple of hours on your hands before you dive in here.
http://www.zine.net/

REAL TEEN
The project of real teenagers Sydney Baird and Kendra Dye! (And "sponsored" by Sydney's dad.)
http://www.cet.com/~bairdst/

BLUESTOCKING
"Fun, controversial, pro-sex, with heart and an open forum." Also has some fun interactive features. Our fave: "submit a neologism for female masturbation."
http://www.teleport.com/~bluesock.html

GEEKGIRL
Groovalicious. Wicked good reading for the geekgirl in all of us.
http://www.next.com.au/spyfood/geekgirl.html

YONI: GATEWAY TO THE FEMININE
A webzine "in celebration and exploration of the feminine." Very well-done, uses hypertext in fun ways. Those Aussies!
http://www.ion.com.au/yoni

CATT'S CLAWS: A FEMINIST NEWSLETTER
This political newsletter/site lives up to the vision and aims of its spritual godmother, Carrie Chapman Catt, a tireless crusader for suffrage and other women's rights.
http://worcester.lm.com/lmann/feminist/cattsclaws.html

PLOTZ (THE ZINE FOR THE VACLEMPT)
A little e-publication from the same wits who brought you *Hey There, Barbie Girl!*
http://www.zine.net/plotz/index.shtml

SISSY (THE LOST ISSUE OF *SASSY*)
More fun from those boys at Blair. Yes, grrrls will be boyz and boyz will be grrrls . . .
http://www.youth.org/zines/blair/sissy or http://www.io.org/~medusa

but not ever "talking" to me. Anyway he got my e-mail address from someone I used to work with by saying that he was my friend, and every day there would be "love" letters from him on my computer. And they were creepy because they said stuff like where I had been the night before, so I obviously knew he had been watching me. Weird. I wrote back and asked him to stop. He didn't. But then a bit later I wrote this very succinct, kinda scary-in-its-own-right letter and he left me alone. End of story. See, not too exciting and not too connected to the whole Net thing. I think the best thing to have done in that situation would have been to ignore it and wait for him to get bored. But my way worked too.

Your best experience as a woman online?

My best experience as a woman online really has been the cool correspondence with various brilliant (femme) minds that I would have never discovered because they are in Vermont or Oregon or NYC or wherever and I'm in sunny Southern Cal.

◊

THEY'RE RAD, THEY'RE POPPY, THEY CHANNEL THE SPIRIT OF OLD SASSY

What is your take on the ways gender gets played out, expressed, discussed online? What are your experiences of online spaces made by and/or maintained for women? Is interaction in these spaces different from that taking place in mixed forums or "guy sites"?

What I like about the more "women oriented" sites is the personal gunk. I just love when people of both genders write from the guts, tell us who they really are, humor me that I'm not the only self-obsessed person on the Web! And you just plain find more of that on women's sites than others, but I find great stuff out there everywhere. I just seem to meet more interesting women on those sites.

Why do you think it's important for girls and women to get online and participate in the imagination/realization of what we call "the cyberscape"? What hopes do you have for the future and impact of feminism(s) online?

Well it's a great place to speak your mind and have full-blown discussion/arguments/rallies even without having to gather people be in a specific geographical location. Also, no one judges you for anything other than your words. I think it's a key outlet for (especially) young women to discover fab things about being a girl, I mean *Sassy*'s gone, there aren't a lot of places for gals to take their cues from, no one at the very least pointing them in the right positive directions, and I think that the Web has that to offer, just by virtue of the young women online who are already doing fab pages—it's real-time zine revolution NOW!

How was the idea for *Foxy* born? How did you go about setting up your business? How are you doing? What are your plans/dreams for the future? What is the philosophy behind your business?

I'll let Keva tell you about *Foxy* because she started it as a printed zine. I came in to do the Web part, and in fact, it was already up when I came, but it was exactly the same as the printed version—now they are unique unto themselves. It was an extension of the existing site, Skateboard.com, same equip and all. It's going better than our wildest dreams. Our plans are to get bigger! Better! More solid women stuff, less "boy" gunk. More women in sports, women working, women writing, women power than anything else. I want to be a launch pad for uninitiated girls who come to the Net and wanna know what to do next. I want to be a pointer and send them on their ever-discoverin' way, and hopefully they will check back with us, maybe write something up for us, but also, DO THEIR OWN THING!

How do you feel about the ways the Internet has been "sold" and "explained" to the public? Would you do it differently?

Kinda a joke in many ways, eh? Either my friends who aren't hooked in think they know so much because they read a cheesy article even though they have NEVER cruised the Web, OR they are totally scared of it like it's some foreign thing. I think it's so basic its scary, but I hate it when people talk about something they have never tried. It's akin to people who read lit crit about a book they have never read and then talk about it like they READ THE DAMN BOOK! Well, I just wish there was more basic info. I wish the mags talked about how easy it is to get online via a local provider and how the software is all free and all that.

Any final tips and words of encouragement for our readers?

Communication can be FUN! (Oy vey.) Seriously though, I do think it's wonderous and especially important for high school/college-age chicks to get on it; I mean at school, it's FREE! And I really do think there can be real clues and inspirations as far as HELPING young women discover who and what they wanna be. Certainly more so than what is offered in mainstream press, so spread the word. Zipadedooda!

And now, Clea's bud and partner in crime...KEVA!

Name: keva marie
Age: 24
Geographical location: Del Mar and San Diego, California

Profession?

girl on the go—ferever

Other personal info you want to share?

i got new shoes today. red suede tennies with white stitching. somedays when things are lame and icky, new things rilly 'kick'

How was the idea for *Foxy* born?

born actually first as a paper zine. from the fact that *poot* got so much rad fan mail, and it seemed like the girls were out there just waiting. plus i've always wanted to work for *sassy* (but...not anymore...)

◊

How did you go about setting up your business?

tod swank rules

How are you doing?

rockin'

What are your plans/dreams for the future?

remove things (from myself or not allow other people with these
habits to affect me) in my life like: judgemental attitudes/talking
shit about people you don't know/negativeness/noncompassion/self-
defeating attitudes/closemindedness/racism...that kinda thing plus
i don't want to be affected in a negative way by what people think
about something i do that i feel good about....not to let it make
me be insecure and/or not do it

What is the philosophy behind *Foxy*?

fffuuuuunnnnnn

So far, what has been your best Net experience?

looking up foxy pages and poot pages and being satisfied and stoked
(way more than when i look at the clothes, sometimes) checking my
daily horoscope/getting film clips from friends i meet via
internet. alex/dear boy once sent one that said something like "hey
keva what's up" like a movie. it was rad.

Your worst?

when my computer freezes/or the pictures don't come up

Online sexism—problem or not?

oh i dont know...i'm sure just the same as anywhere

Your most heinous or unsettling experience?

in life? or online? oh but even unsettling stuff is good sometimes—
shakes ya up. good for jokin and laughs

Your best experience as a woman online?

meeting other online chicks/meeting them faster. getting things
done faster. not having to deal with boys if we don't want to/
having the ability to bypass thru red tape and get straight to who
you want to deal with (so far...)

◊

What's the best way to deal with sexist trolls/flamers and unwanted sexual attention?

love em

What is your take on the ways gender gets played out, expressed, discussed online?

expression is beauty

What are your experiences of online spaces made by and/or maintained for women?

same as boys/sites done by rad human individuals with visions...

Why do you think it's important for girls and women to get online and participate in the imagination/realization of what we call "the cyberscape"?

just like any forum, girl-powered ANYTHING IS necessary to express ourselves and give other girls a place or inspiration to do it themselves...as well as let boys (and everyone else fer that matter) know what we're all about. working towards understanding— this is just another wonderful way to get it....

What hopes do you have for the future and impact of feminism(s) online?

everything and anything, of course

AHHH, CYBERGRRL!

Name: Aliza Sherman
Alias: Cybergrrl
Age: 30
Geographical location: New York City, New York

Aliza Sherman is known in the online world (and off!) as Cybergrrl. Frankly, we can't think of a better woman to officially hold that title. After nine years in the music biz, Aliza spent a year running a domestic violence nonprofit organization, and then left that project to write books for teens on subjects like violence against women and adoption. After that, she started her own business: online marketing and interactive products for women and girls. She also runs the Cybergrrl Webstation (http://www.cybergrrl.com/), Femina (http://www.femina. com/) and Webgrrls, a loose affiliation of women on the Web, with real-life groups that meet in New York City, Los Angeles, Washington

D.C., Seattle, Boston, San Francisco, London, Australia and New Zealand. More Webgrrl groups are in the works, so if you are interested in joining one (or starting your own!), feel free to contact Aliza at aps@cybergrrl.com.

Why do we love Cybergrrl? Read this, dig the projects with which she's involved and count the ways for yourself. It's so neat to see a member of your community (now your community, too, dear reader) tapped by some national newsmag as one of the primo movers and shakerettes of the info-millennium. What took those folks at *Newsweek* so long to figure that out? We've long known she is one of the hardest-working, grooviest chicks in Netbiz, a veritable reverse-piranha of good works and healthy self-interest. We'll stop now before we get effusive or anything.

How old were you when you started messing around with computers?

When I was a temp at about 20 years old. I was told I could make more money with computer skills so I learned . . . it was work related.

Did you ever have to deal with any sort of techno-sexism in labs, computer stores or wherever?

Not really. A very little bit online, but in real life, I'm surprised at how cool everyone has been.

Do you think you had a different approach to computers than your male counterparts did?

Actually, in the music biz, the men were computer incompetents—thought it was for secretaries. They sure missed out and are scrambling now to learn.

When did you discover the Internet? Why did you first go online?

I went online eight years ago—on BBSs and played games. Really got going on AOL and the Net about three or four years ago. Wanted to see what was out there. From the start, I saw it as a place to create anything I wanted—and I've been building forums, resources and Web pages ever since!

What really blew your mind about the Internet and convinced you to get involved in this "revolution"?

I have incredible power at my fingertips and can create communities, reach people around the world and build things! The payback is so satisfying—I see it happen and then get the feedback from others—amazing communication. I knew my mission was to get more women and girls into this powerful medium—to empower them with possibility, information and contact.

How did you go about becoming a fully functioning netizen? What resources and people were useful to you?

Eva Shaderowfsky (EvaS@aol.com) was my mentor on AOL—a brilliant woman who has led several online conferences for women and is now building the beginnings of a women's forum on AOL.

So far, what has been your best Net experience? Your worst?

Best: Webgrrls in NYC—we met via e-mail, met in April [1995] (eight of us), then this past week there were over one hundred women!

Worst? No really bad experiences. Some mindless blather from silly men, but nothing unmanageable.

Online sexism—problem or not?

As much of a problem as anywhere else.

What's the best way to deal with sexist trolls/flamers and unwanted sexual attention?

I am polite or ignore yucky e-mails. Like someone e-mailed "where are the naked girls?" and I just said "oh, you must have the wrong site. Sorry!"

BTW, www.cybergirls.com *are* naked women—hope women do not get confused and go there instead. And www.cybergirl.com is a company called Networks Wizards who only picked the name because it was close to cybergrrl.com and cybergirls.com and would attract folks. (My mistake for not reserving them all!)

What is your take on the ways gender gets played out, expressed, discussed online? What are your experiences of online spaces made by or maintained for women? How is interaction in these spaces different from that taking place in mixed forums or "guy sites?"

I don't pay much attention to gender issues in cyberspace or the real world—I'm a woman with my own business now and won't let anything stop me. When on Women's Wire, the first year was amazing— great women, great support—but when the new president took over she destroyed the spirit of the service, and it might as well be just another service. Very lame.

In mixed areas men tend to dominate conversations and tend to be condescending to women—but isn't that often the case?

Why do you think it's important for girls and women to get online and participate in "the cyberscape"? What hopes do you have for the future and impact of feminism(s) online?

Women and girls will gain immense power from being online—from gaining support from other women to being able to self-publish, create places, build businesses and have a voice. I'm starting a nonprofit—Digital Women—to bring technology, training and equipment to women and girls through the organizations that serve them— it is essential for them to get up to speed and not fall behind.

How were the ideas for Cybergrrl and Femina born? What are your plans/ dreams for the future?

Cybergrrl was my personal homepage, and she was created to represent me. Now she represents all women and girls online and the page is growing into an essential resource for women online. Femina came about because nothing like it exists, and women have particular interests and online needs that won't be met by male-created Web resources (such as the latest Women's Wire homepage—designed by a man and pretty weak).

How did you go about setting up your business? How are you doing?

My business is CG Internet Media—online marketing—and at eight months we are doing well—moved out of my studio apartment to an office. We have many great clients including Avon's Breast Cancer Awareness Crusade.

What is the philosophy behind your projects and business?

My philosophy is that women and girls should embrace technology, and my company will help bridge gaps, pave the way and bring them along to where they need to be. My fave saying is "For women, being online is like having the world at your fingertips…or better yet, holding it in the palm of your hand."

What is your utopian fantasy (or worst nightmare) of the impacts the Internet will have on culture and society as we move into the next millennium?

Fantasy: Women are a dominant force on the Net (and why not the world) and we have peace, harmony and happiness!

Any final tips and words of encouragement for our readers?

Cybergrrl says: Get Online, Grrl!

Outro

SurferGrrrls AfterFAQ

Why did you finish the book?

Laurel: Because the more time I spent online, the more I learned and the more excited I got about the radical potential of the Internet-at-large. I get called bad names a lot . . . like, utopian. And evangelical. And yeah, I *am* evangelical about the Internet, and I'm not really interested in discussing the question of *if* the Net is radical: It is. It's forcing questions I'm not sure we're ready to answer yet; the different cultures of the world are realizing they have to deal with each other, the United States has to rework all sorts of free speech/information assumptions and the way people form their identity won't ever be the same. Personally, I find all this to be *a good thing*. It's great to have these major paradigm shifts every couple of centuries (and I do think the development of human-computer interaction is a paradigm shift of printing-press magnitude) to keep us on our collective toes.

✧ *Crystal:* I'll second that, but, except philosophically, I don't harbor utopian illusions about the Net anymore. When you get down to it, the

Net is just a medium: a radically different sort of medium, potentially a very empowering medium, but a medium all the same. That's why *I'm* so invested in getting women and girls interested in constructing the Net and/or weaving the Web. Finally, here's a widely affordable opportunity to represent ourselves in "the media" and to network with one another.

However. The current repressive political climate in this country scares the hell out of me, and the "decency" provision in the Telecommunications Act of 1996 is proof that all this talk about "power to the people" and decentralization of government is just a bunch of smoke and mirrors cloaking a peculiarly American brand of emergent reactionary moralist fascism. It's shocking but true that under the original "decency" provision, online discussions of abortion, birth control and even breast cancer would have been prohibited! Welcome back, Anthony Comstock!

That said, one of the things keeping me going throughout this project was the massive online resistance to the calls for across-the-board censorship of Net content. It seems that almost every Website I visit is flying a blue ribbon in a show of anti-censorship solidarity. In the dark days of early 1996, the smart and amusingly dissipated folx who hang out in the alt.showbiz.gossip "trailer park" (Usenet group) saturated their posts and subject lines with every gratuitous "indecent" word they could think of, and all but dared the authorities to come and get them. For two weeks, a group also kept track of the unenforced fines the pottymouth members were racking up at $250,000 per post. The total was $180,500,000 and change.

⬦ **What did you learn that you didn't know before?**

⬦ *Laurel:* Most of the technical material was already familiar to me. I've been helping people get online for a couple of years, and have a stock, forty-minute "this is how to get online" spiel. Thinking about the cultural implications was fascinating, though, because as the Net changes (and it has changed dramatically during the year we worked on *SurferGrrrls*), both online and mass media perceptions of it change, too. Crystal was really amazing to work with and she has the ability to hang out in the strangest places online and then fuse whatever she's gleaned into a coherent narrative of "Net culture." I am amazed at her ability to think "culturally" and sometimes felt my own understanding lagged behind, but then I'd ask her a question about processor speed or ISDN and her blank look assured me we simply had different areas of "specialty."

✧ *Crystal:* I came to the boggling conclusion that the Internet really is "alive," and that its totality is beyond human comprehension. From thinking intensely about the emergence of cyberculture, I've cultivated a much deeper appreciation of brave, out-there, guerrilla-cyborg visionaries. My people! My people! As this fortune cookie I got the other day reminded me, "The philosophy of one century is the common sense of the next." If we can get past this millennial panic without exterminating ourselves, The Age of Aquarius is going to be one wild party! As disaffected as I pretend to be sometimes, I feel really privileged to be alive at this time in history.

✧ So where can we find more information?
✧ The *SurferGrrrls* Website, of course! http://www.sealpress.com/surfergrrrls/ has hotlists, more interview texts and other fun resources for online women.

✧ Any final tips?
✧ Remember your CyborGrrrl Oath!

> **We are wired women. We would rather be cyborgs than goddesses. We have made a special vow to help guide our sisters, our mothers, our daughters and our friends into a cyberscape of their own. We promise to support them— however initially technophobic—as they apprentice themselves in that realm. We live by the geekgirl code: "The keyboard is a greater equalizer than a Glock .45." We are wired in to Chaos and Gaia. We swell the listservs, we proliferate in the Usenet groups, we weave the Web, we chat and MOO, we upload and download, we help build and nurture our chosen online communities. We help imagine and create new applications and forms, always looking to that next horizon, always thoughtful about the interface of embodied humankind and the electronic projection of the highest mental faculties of our species. In the name of global good and human freedom, we vow**

never to surrender the Internet and its successors to dangerous, self-perpetuating myths of the technological incompetence of women.

LAUREL GILBERT has just returned to her hometown of Salt Lake City, Utah, after almost five years in the English and American Culture Studies Departments at Bowling Green State University in Ohio. She wishes only for a quick and painless dissertation.

HOTLIST

Laurel's Little List of Luscious Online Hotspots

NEWSGROUPS DEAR TO MY HEART:
alt.tv.er, rec.equestrian, comp.infosystems.www.authoring.html, rec.drugs.smart, and rec.pets

LISTSERVS I HAVE KNOWN AND LOVED:
Ferret-l, Equine-l, Spiderwoman and ROCK (a small mailing list for Violent Femme's fans).

And finally, those Websites that have top billing in my bookmark file:

EDUCATION CENTER: NO GIRLS ALOWED
One of the first places to check if you want to get a girl turned on to computers . . . a fun and thorough study of how we grow up female, how growing up female discourages our use of technology and what to do about it.
http://www.gnn.com/gnn/meta/edu/features/archive/gtech.html

SANDY STONE'S HOMEPAGE
My idol, Ms. Stone is former recording technician for Jimi Hendrix, old hand at Olivia Records, reining mistress at the ACTLab at University of Texas at Austin and sexy theory-head. Whoo! Whoo!
http://www.actlab.utextas.edu/~sandy/

TIMOTHY LEARY HOMEPAGE
What's to be said? Leary's great.
http://www.leary.com/

THE WEB DESIGNER
Massive list of resources for anyone who wants to build spaces in the cyberscape. Levels range from beginning HTML questions to the cutting edge of VRML and Java programming, with backgrounds, textures, and imagemap help in between.
http://www.kosone.com/people/nelson/nl.htm

CRYSTAL KILE is completing her Ph.D. in American Culture Studies from Bowling Green State University in Ohio. Now repatriated to her native South, she lives in New Orleans and works as Education Coordinator at the Newcomb College Center for Research on Women at Tulane University. As God is her witness, she will never shovel snow again.

Net Profile: PopTart

SOME PLACES I HANG OUT AND LURK ON USENET:
rec.arts.tv.soaps.cbs, alt.showbiz.gossip, alt.folklore.urban, alt.history.what-if, alt.tv.x-files, bit.listserv.cinema-l, alt.appalachian, alt.music.alternative.female, bit.listserv.mla-l, alt.feminism, comp.infosystems.www.announce and a bunch of Macintosh-specific newsgroups

A HANDFUL OF LISTSERVS I HAVE LOVED:
Bad Subjects, WMST-L, Bubba-L, Spiderwoman, FutureCulture, the Trooper-run riot grrrl e-list, Keanu-L, Campus Activist Network: Right Wing Alert (CAN-RW)

A few women/homepages I really think you should meet:

MUFFY BARKOCY
One of the ex-moderators of alt.feminism and soc.women, Muffy is endlessly patient, passionate and lots of fun.
http://www.fish.com/~muffy/

EMILY WAY (SPAMILY)
First encountered this chica hanging out on alt.generation-x. As of this writing, the title of her page was "I can stop whenever I want to!" Fun and literate.
http://www.io.org/~spamily/

KEEVAH
Beaming out to the world from my hometown of Chattanooga, Tennessee, she and her hubbo are the Carol and Mike Brady of the information age. Seriously.
http://caladan.chattanooga.net/~keevah/

MEDUSA
"A woman's place is in your face." 'Nuff said. She's such a bitch, she's such a gorgon, she's such a bitch! And she's sooooo witty. And that makes her a fantastic Usenetter! Especially on alt.showbiz.gossip.
http://www.io.org/~medusa/medusa.html

THE GHIRLEE BANDS PAGE
Enough said!
http://members.aol.com/corinangel/index.htm

JANE PROPHET'S IMAGINARY INTERNAL ORGANS OF A CYBORG
Artsy and fun.
http://www.lond-inst.ac.uk/Cyborg/

ELLEN FORNEY is an illustrator/cartoonist in Seattle. She has published a solo comic book, *Tomato* (Starhead Comix) and her comic strip "I Was Seven in '75" is serialized in *The Rocket*. Her work appears regularly in *The Stranger* and *Seattle Weekly*, and has also been published in *Mirabella*, *Mademoiselle*, *Dyke Strippers*, *What Is This Thing Called Sex*, *Seattle Laughs*, *Dark Horse Presents* and other comic books and anthologies. Her Website is http://www/ qinet.com/ellen. She's on a swim team, recently switched from bleached-blond to purpley-red hair and her platform choice is Macintosh, hands down.

http:// cs.yale.edu/homes/tap/tap.html
(Womyn's resources)